VOLUME 1

Perspectives on Community College ESL Series

Pedagogy, Programs, Curricula, and Assessment

Edited by Marilynn Spaventa

Craig Machado, Series Editor

Teachers of English to Speakers of Other Languages, Inc.

Typeset in Galliard and Kabel
by Capitol Communication Systems, Inc., Crofton, Maryland USA
Printed by United Graphics, Inc., Mattoon, Illinois USA
Indexed by Coughlin Indexing, Annapolis, Maryland USA

Teachers of English to Speakers of Other Languages, Inc.
700 South Washington Street, Suite 200
Alexandria, Virginia 22314 USA
Tel 703-836-0774 • Fax 703-836-6447 • E-mail tesol@tesol.org •
http://www.tesol.org/

Publishing Manager: Carol Edwards
Copy Editor: Marcella F. Weiner
Additional Reader: Sarah J. Duffy
Cover Design: Tomiko Chapman

ISBN 9781931185349
Library of Congress Control Number: 2006906800

Table of Contents

Series Editor's Preface

I am pleased to introduce Perspectives on Community College ESL, a three-volume series designed to bring into practical focus a wide and diverse array of reflective work on ESL education in community college settings. The idea for this series initially grew out of numerous discussions and meetings I had with community college ESL practitioners at TESOL conventions and other venues. Because of the complexity and variety of ESL offered at community colleges, it was readily apparent that a series focused on this topic would undoubtedly be beneficial and useful. While community college interests and concerns within TESOL have found expression through other TESOL publications and events, no single one has been devoted entirely to this important educational milieu.

The project came more clearly into focus when I brought it before the TESOL Publications Committee, whose members helped me shape and refine its purpose and scope. I am deeply indebted to the committee, Past Chair Julian Edge, and, in particular, former TESOL Managing Editor Marilyn Kupetz, whose unflagging assistance, patience, and expertise carried me and the project forward.

Volume editors Marilynn Spaventa (*Pedagogy, Programs, Curricula, and Assessment*), Amy Blumenthal (*Students, Mission, and Advocacy*), and Jose Carmona (*Faculty, Administration, and the Working Environment*) have done an admirable job of evaluating manuscripts, working with contributors, and giving me timely and incisive comments and feedback. I could not have done this without them.

As the reader will note by glancing through each volume's content, this is an eclectic series—as it should be—drawing on the broad mission and constituencies that a community college must embrace. Topics range from the role of workforce ESL in an Oregon fishing community to training non-ESL faculty working with immigrants in a technical college in the Midwestern United States, from how the Smithsonian Institution provides an opportunity for ESL faculty and students to engage its museums as classrooms to what it means to be a blind ESL instructor working with sighted students.

Volume one, *Pedagogy, Programs, Curricula, and Assessment*, focuses on three main components of instruction: the kinds of courses offered, the organizational and programmatic structure through which courses are delivered, and the means by which students are evaluated. The latter includes discussion of placement tools for students entering a given program; the kinds of evaluation tools used in specific courses (e.g., grades, tests, portfolios); and assessments, such as exit or proficiency tests, that are administered when students complete a program or a series of courses. ESL is taught in many types of community college settings, and it varies based on the nature and purpose of a program— credit or noncredit, academic or vocational, and so on. Reading the chapters in this volume, one is struck by the creativity, resourcefulness, determination, intelligence, and wit that the writers bring to bear in what are often challenging conditions.

Students, Mission, and Advocacy, volume two, considers the experiences and needs of the immigrants, refugees, and international students who pass through the doors of community colleges. It explores the college mission to educate and advocate for ESL students individually and as parts of distinct, diverse, vibrant, and changing communities. This volume also looks at who community college ESL students are, how they fit (or perhaps do not fit) into a college's overall mission, and the roles that ESL and other college professionals play as educators and advocates. Contributors to this volume underscore the importance of building collaborative relationships among ESL programs and other college entities, and highlight the critical need for ESL educators to promote their students' welfare and success by helping to challenge and shape the college mission over time.

In response to the growing awareness of the difficulties that ESL practitioners face daily in making a viable living, volume three, *Faculty, Administration, and the Working Environment,* explores various aspects of the community college work environment in which ESL professionals function and interact. Given the large numbers of part-time ESL instructors, many of whom work multiple jobs in different programs at diverse institutions, it is more crucial than ever to understand the impact this state of affairs has on classroom effectiveness, professional standards, burnout, employee-employer relationships, and program management. This volume looks at workplace issues realistically and offers suggestions and strategies for improving the longstanding inequalities that have beset ESL education for some time.

The breadth and depth of the work presented in this series is a lasting reminder of all the accomplishments that community college ESL practitioners have made in terms of creative curricula, innovative program design and management, successful collaboration across disciplines, and unwavering devotion to the betterment of their students' lives and livelihoods.

I hope the reader enjoys reading this series as much as I have enjoyed bringing it to fruition.

Craig Machado
Norwalk Community College
Norwalk, Connecticut USA

Volume 1:
Pedagogy, Programs,
Curricula, and Assessment

##

Marilynn Spaventa

The field of English as a second language (ESL) provides a mélange of organizational models to serve students with diverse vocational and academic goals in both credit and noncredit programs. Faculty and administrators design programs and curricula and select assessment instruments customized to the mission of their institutions and to serve the needs of their student populations. There is much for ESL professionals to learn from each other in a dynamic discipline, which is influenced as much by global as well as local events. The authors in this volume contribute their perspectives and personal experiences related to pedagogy, program organization, curricula, and assessment, providing the reader with theory and experience for reflection.

In the section on pedagogy, Venkatesh, Berman, Caballero, Carroll, and Gaines (chapter 1), from Montgomery College in Maryland, describe the insights gained from their participation in a Smithsonian Faculty Fellows Program and recommend application and replication by ESL faculty teaching near any museum or by accessing museums with the Internet. In chapter 2, Ramírez shares his personal journey as an instructor of language, examining very thoroughly the ideological basis for what occurs in the classroom through an instructor's choice of curriculum. He demonstrates that reflection can create profound change in the roles of instructor and student, affecting both curriculum and methodology.

The chapters related to programs, to no great surprise, demonstrate the diversity of structure and mission of ESL programs in community colleges. Allison (chapter 3) describes the evolution of an ESL program for Generation

1.5 students at Gainesville College in Georgia, a location that had not had an immigrant population. Babbitt (chapter 4) shows how students in Brooklyn, New York, benefit from learning communities, which result in greater persistence, more rapid entry into other academic courses, and an increased rate of graduation. Two chapters focus on vocational instruction: Lenhardt, Purcell, and Tyson (chapter 5) describe the development of a workplace-based bilingual program in the Pacific Northwest, and Thomas (chapter 6) details the daunting challenge of developing and implementing an ESL program for displaced workers in Texas within a very short time frame. Creativity and flexibility clearly remain prime character traits for ESL professionals.

In the section on curricula, Ayala and Curtis (chapter 7) focus on curriculum revision at Queen's University School of English in Ontario, Canada. The authors describe the process they undertook and make recommendations for administrators and instructors considering curricular revision. In a chapter focused on technology and ESL, Brutza and Hayes (chapter 8) describe their concerns and successes with using computer writing programs for ESL instruction. Thomsen (chapter 9) also focuses on writing as she details the development of an integrated skills writing project for immigrants in a vocational program, which provides students with skills applicable in future job searches. Finally, Lieske (chapter 10) takes readers inside a community college in Japan for a rare, insightful, and somewhat surprising view of English as a foreign language instruction.

The final section of this volume addresses issues of assessment, an area of ongoing interest, development, and research. Connell and O'Leary (chapter 11) describe the approach they took in developing student learning outcomes for their ESL courses. Machado and Solensky (chapter 12) explore many of the issues involved in shifting responsibility for providing accurate and efficient computerized placement for ESL students from the ESL department to the college's testing office. In the final chapter in the volume, Sheppard and Crandall (chapter 13) compare two programs in very distinct institutional settings, emphasizing the role of assessment in each program.

I hope that the experiences shared and lessons learned in these practical and thought-provoking articles provide new perspectives or, at the very least, raise new questions that are of value to readers. In closing, I extend my sincere appreciation to all of the authors who contributed to this exploration of the varied, interesting, and always evolving discipline of ESL in community colleges.

▦ CONTRIBUTOR

Marilynn Spaventa is dean of educational programs at Santa Barbara City College (SBCC) in California in the United States. She oversees the School of

Modern Languages, the Sciences and Mathematics Divisions, the Disabled Student Programs and Services, and the SBCC Online College. Before discovering community colleges, she taught ESL and trained teachers in more than six countries and proudly served as a Peace Corps volunteer in Korea. Along with her husband, she coauthored an ESL writing series and contributed to a grammar series.

PART 1

PEDAGOGY

CHAPTER 1

A Funny Thing Happened to Me on the Way to the Museum: From Collaborative Inquiry to Transformative Pedagogy

Usha Venkatesh, Michael Berman, Henry Caballero, Sherrie Carroll, and Judith Gaines

"So, what I get is not what I see?"
"No! What you get is what you make of what you see."
"And what do I see?"
"What someone wants you to see."
"So someone controls what I see, and I control what I make of it?"
"Precisely."
"What is that called?"
"Reading."
"Reading what?"
"Reading anything—including my face."

FRAMING THE ISSUE

We, the authors of this chapter, Usha Venkatesh, Mike Berman, Henry Caballero, Sherrie Carroll, and Judith Gaines, teach English as a second language (ESL) at Montgomery College in Rockville, Maryland, in the United States. Montgomery College, Maryland's largest community college with three campuses, has a well-established ESL program for more than two thousand students from more than 170 counties. We are also members of a faculty cohort participating in a Smithsonian Faculty Fellows Program, which is a partnership between the community college and the Smithsonian Institution.

The fellows program enables the multidiscipline cohort to participate in a series of seminars in which museum curators discuss the curatorial process of a particular exhibit and relate it to a theme chosen for each year. Faculty engage in critical discussions with the curators and then transform the curriculum in one or more of the courses they teach to include a museum visit as well as pedagogy emerging from their participation in the program. Although we experienced the program differently from our different positions at the college and in our own professional lives, there is overwhelming consensus among us regarding one outcome—the tremendous pedagogical implications of such a program and the wealth of teaching and learning opportunities provided by the use of museums as extended ESL classrooms.

In this chapter, we use excerpts from our individual narratives to tell a collective story of the Smithsonian partnership as a professional development model and describe the pedagogy generated by this professional development activity. We also look at how the pedagogy works in the classroom and discuss ways in which other community colleges may build collaborative partnerships with cultural institutions in their communities.

∷ NARRATIVE

A Museum/Community College Partnership

Why a partnership between a community college and a cultural institution? What happens for faculty during their fellowship year? What specific implications does this type of faculty professional development have for ESL faculty in higher education?

In 1997 Montgomery College and the Smithsonian embarked on a visionary project, joining resources and talents to establish the first partnership in the country between the Smithsonian Institution and a community college. Funded by a National Endowment for the Humanities Challenge Grant, the Smithsonian's Center for Museum Studies and the college's Paul Peck Humanities Institute created the Paul Peck Humanities Institute/Smithsonian Faculty Fellows Seminars, offering faculty at Montgomery the opportunity to participate as members of a community of scholars in a yearlong seminar on a single theme.

Each year since then, twelve to fifteen faculty members from different disciplines have participated in yearlong seminars covering a broad range of scholarly topics. Using the primary source materials of the Smithsonian complex of museums and working directly with scholars who are conducting research using museum resources, faculty pursue studies and new approaches to teaching and learning designed to provoke thought and action, inspire values, and develop new insights and knowledge.

In her narrative, Gaines, the current director of the Paul Peck Humanities Institute at Montgomery, offers the following reflection:

In 2003, I was appointed as director of the Montgomery College Paul Peck Humanities Institute (PPHI). With its mission to offer faculty, students, and the public programs designed to strengthen the teaching and learning of the humanities at Montgomery and in its larger community, the PPHI is a vibrant intellectual resource. Its centerpiece and treasure is its Smithsonian Faculty Fellows Program, a partnership between the Smithsonian Institution and Montgomery College to develop an innovative, yearlong seminar for Montgomery faculty (fellows). As a former fellow, I knew firsthand the tremendous opportunity for scholarly renewal and pedagogical growth the seminar offered faculty. Now as its director, I would begin to recognize my own commitment to the professional growth and development of my colleagues and, by extension, Montgomery College students.

Faculty apply for the fellowship for different reasons and with varying goals, as Venkatesh, the coordinator of the Faculty Fellows Program, notes,

> I came to the fellows program looking for a new way to extend and consolidate theories and practices that I had been working with and through in recent years.

In her narrative, Carroll recalls how being part of a cohort attracted her to the program:

> The theme was to be inclusion and would be centered on the upcoming *Brown v. Board of Education* exhibit. I was immediately seduced. I loved the theme . . . and yet, I was perhaps even more attracted to the experience that I could have. I loved the idea of being a part of a cohort of faculty who were both following the path of individual inquiry and supporting one another in the development of our pedagogical projects. My day-to-day work at the college, largely administrative, did not lend itself to these kinds of scholarly collaborations. In all honesty, it was this process, the fun I would have as part of a group of faculty going behind the scenes of the museum with the curators, which propelled me into the fellows program far more than the thought of the pedagogical product that I would create.

Caballero, in his narrative, notes the difference between the growth possible through this professional development model and those commonly available:

> Most professional development programs at our institution consist of workshops and seminars that an education major takes in graduate school to prepare for working as a professional educator, what I call the nuts and bolts of teaching (i.e., lesson planning, classroom management, teaching in a multicultural environment, assessment techniques, integrating technology, educational psychology). Although I attended these workshops with a plan to use what I learned, I rarely gained any "new" insights. I discovered that the Humanities Institute on our campus offered a unique professional development opportunity called the Smithsonian Fellowship. I immediately became interested in participating as a Smithsonian Fellow. Although I did not completely understand the work involved, I knew that the fellowship involved a one-year commitment with an obligation to incorporate museum visits in the curriculum. What I did not know was that this fellowship

would tremendously influence my teaching. During the second semester of the fellowship, my teaching paradigm was altered in a positive way.

ESL Teachers as Culture Brokers

As faculty engage in the seminars during the first semester of their fellowship, they begin to understand the structure of the museum as an educational institution, the curatorial process, and the complexities involved in *culture brokerage*. The organization of cultural institutions (e.g., museums) differs dramatically from the discipline-based scholarship model of higher education. While college offerings are organized departmentally to engage students in discipline-based knowledge, cultural institutions are places of self-initiated learning where ideas, information, and knowledge are available to be assimilated at will, with no prescribed sequence. Museums do see themselves as educational, and curators consider themselves to be part of academia. However, the freedoms and constraints imposed on this particular form of organization are very different from those that we, as academics, are used to. For example, the curator may or may not have the academic freedom to include or exclude materials used in the exhibit. Moreover, once the exhibit has been put together and opened up to the public, the curator, like an author and unlike a teacher, is not present to direct the course of interpretation. During the seminars, faculty interact with curators to discuss issues of representation, authenticity, authority, funding, external control, and so forth as they apply to the curatorial process. These discussions give the multidisciplinary faculty much on which to reflect as they begin to conceptualize their pedagogical projects.

Faculty also come to understand the role of curator as *culture broker.* In Kurin's (1997) book *Reflections of a Culture Broker: A View from the Smithsonian* (a mainstay for the fellows), the author notes:

> Representations of peoples, culture, and institutions do not just happen. They are mediated, negotiated, and, yes, brokered through often complex processes with myriad challenges and constraints imposed by those involved, all of whom have their own interests and concerns. In the end, a series of decisions is made to represent some one, some place, some thing in a particular way. (p. 13)

He explains that while brokerage is not a term many professionals like to have applied to what they do because it somehow seems to cheapen their lofty goals, good brokering is, in fact, a difficult, complex, and necessary means of representation. He suggests that there are many models of representation, ranging from the extractive model in which the scholar takes elements of culture from others, studies them, writes about them, and displays them, to a "flea market" approach in which anyone who in some way qualifies as being from or of the culture gets "a table, or stage, or room, or lectern, or home page into or onto which he or she can put out the stuff of the culture" (p. 19).

However, "if there is to be any type of mediation in representing culture, any agency involved on behalf of the represener, the represented, and the audience to whom they are represented, brokerage is involved" (p. 19). As Kurin half jokingly points out, if we can have everything from peace brokers to pawn brokers, why not culture brokers?

Herein lies one of the program's links to the field of TESOL. As ESL instructors, we are keenly aware that learning a target language is intrinsically linked to understanding the workings of the target culture, and, as such, language teachers inevitably become culture brokers. As Caballero explains,

> I have become acutely aware that I interpret and represent not only the American culture but also the American academic culture for my students. Since inquiry, constructing knowledge, and critical literacy are key components to our higher education system, I attempt to give my students opportunities to build their own knowledge and not directly tell them what I want them to think. I ask them to make judgments and opinions about the exhibits and how the artifacts, documents, and subjects are represented. Some students complain because they would rather I tell them what to think. This student mentality results from the student being accustomed to educators thinking for them and their own lack of confidence. When ESL students "think" through an exhibit, they learn how to better express their ideas and gain more confidence in their ideas. As ESL professors, we are all responsible for "brokering" our course content and empowering our students.

Berman, in his narrative, extends the notion of culture brokerage to encompass not only the role of instructors but also the learners in a multicultural ESL classroom:

> Not unlike curators at the Smithsonian, we ESL teachers are also culture brokers. We shape meaning. We represent the "culture" of the English language within the walls of our classroom. In fact, our students typically expect this sort of representation. That being the case, our social and political ideologies, however we may try to suppress them, flavor our examples and our explanations. However, in dealing overtly with museum studies—that is, with the ideas of representation and bias in public spaces—I myself have become reminded of and sensitized to the power of my own leanings in the classroom, and, in turn, have sought to sensitize my students to these biases . . . and to their own. That is, just as I may broker U.S. culture in the classroom, my students are representatives of their own cultures, shaping the way I and their peers view their homeland or other elements of their identity. Consequently, I may gently nudge the student who maintains that issues of gender, racial, and ethnic inequalities do not exist in his or her home country. "Would anyone in your country disagree with you?" I ask. "Are there alternative experiences?" This can be touchy stuff indeed. Museum studies provide a tangible, intellectual, nonthreatening entryway into such topics, and it empowers students to "read" and question their surroundings, their teacher included.

For Venkatesh, cultural brokerage is related to varying interpretations students make of her identity:

> What I represent to my students has always intrigued me. Some see a nonnative speaker, an immigrant, who has mastered the target language sufficiently to have convinced "them" (native speakers) to "let me teach their language" (quotes from teaching evaluations). They also see me as able to better comprehend the struggles of language learners, even be more sympathetic to their failures. Some may see my demands for accuracy or higher standards as somehow more unreasonable than those coming from my native-speaker colleagues. Others see my classes as learning the language secondhand, and a student once told me, "No offense, but if I am going to learn this, I would rather it was from the Original." The multiple ways in which my students see me as an English teacher allow me to problematize the notion of representing identities and cultures in essential ways. By bringing into play my own multiple identities as Indian, immigrant, American, English teacher, and so on, I feel I am in a great space from which to broker the language and the culture and allow students to see the complexities involved in the process. Museum studies gives me a deliberate way to do this—it is not always "international night"!

Pedagogical Transformations

While the professional seminars are undoubtedly intellectually challenging, the question remains: how do they manifest in pedagogical practice? In attempting to incorporate the museum experience into our curricula, we have discovered that it lends itself to a variety of pedagogies, strategies, and activities. For example, several of us have found the incorporation of museum studies into our courses to be a useful venue for our critical practice, in which we help students contextualize their experiences and their understandings of self within greater understandings of larger social and cultural structures.

> The fellows program has become a place for me to develop my pedagogy in the direction that I want to take it. In my course, I have found great value in constructivist approaches in which students explore their experiences through autobiographical writing, leading them to develop greater understandings of their lives and themselves. I have wanted to combine this approach with transformative pedagogy, a pedagogy that would encourage them to see beyond their personal experiences and question larger societal structures that result in power, privilege, and oppression, integrating their experiences within this newfound understanding to ultimately see themselves and their worlds differently. My Smithsonian Fellows project has given me the very concrete opportunity to try to put into practice these abstract goals that I have been developing for my pedagogy. (from Carroll's narrative)

> My classroom pedagogy has been shaped by critical and transformative pedagogies. My adult nonnative students of English critically examine texts, and, applying insights gained through the analysis, draw upon and reflect on their own life

experiences, thus expanding experiential knowledge to a larger context. The potential for language use generated by this activity is stupendous and very rewarding for the learners as it provides a framework in which to understand a culturally different world around them and be able to express thoughts and opinions about the same with grounding in their own worldview. It also allows for the teacher and the students to accommodate different learning styles and levels of language proficiency. In this context, using the museum exhibit as "text" has done wonders to my pedagogy and my students' course experience.

"Reading" a museum exhibit as "text" fits very well with the basic concept of reading as an interpretation or decoding of subject material that has been "represented" or encoded. An exhibit is the representation of some cultural material and automatically becomes a coded text. The process of decoding this text provides an interesting and challenging arena for language use. For adult nonnative speakers, it provides a ready forum to decode verbal and nonverbal coding applying analytical skills that they, in most cases, already possess. Classroom pedagogy can take them further into decoding and understanding their own cultural experiences through the new lens of interpretation. (from Venkatesh's narrative)

In practical terms, it has led to some very creative and productive activities, the most significant of which is an activity we call "My Life in a Bag." In this activity, a variation on a commonly used school activity, students are asked to place five artifacts that represent their lives or identities in a brown paper bag and present these to their classmates. Classmates attempt to "read" the identity of the student as represented by the artifacts in the bag. From this point on, what the students do with the "reading" depends on the goals and motivations of the teacher. Uses have ranged from a simple icebreaker to detailed demonstrations of the complexities of representation and interpretation. In the ESL classroom, this activity has led to oral and written narrative assignments as well as comparison and contrast studies of the intentions of the "author" of the bag and the interpretations of the "reader" of the artifacts.

In addition to serving as a highly entertaining way for students to learn about each other (and themselves), My Life in a Bag has proven to be a spectacularly effective introduction to the complexities of curatorial choice, representation, and spatial limitation. That is, on top of reinforcing the basic academic oral skills of clarity, organization, and confidence, students must analyze themselves and subsequently select artifacts that fit in their bag to represent chosen facets of their identity . . . or vice versa: define facets of their identity that explain central artifacts in their lives. This is truly a curatorial exercise. Moreover, during the presentation stage, as students proudly, sometimes apprehensively, present their artifacts, other students guess the meanings of the objects before the true significance is revealed. Surprise! Representation isn't easy! The cell phone did not represent the student's proclivity to make phone calls; it was the device with which that student called his mother every day, a symbol of the importance of their relationship. The spiral writing book did not represent the student's interest in prose or poetry or mathematics or school in general; it was the tablet on which the student wrote letters to prison inmates. Car keys did not turn out to represent a red sports car or a passion for driving; they were a metaphor for the student's freedom. I almost cried during that one. (from Berman's narrative)

And so begins the unsuspecting students' orientation to the museum-based assignment that serves as the centerpiece of the semester. It is also the initiation into the cross-cultural element of the course. The My Life in a Bag exercise, for example, is supported with the inside-out approach to cultural awareness, whereby students begin with cultural self-awareness and move to other-culture awareness (Levy 1995). That is, by selecting artifacts of importance to them—a religious text, a favorite piece of traditional clothing, a music CD, a family photo—students necessarily interweave elements of their cultural values including not only elements of ethnicity but also other elements of identity such as gender and age. Students then move to assessing the artifacts of others, first applying their own assumptions to the artifacts and then learning the true significance of the items. Once one includes artifacts in the curriculum, "[they] are always present and available for exploration to help deepen one's understanding of language/culture" (Fantini and Fantini 1997, 57).

While My Life in a Bag is a great starting point, it also becomes rich ground for the concepts of representation, interpretation, and narrative voices to take root. It brings to focus identity issues: issues of whose story and who gets to tell it are important in the process of critical reading. Students begin to question not only what they see but also their own interpretation of it—their lenses, so to speak.

Integration into Curricula

We have used the museum component in many different ways, depending on the theme and course. In the first example, Berman constructs the museum experience for his students along similar lines as the My Life in a Bag activity:

> Students move from predicting vocabulary, verb tenses, specific themes, and artifacts of an exhibit to evaluating their predictions to reporting on the accuracy of their predictions and on what particularly surprised and engaged them. Students also must comment on the meaning and effectiveness of particular artifacts within the exhibit.
>
> In leading students through the assignment a number of times, I have been struck by several pedagogical benefits of this extended-classroom exercise. First, the teaching of prelistening or prereading strategies comes across with particular resonance when done with museum exhibits. In preparing vocabulary lists and devising questions that students think the assigned exhibit(s) will answer, students are palpably buoyed by the innate authenticity of the museum. They are not applying these strategies to a textbook reading or a canned audio lecture; they are preparing for a brick-and-mortar exhibition, an 8,000 square-foot, three-dimensional,

multimillion-dollar product of a team of social scientists. They are preparing to engage an American institution, and, in this case, an institution many had heard of even before moving to the area. Furthermore, this inherent real-world aspect of the museum experience is especially important in the community college setting, where most students are in a hurry, anxious to dive into their content-area interests. The museum gives a true taste of intellectual vigor and substance across the spectrum of academic fields. In sum, it partly satisfies their need to throw off the shackles of preparatory language study and work in the type of authentic environment they have envisioned for themselves.

Second, the very tasks of preliminary research; vocabulary development; and, finally, prediction of an exhibit's themes, central questions, and material artifacts lead naturally into the core ideas of museum study. Did the exhibit address the issues I thought it would? If not, why? What does this say about the biases or limitations of the curators?

Third, like the My Life in a Bag exercise, students learn to handle surprises. Many of their predictions will not be correct, and they will need to revise their paradigm as they walk through the exhibit. If they see some of their vocabulary words they had predicted, these words will often be sandwiched between academic terms they had never seen before, forcing students to apply their guessing strategies on the spot. Also, rather than being drawn to the major aspects of the exhibit(s) they had thought would interest them, students frequently find themselves sucked in by completely unexpected elements, such as music or a photograph.

In Venkatesh's practice, the museum experience becomes one of several components of a multimodal pedagogy:

> The theme of the program that year was "E Pluribus Unum: *From the many, one.*" My students were examining the obstacles to assimilation/acculturation especially with reference to the treatment of immigrants during times of political and economic strife. I had designed the course to use multimodal content. The students were to read a novel pertaining to Japanese internment; watch a documentary related to changes in immigration laws around pre- and post-Depression era; and visit A More Perfect Union, an exhibit at the Smithsonian, depicting the treatment of Japanese immigrants in internment camps.
>
> After several analytical essays on the various "texts," students had to do a term project examining the treatment of Arab Americans in post-9/11 America using the models they had examined in relation to the treatment of other ethnic groups in the past. This project could take the form of an essay, a video, or a poster exhibit. I have no hesitation in saying that in my fifteen years of teaching at the college, these projects produced some of the most outstanding work I have seen from the students. Several factors seem to have contributed to this difference, including
>
> - the challenge presented by the task of relating a portrayal of the past to the reality of their own lives in the present;

- the understanding of the implications of constructing a cultural identity in a multicultural world;

- the impetus they felt to use images, words, and notions gained from an experience so unlike any they had experienced in their traditional classrooms.

When a visit to the museum can be complemented by a written text and a film or other modes of telling a story, students begin to see that they are, in fact, engaged in the act of "reading" almost on a constant basis in life. This realization changes the analytical skills and vocabulary they then employ in writing about their life experiences.

Museum exhibits also lend themselves to discussions of minority and dominant discourse. In the exhibit Separate Is Not Equal: *Brown v. Board,* for example, students were at first tremendously struck by the central display of the Ku Klux Klan (KKK) robe in the entry hall. It impressed them and aroused curiosity, fear, and misgiving, as it was intended to do. When we started discussing their understanding of the events surrounding *Brown v. Board* as portrayed by the exhibit, however, they began to see that they were automatically attributing all anti-black sentiment in the society to the KKK. One of them remarked, "But the exhibit seems to show that all the bad things that African Americans experienced was because of the KKK and that the Supreme Court made it all right again and there are no more KKK problems." Another picked up the thread and pointed out the following:

> They never really say that, but by putting the KKK robe right there in the front and the Supreme Court structure in the beginning of the section on the solutions, they make us think that, if we don't know the rest of the history. I am sure the Blacks didn't see it that way. The KKK was bad, but so was the rest of the society in this matter.

This was followed by the most fruitful discussion I have had with students regarding "othering" and suggestive representation as well as the concepts of dominant and minority discourse.

In Carroll's pedagogy, the museum experience becomes a springboard for examining how individual experiences are situated within larger sociocultural contexts:

> I wanted to take the theme of inclusion, of segregation/integration in education, beyond the historical moment in the United States. I thought this theme of educational inclusion could be quite provocative if looked at from various angles both within the contemporary United States and the students' cultures of origin. We could look at various kinds of segregation and integration (based on race, gender, linguistic ability, class, religion, etc.) and examine what is lost as well as gained when one moves to more inclusive models of education. We could also look at how the education system in the United States (both in higher education and within the public school system) responds to the students and their children as linguistic minorities and how it accommodates their linguistic needs and cultural

identities. I've revised my course so that my students and I can explore the follow-ing questions:

- How does an education system respond to differences?

- What are the results of treating different groups differently in education—of providing differing educations?

- How does this affect the society?

Students explore these questions initially by learning how the education system within the United States has dealt with racial, ethnic, and linguistic differences. They then explore how other cultures (including their culture of origin) address various categories of difference within education and the larger societal ramifica-tion of such inclusive or exclusionary practices. The course culminates with the students writing and revising their educational autobiographies in which they not only tell of their personal experiences within education but also locate these experi-ences, their story, within a larger discussion of the context of schooling in which they were educated. Through this, students are encouraged to explore the nature of both privilege and oppression within education and how this has played out in their lives.

While I have been exploring this transformative pedagogy (both a constructivist and social reconstructivist approach) theoretically through my doctoral work, the fellows program has given me a chance to develop my emerging pedagogy in very concrete terms. In this way, it has helped me move from theory to praxis, to make this transformative pedagogy my own.

What do students think of all this? The true value of the experience can be found in the comments students have made with regard to their understanding of content based on museum visits as extensions of their classroom activities. The following excerpts are from statements made by students in the fall of 2004:

> The Smithsonian gave me a lot of information about discrimination which helped me realize that, as an immigrant, I am in a vulnerable position in this country. Discrimination is a problem that has not been resolved for people are still experi-encing this unfair treatment. These people have many dreams and goals just like me. I belong to this group and I will have to struggle much more than others who don't belong to this group. I had not realized how serious this problem was until I went to the exhibit. Also, this experience has made me tolerate people who look and think differently than me. I learned that tolerance is the way to achieve world peace.

> The Smithsonian exhibit was the first visual lesson I had about racism in America. I now understand why and how black and white people were separated in the past. I think the racial discrimination was wrong. Some of the pictures of the very poor, tired faces of the black children impressed me.

I knew little information about discrimination in the USA. Since I went to see the Smithsonian exhibit, I've changed my way of seeing discrimination as [not only] a racial issue and I started to see it as a trouble that affects everyone that doesn't belong to the dominant class in this country. . . . Particularly, I am impressed by all the different sights of the exhibition because they showed me the reality of segregation at that time in the U.S. Every ambient conveyed the pain, terror and frustration that defined the African-American's regrets. . . . People are still wounded and probably fed up because of all those years of segregation and humiliation.

⠶ PROFESSIONAL RESONANCE

The Smithsonian Faculty Fellows Program and its pedagogical implications go beyond the professional revitalization of faculty in one community college in metropolitan Washington, DC. Its beauty is that it can be duplicated in almost any community college and modified to suit most teaching styles. Most communities have museums, galleries, and other similar institutions that broker culture and are willing to partner with educational institutions to bring about learning experiences. Community colleges typically are rooted in the community and take pride in using local resources. In a cyber world, most exhibits of the Smithsonian Institution are also available online in a virtual gallery. Thus, museums provide

- culturally rich and intellectually challenging materials;

- authentic verbal text;

- artifacts and visuals that help both high- and low-proficiency learners;

- concrete examples of coding, decoding, and recoding;

- ready access to materials.

Moreover, taking our students into the museums empowers our programs and puts ESL instruction on a different playing field in higher education. For too long, ESL instruction has held a marginalized place in higher education, and the students are often seen as underprepared for college work. Professional organizations like TESOL have argued for the place of ESL alongside other foreign language programs. Transforming our curricula to include such activities as museum visits draws attention to our students as intellectually competent and capable of handling complex materials.

As a professional development program, the fellowship has many advantages. Being a fellow is like having a mentorship with educators from many disciplines. A single mentor or multiple peer mentors have a significant effect on a faculty's productivity and growth. Mentoring also empowers faculty members in that they are better able to analyze and solve complex problems (Luna and Cullen 1995). Because the fellowship involves participation in a cohort of faculty from different disciplines, one can garner valuable ideas from several more experienced professors. In other words, the knowledge gained is more than just ESL specific. Subsequently, fellows also learn from the curators.

From the very beginning, the seminar discussions have provided much food for thought. A true teacher-learner is constantly reflecting on theory and practice and perfecting one's teaching. The fellowship gives us an opportunity to be teacher-learners. In the beginning I was shy and quiet like an outsider because I still grapple with feeling out of place, that is, being a minority teacher who teaches a minority subject. Mentoring programs for minority faculty members should consider:

1. Pairing minority faculty who need to build their research and scholarship with senior scholars

2. Developing parameters and including goals that address nontraditional protégé concerns

3. Not assuming that minority faculty know the "rules of the game"

4. Exhibiting cultural sensitivity and learning about the backgrounds of the minority faculty (Luna and Cullen 1995, 60)

For me, the fellowship puts this advice to practice. Now I feel more empowered and confident about what I want to do in the classroom. In a way, being involved in the seminars is like going through an acculturation process. (from Caballero's narrative)

The ultimate beneficiaries are, of course, the students. Research and theories have exalted the use of culture-rich, authentic, content-based texts that students can relate to as the most productive in second language acquisition. When adult learners of a target language are engaged in activities requiring higher-level thinking skills in the target language, they are more likely to attempt complex structures and take risks in the use of the language. It is through this risk taking, which does not come easily to adult learners, that language is best acquired. The museum experience puts students in the middle of the action, whether they are simply reporting on what they see or questioning the dominant or minority nature of the discourse presented to them.

▪▪ INSTITUTIONAL CHALLENGES

Whereas an individual instructor could incorporate the museum experience into a particular course with relative ease, instituting the larger program complete with its collaborative professional development component presents some institutional challenges. Cultural institutions and community colleges may be found in thousands of communities across the nation. The Smithsonian Faculty Fellows Program established for the first time a model for working relationships between community colleges and museums. With the seminar firmly established at Montgomery College, its replication and dissemination to a national audience of community colleges is a natural extension. Through distance learning, community college faculty can either join the seminars for Montgomery College faculty with Smithsonian curators using Smithsonian online exhibits or adapt the existing model to develop their own collaborative partnerships with local cultural institutions.

Crucial to the success of a collaborative partnership between a community college and a cultural institution is the determination of institutional readiness. How will a professional development seminar that intellectually revitalizes community college faculty benefit all segments of the community college and the wider community it serves? What important administrative and programmatic challenges need to be addressed when developing an innovative collaborative initiative between a community college and a cultural institution? With heavy teaching loads leaving little time for scholarly renewal, how can community college faculty continue to teach and participate in an important professional development seminar? What level of in-kind support is the community college willing to provide, including partial release time for its faculty, additional staff support, and the reallocation of program resources?

Recognizing a mutually reinforcing relationship between college attendance and learning in the informal setting of museums, Montgomery College has agreed to provide annually up to twelve faculty members with release time from one class for two semesters to participate as fellows in the Smithsonian seminar. Every spring and fall, the faculty fellows receive release time from one three-credit class. Though the number of faculty fellows varies from year to year, the college provides approximately thirty-six hours of faculty release time each semester. The seminar meets the college's priority to develop innovative, challenging curricula for all its students, thereby justifying faculty release time. By bringing Montgomery students in contact with the museums of the Smithsonian, the faculty fellows continue to exceed the expectations of the college to encourage higher academic endeavors and aspirations in its students. With more than seventy former and current faculty fellows teaching courses with Smithsonian components, at an average of twenty-five students per course, the college sends approximately one thousand students each semester to the Smithsonian.

The annual seminar is planned and developed by a former faculty fellow serving as a program coordinator on partial release time. The coordinator is responsible for the design and development of the annual seminar and the coordination of the program between the college and the Smithsonian Institution. The coordinator works with the Smithsonian to develop a seminar theme, selects seminar readings, and oversees the Smithsonian's development of the individual seminars with college faculty and museum curators. In the fall, the coordinator plans six on-campus meetings of the fellows to discuss the spring seminar and its impact on the fellows' scholarship and pedagogy and to present museum-based classroom projects. Five percent of one full-time administrative associate's position is allocated to the administrative support of the seminar. Other support includes the purchase of books and materials for the fellows and stipends for independent research during the summer.

⊞ EXTENDING THE DIALOGUE

The intellectual challenges of the Smithsonian Faculty Fellows Program and pedagogical innovations inspired by it have reshaped our understandings of representation, of interpretation, and, indeed, of language teaching. As teacher-learners, we have benefited from looking at a nontraditional modality (i.e., exhibit as text) and examining the complexities of encoding and decoding text in that modality. In teaching our students to "read" all kinds of texts, especially on the subject of culture, we have, as a faculty, learned to critically examine our own lenses and make students aware of theirs. Incorporating a multidimensional text (like an exhibit) in the ESL classroom provides an accessible way to have students examine and practice complex concepts such as representation, interpretation, and identity. We hope that our fruitful experiences with this program will prompt other explorations of nontraditional venues to enhance ESL curricula. The irony is that as teachers most of us go into the task seeking to transform our students, and, in the process, it is we ourselves who become most transformed.

⊞ CONTRIBUTORS

Usha Venkatesh is a professor in the Department of Reading, English Language, Foreign Languages, and Philosophy at Montgomery College in Rockville, Maryland, in the United States. She has been teaching English to nonnative speakers for more than twenty-two years in a variety of learning environments. She is currently the coordinator of the Faculty Fellows Program for the Paul Peck Humanities Institute.

Michael Berman is associate professor of English as a second language at Montgomery College and is coordinator of the college's American English Language Program. In addition to writing numerous books and articles, he has authored the award-winning ESL software series Advanced Listening (DynEd International).

Henry Caballero has presented workshops and teacher training on integrating technology; learning language in early childhood, in adult literacy, and as a second language; creating parental involvement opportunities; and discovering techniques to bridge the culture gap. He holds a master's degree in bilingual education from Texas A&M University–Corpus Christi in the United States.

Sherrie Carroll is senior program director for the noncredit ESL program at Montgomery College. She has taught ESL and EFL in university and community college settings since 1987. She is a doctoral candidate at the University of Maryland, where she studies multilingual identity (re)construction, TESOL, teacher education, and transformative pedagogy.

Judith Gaines is director of the Paul Peck Humanities Institute at Montgomery College, where she has been a faculty member in the Department of Reading, English Language, Foreign Languages, and Philosophy since 1991. She has developed numerous faculty professional development projects and public programs in the humanities. She is the managing editor of Potomac Review: A Journal of Arts and Humanities.

CHAPTER 2

Caminante Si Hay Caminos: Toward a Postcritical ESL Approach for Community Colleges

::

J. Andrés Ramírez

:: FRAMING THE ISSUE

Formal schooling, in its mainstream form, has traditionally functioned as an ideological state apparatus consciously created to regulate social order and maintain current social arrangements (Althusser 1971; Aronowitz and Giroux 1993; Bowles and Gintis 1976; Resnick and Wolff 1987; Willis 1981). In the United States, this assertion is usually backed up historically by a series of events during the so-called Age of Reform or the U.S. Progressive Era (1880–1920), which roughly coincides with the first stage of the development of so-called junior colleges (Deegan, Tillery, and ERIC Clearinghouse for Junior Colleges 1985).

Historically, class stratification at the community college level can be seen as a struggle between two missions: transfer and vocational. In this context, the junior college focus on providing "junior" access to four-year institutions began to be challenged in favor of terminal and vocational education that provided "work training." This mission transition has been explained as a "topdown leadership conspiracy to promote vocationalization" (Richardson and Richard 1990, 53; see also Brint and Karabel 1989).

One important example of this top-down tendency was a report by the

---

The Spanish title means "Traveler there are roads." This chapter evolved out of the presentation "Exploring Connections between ESL and Critical Pedagogy" delivered at the 38th Annual TESOL Convention and Exhibit in Long Beach, California, in the United States, March 30–April 3, 2004.

Carnegie Foundation for the Advancement of Teaching in California. Members of the Carnegie panel (called the Commission of the Seven) led what was essentially a class struggle to vocationalize junior colleges, hoping to impede the intuitive historical student resistance toward terminal education. Not surprisingly, the report rejected the transfer function as the main function and unanimously endorsed the provision of "terminal education for the majority of students" (Brint and Karabel 1989, 48). Indeed, the panel went further and rejected the label "junior colleges" because these colleges were not really part of the system of higher education but the last stage of secondary education; they were senior to all common schooling below it (Brint and Karabel 1989).

This deliberate attempt to create a two-tiered educational system that provides vocational school for the lower or less capable classes and classical school for the dominant classes and intellectuals has been pursued vociferously and openly by leaders in community colleges and privileged universities. Sociologist Amitai Etzioni from Columbia University writes, "If we can no longer keep the floodgates closed at the admissions office, it at least seems wise to channel the general flow away from four-year colleges and toward two-year extensions of high school in the junior and community colleges" (quoted in Bowles and Gintis 1976, 204). In this view, community colleges were to take charge of the youth problem. This remedial focus destined colleges to assume "the residual responsibility for youth" and, thus, to enroll disproportionate numbers of minorities and students with poor academic skills and historic trends of poor retention (Cross 1985, 44).

As a consequence, many authors consider that terms and missions associated with community colleges such as *open door, people's college, democratic institutions,* and so on are just part of rhetoric that is not backed up by the history of this institution (Bowles and Gintis 1976; Brint 2003; Brint and Karabel 1989; Clark 1960; Dougherty 1994; Karabel 1972; Richardson and Richard 1990; Shaw and Jacobs 2003; Zwerling 1986). In fact, in the past fifteen years, the educational discourse in general has shifted from education as a human right to education as a government investment (Comber 1997). The already described initial impetus that brought the community college to life persists today in the form of managerial discourses such as "lifelong learning" (Bagnall 2000; Collins 1991; Martin 2001). Under such a philosophy, and under present conditions of teachers' work intensification (Hargreaves 1994, 2003) and deskilling of teachers' work (Luke 1998), traditional English as a second language (ESL) pedagogy ends up being the most common pedagogy in the ESL community college classrooms. As I demonstrate in this chapter by showing pedagogical practices that are anything but traditional, nontraditional classroom practices acknowledge students' differences, needs, strengths, and decisive role in shaping the curriculum; furthermore, these practices may help students attain higher educational levels.

Because the community college is a preferred institution for minority students, and since many of those minority students do not have English as a first language, ESL classes become a logical first option for these students to have contact with the institution. In the following section, I map out how the ESL field has been influenced by broader ideologies outside of the field as well as by internal conditions or *thought collectives* pertaining to its academic roots and purposes to argue in favor of a postcritical approach for community college ESL.

Thought Collectives: Shaping English Language Teaching and Learning

Thought collectives refer to a relatively stable disciplinary community, to an individual program or discipline of teachers in training, or to strategic patterns of thought that originate in group existence and collective action. They are defined as "a thought structure that belongs to the collective" (Ramanathan 2002, 5). In recent years, some researchers (Block 2003; Bloome 1989; Canagarajah 1993, 1999a, 1999b; Egan-Robertson and Willett 1998; Gebhard 1999; Gee 1992; Larsen-Freeman and Long 1991; Rodby 1992; Willett 1995) have challenged the field of second language acquisition (SLA) and its dominant patterns of thought. One of the main criticisms deals with SLA's focus on the individual to explain second language learning and its consequent treatment of social context as a mere variable that influences individual learning that is located in the individual's mind (Rodby 1992). This has caused an overreliance on the individual as opposed to the social, the objective as opposed to the interpretative, and the nonpolitical as opposed to the political. According to Rodby, this has been, in part, a result of linguistic theory. Linguistics has contributed, as no other discipline, to the confusion that many ESL teachers face when dealing with the teaching of reading and writing.

Linguistic tradition (at least in the United States) has been responsible not only for the individual and mentalist character of SLA theory but also for the overreliance on language teaching that defines language as a set of prescriptive rules and not as a set of choices that are functional to communicative purposes in different situations (Eggins 1994; Halliday 1994). This prescriptive pedagogy sees language as an end and not as a means as it prioritizes form over content. More important, it prevents students from acquiring anything beyond what Dell Hymes calls communicative competence and leaves students with no sense or possibility to question the world around them (quoted in Canale and Swain 1980). Unintentionally, well-meaning ESL teachers end up educating in a vacuum and thus contribute to the reaffirmation of the status quo because this lack of content (other than the one related to the "right" language proficiency) prevents students and teachers from accessing critical positions to work toward the construction of alternative social class arrangements (Benesch 2001).

By making use of sociocultural, critical, and postmodern theories that inform their research agendas, these researchers began redrawing the boundaries of SLA theory and practice, moved it away from the individual's mind, and broadened the scope of the SLA field to a social practice. Along with the criticism of the SLA field, a challenge to the agencies that have traditionally studied second/foreign language teaching and learning, in particular TESOL, has also been carried out. Specifically, this organization has been questioned for the supposed "apolitical" nature of its instructional objectives and goals, which have, more often than not, uncritically engaged with English language teaching and very little with the sociocultural impact of its spread around the world. Until recently, challenges came from isolated theorists drawing on critical theory and postmodern studies (Canagarajah 1999a, 1999b; Ramanathan 2002) who have more vigorously carried out this criticism by demonstrating TESOL's political agenda. Recently, however, challenges have been carried out from inside TESOL by members of the TESOL caucus known as TESOLers for Social Responsibility.

Yet, and despite the need to study all sorts of ESL practices in detail, these initiatives are in need of academically sound studies that link these alternative theories with educational settings. They need studies in English language teaching that build not only on publications that approach the subject from a macroscopic perspective as is the case with Pennycook (1994) and Phillipson (1992) but also from the everyday classroom practices of ESL teachers and students such as the one I am proposing. More important, there is a need for studies that emphasize the connection between content and language practices at the micro level (i.e., the classroom) and broader historical, economic, and political forces as mediated by institutional practices. (Good examples are Canagarajah 1993, 1999b.)

By engaging in the kind of research that connects the micro and the macro and that favors a pedagogical approach that goes along with such a research agenda, teacher-researchers can begin to uncover and successfully challenge traditional ESL pedagogy and the ideology upon which it is based. To do so, practitioners and researchers alike need to reject positions that lead to thinking about the educational institution (and the community college in particular) not only as an open canvas where masses are uncritically trained and domesticated into accepting their subordinate destiny but also as contested terrain where ideological struggles are and should be fought. As ESL teachers in an institution that traditionally considers ESL curricula at best developmental and at worst remedial, we should regain our role as intellectuals (Giroux 1988) by finding ways to fight the powerful inertia of falling into traditional pedagogies.

Thought Collectives in Action

In this chapter, I demonstrate a nontraditional pedagogical approach and explore some of the problems I encountered. My underlying assumption is that action research is an extension of any critical literacy attempt. In this approach, I applied critical pedagogy principles to the traditional language and function objectives of an advanced ESL listening and speaking class that serves (along with a reading and writing course) as a transition into mainstream classes at a community college and documented practices through action research methods. I used this combined approach and reflected upon it using action research principles during several semesters in a three-year period. Representative pedagogical examples from the classroom revealing curricular, language, and content adjustments show how students positioned themselves in different ways than they had in more traditional classes.

In addition, these examples show how the framework had a positive influence on students' learning by making explicit how students appropriated, built awareness, and changed many of their attitudes on academic topics dealing both with social justice issues and language goals that pertained to the course. Finally, I conclude with a self-critique addressing the dangers and limitations of this approach in the hope of making a statement against essentialist proposals. Instead, this experience should be seen as an open invitation to teachers to conduct their own examination of the specific conditions and faculties of their students and to adopt a postcritical approach that best suits their own context. To be sure, the postcritical approach proposed here not only has the reflection component inherent in traditional critical approaches but also is informed by continuous action on such reflections.

∷ NARRATIVE

Context

Holyoke Community College in Holyoke, Massachusetts, in the United States, has a long history of immigration. The most recent immigrant ESL students are Puerto Rican and Russian. The ESL program at Holoyke can be described as transitional but without any native language component. The purpose of this five-level program is to provide ESL learners with enough English so that they can enter into mainstream programs at the college. Each level provides a listening and speaking class and a reading and writing class. There are also three grammar classes and one pronunciation class.

Although the ESL classes at Holyoke are tailored to make use of language that is comprehensible to students (or at least at their language level), the focus is not on academic content. The program focuses on language skills such as understanding classroom instructions and speech phrased in the grammatical structures of the level, understanding simple material with the aid of a bilingual dictionary, organizing and giving short planned presentations using structures appropriate for the level, and so forth. In many cases these courses do not provide students with subject matter that prepares them to cope with the academic content they will find in mainstream programs (Faltis and Hudelson 1998; Kelley 1993).

(Re)Appropriating Catastrophe

Before becoming familiar with the principles guiding critical pedagogy, I was the perfect example of a traditional ESL teacher; I was in an "alignment" mode with traditional teaching English as a second language (TESL) thought collectives. During my undergraduate years, I was trained to teach language skills in an integrated way and to train students in word-, sentence-, and paragraph-attack skills such as predicting from context, guessing meaning from lexical and syntactical clues, and using reading comprehension techniques such as skimming and scanning. During these years and after completing a specialization in language teaching in Colombia, my native country, and receiving a master's degree in TESL in the United States, I saw the teaching of content along with language as an elective subject just like the use of language and technology or literature for language teaching.

After finishing my master's degree in 2001, I began exploring the North Americanized[1] idea of critical pedagogy influenced by Freire and followed by Shor, Giroux, Apple, and McLaren, among others. I soon realized that critical pedagogy of this kind was impossible to realize having only language as the content. Soon after, the events of September 11 interrupted my traditional skills-based course. By the middle of the semester we were right on track again with the content we were to cover. Without even noticing, we had created a safe place in which we could concentrate on learning English without outside noise, even when such a phenomenon was constantly whistling into our ears. By the end of the course, it became evident that the course as it was designed did not enable us to even respond, let alone analyze our silence and paralysis, to the current events affecting our lives. This is when I decided to appropriate this catastrophe as a pedagogical turning point and transformed it into the project described here. I was entering a "creative alignment" mode (MacDonald 1987, 5) characterized by my individual appropriation and adaptation to TESL thought collectives.

---

[1] It is necessary to differentiate this topic or field-based critique version of critical pedagogy from the Australian one. The Australian school has criticized the North American school on the grounds that it treats critical literacy as a possession and thus may be as reproductive as any other type of literacy. Australians give priority to genre appropriation (frequently written texts) and consider that "what really matters is what is done with a text rather than the kind of texts you own or choose to read" (Veel and Coffin 1996, 226).

Critical Pedagogy and Saving the World

Right after that moment, I was fortunate to attend a seminar on reading at the University of Massachusetts Amherst, which concentrated on critical pedagogy and literacy. I decided to try this approach with my students and to follow action research principles to document my analysis and change. In this section, I comment on some selections from different journal entries that capture my initial "saving the world" approach to critical literacy:

> I became engaged in critical literacy in my classroom by chance. Nothing around me was really pushing me to change. . . . I stopped seeing myself and the English I taught as natural and beneficial; I began seeing myself and my English instruction as carriers of ideology and as agents of the status quo. . . . Then, while reading Freire's (1998) book *Teachers as Cultural Workers,* I came across two ideas that gave me strength to just go ahead and begin my daring project. The first of them was a phrase from Antonio Machado's poem: "Caminante no hay camino, se hace camino al andar [Traveler, there is no road. The road is made as one walks]." This idea taught me that it would be impossible to have everything planned a priori because my students needed to be part of the process in shaping the curriculum.

The idea of mutually constructing the "classroom practices road" with students was an important advancement in my philosophy because in making the road as one walks, one is engaged in not just a constant creative process but one that is also shared with others. I knew that this process would involve showing the limitation of my knowledge, but I was glad to take the chance if it was instrumental in acknowledging and recognizing students as equally important in the construction of the road. But one question still remained unanswered. Why bother?

> The second idea was taken from Freire himself. He contends that "We must dare, in the full sense of the word, to speak of love without being called ridiculous, mawkish, or unscientific, if not antiscientific . . . we must dare so that we can continue to do so even when it is so much more materially advantageous to stop daring." . . . In reading Freire's words I felt the strength to express that it was the love for my students that was really pushing me to do something differently.

The co-construction of the road approach, paired up with my sense of hope and love, led me to suggest social justice topics that my ESL students would be interested in pursuing and from which I would be learning as well. This is what I wrote in my journal about the issue:

> Now I had a real dilemma since I knew nothing about social justice issues. It was then when hope, love, and my eyes set on the stars kept me going. I found *Teaching for Social Justice* (Ayers, Hunt, and Quinn 1998) and in it an encouraging article by Bill Bigelow (1998) called "The Human Lives behind the Labels: The Global Sweatshop, Nike, and the Race to the Bottom." That article set the beginning of my interest in global economy and its consequences in our daily lives.

In sum, my deep sense of social responsibility and love for humankind led me to transitorily abandon the pedagogical terrain in which I felt most secure and enter into the uncertain but fulfilling proposal I was envisioning: I wanted to empower students and myself so that we would know a little more about topics that have been considered tough and exclusive (such as the global economy) and how they touched every aspect of our lives. The following section looks at how the course developed and how this initial perspective on critical literacy evolved into what I call a postcritical ESL approach.

Reaching Out: Taking Action

At the beginning of the semester, and following the direction of critical literacy theorists, I began stressing that we, as a class, were to learn about the global economy and take some kind of action. This was essential because, as the next examples make clear, it was through this project that we could see how students needed to explore topics in a critical and meaningful way and invest themselves in collaborative ways with peers to reach a common goal. I made sure they understood that in looking for a way to take some kind of action, I was not looking for anything in particular and that the actions we took needed to be co-constructed. As a requirement for the class, I wanted them to prepare, practice, and deliver a fifteen- to twenty-minute presentation in front of an audience.

As a result, students engaged in different critical projects to reach outside the classroom. One project was to find out why the clothes sold in the college store were made in countries other than the United States. After creating questions in class, three students interviewed the store manager, took notes, and recorded the interview. The following is an excerpt:

> He said that before those people start to work for the college they do an investigation and if they see that they work for sweatshops, they don't take the factories. I believe that maybe he was saying the true but you never know what is there. I am not saying that he is lie but I believe they work with sweatshop because they have a lot of clothes that are made in Mexico and other clothes that have to be with sweatshops.

As part of the minipresentation that every student had to prepare for the final presentation, these students reported back to the class and were excited about the interview. Once the group heard this information, we decided that a good way to reach out was to conduct two major oral presentations outside of class: one was done in a friendlier environment (ESL groups that included teachers and students they knew), and the other was in front of an open college audience. This later presentation included showing the video *Sweating for a T-Shirt* (Mendonça and Franco 1998), which was familiar to the students because we had seen it in class. Student investment and willingness to engage in this project is captured in the following quote from a student:

30

The most hard part for me is to hear about this, and sit here in my bed thinking what we can do to stop this. It is really hard for me to understand what is happening in this world. A world that everyone do whatever they want without any concern. If I can do something for this is to let people know about this and ask them what they think about this. I feel really bad about those kids but I really understand why they do this hard work, but is not heart in these people who don't care about these children's future.

An excerpt from the first presentation delivered in one of the three ESL classrooms they visited follows.[2] It is important to note that presenters distributed roles and presentation parts for both presentations based on their own expertise or competency to accomplish a common goal. This rough transcription is followed by a student's vivid comments on her experience in delivering the second presentation to the whole community.

The Global Sweatshop Presentation

ANDREA: We are going to talk about children who are working outside [the home]. Do you think that it's fair for these 10-year-old children to work in this factory?

No? [*Students nod negatively.*] Why?

STUDENT 1: I think at that age, they need to go to school first.

ANDREA: Education and their childhood. Why children? Because they're easy to exploit and really cheap. They do not complain about overtime and they work the hours that their masters tell them. How does the master treat the children? When they cry for their parents they are hit with a bamboo or with any heavy object so that they don't escape. Why? They work too slow. So imagine, your nephew . . . somebody, a little kid tied like a dog to a machine and with no time to go to the bathroom and crying because they don't see their parents.

ROBERTO: You have these papers? [*referring to the cartoon*] Do you? [*shows a cartoon depicting a worker who is being sold to the bidder who pays less instead of more*]

STUDENT 2: It's supposed to go up. [*Student is referring to the cartoon in which the "product" (in this case, the worker) is usually sold to the one that offers more, not less.*]

TEACHER: I think it means that wherever the labor is cheapest, that's where you are going to have the most sweatshops. And that is where countries such as the United States profit because they get a lot of mass production.

---

[2] The edited video of this presentation is available in digital format. To request this video, please send a self-addressed envelope, a money order or check for $10 (U.S. dollars), and a written statement protecting the students' identities and explaining how the material will be used to J. Andrés Ramírez, 829 Mystery Lane, West Chester, PA 19382.

ROBERTO: They are offering less money to pay an employee. I'm going to give you a quick example of what race to the bottom is. Nike was still making their products in the United States. They were paying people $5.50 an hour [*writes on the board*]. People were working 40 hours a week and of course they had insurance, they had benefits. Going to Mexico could represent more money for them, more profits. So what they did was in 1999 [*others utter the number too*] they went from United States to Mexico and they could pay 28 cents an hour a person [*writes on the board*]. Big difference. They went to Bangladesh, they moved all their factories to Bangladesh and now they are not paying 28 cents, they are paying 19 cents an hour and people work 80 hours a week. And Nike didn't have to pay taxes, there were no benefits at all for these employees. What they are doing is getting richer and richer and poor people are getting poorer and poorer.

Let's talk about children. Children who work in these companies in Bangladesh or Mexico. They are working every day, they are working 80 hours a week. That's a lot, they don't go to school, they don't have time to go to school. So, basically they are killing their future. They know all their life in these factories that's the only thing they can do. And their children are going to do the same and this will go on over and over and over. So this is race to the bottom and now we have Nelson.

NELSON: If you compare in the United States the living wage and the minimum wage. If you compare it with Mexico. The living wage is like, what you need to live. The minimum wage is what those companies are paying. It's easier to live there [*referring to Mexico*], to get food and everything like this, but they need more than 25 cents, they need a dollar or something. To have the minimum wage [*the living wage*]. The minimum wage is lower than the living wage. That is when you are earning too little to live, literally . . . you have to pay one dollar or something, that's too low. You have to bring your kids, your parents, your grandma, you know [*laughter*] to earn the living wage [*applause*].

ANDREA: Remember every time when you go to a store to buy a pair of pants, or a shirt. Remember that probably one or two kids were removed from their homes to work in these sweatshops. Now that you know what you already know, pass the voice, you might not change a kid's life but you would be making a difference.

Three students presented the second presentation at the end of the spring 2002 semester. Here is a quote from a student's journal that captures this experience:

> I have learned a lot about sweatshops this semester. . . . I had a wonderful experience doing my presentation during the video about sweatshops. I never thought that my presentation was going to be done in front of a lot of people. There were 58 people in the audience. . . . We were a little nervous but we did a good job.

> After the video finished, everybody was asking a lot of questions about sweatshops. . . . Carlos made people laugh. Sinclair made people angry. He spoke about many interesting points with specific tasks and statistics to teach people what is going on with people who work in sweatshops. I am very proud of my friends. Also, I am very proud of myself. I cannot believe I made people cry during the video. I was looking for a way to convince people that they must not buy clothes made by sweatshops. . . . So, I suddenly got the idea to make all the people cry. I acted in fro[nt] of them. . . . We did a great job. . . . The only thing I am resentful is that there was no camera in this place. . . . I lost nervousness to talk in front of people.

In this same description, the student talks about how the course helped her attain goals that could be applied in her current courses:

> This experience helped me to give good speeches. The next day I had to make a speech in my psychology class and I did a super job. My teacher had told me she had never had a good student giving a speech naturally and freely. I feel proud of myself. . . . [The topic of sweatshops] was an interesting and controversial topic.

This same idea was expressed by a different student upon completion of the course: "Believe me, I really like this class and I know it's becoming part of the basis of my further education at HCC." By this time, I knew that my teaching had gone through a colossal transformation: I felt I owned my teaching; I had finally found a way to creatively align with TESL thought collectives.

Moving Forward: Students' Feedback

Toward the end of the semester, students, in general, reacted positively to the experience and gave suggestions on how it could be improved. Some students felt that although they learned about global sweatshops, the content became dense, overwhelming, and at times repetitive. Other comments noted that the class needed more direction and more accountability. I agreed with the students' comments: I was too engaged in the content objectives and maintained but lost focus on the language objectives. Because of my lack of structure for the class, I found it hard to account for the overwhelming interest of the majority but the passive resistance of some (for student resistance to critical literacy, see Auerbach 1999). These reflections and resources were instrumental in helping me refine the course.

The positive comments about the class are significant because they show diverse ways in which the course prepared these students to deal with and master short- and long-term educational goals that went beyond merely reaching the objectives of the course:

> I am getting new ideas with the help of this class. I gain new ideas for example about sweatshops, child labor, global economy. I gained knowledge about computer technology. I gained knowledge about distribution of wealth, how rich countries are becoming richer and poor countries are becoming poorer.

Moving Forward: Backward Design

Because I could see specific effects on student learning, awareness, and attitudes, I felt positive about my first experience with critical pedagogy. However, I was determined to incorporate student comments and my own critique into course revision and had the opportunity to do so a year later, in the fall of 2003, and again in the spring and fall of 2004. During this time, I went over my notes, reviewed the videos and other data collected, and evaluated the project with less personal involvement and a more critical eye.

My reflections led me to reluctantly drop the idea of imposing a topic on the students in favor of helping them analyze a critical social issue on their own—an issue close to their lives, cultures, and communities. At this point I was convinced that I needed to show my trust in students by letting their backgrounds, interests, and experiences shape the class in a more direct way. Thus, instead of the traditional needs analysis usually conducted by an expert outside (i.e., the teacher and his or her own topic of interest), I decided to conduct a rights analysis that was instrumental in conceptualizing a more active role for students in shaping the class. According to Benesch (2001), a rights analysis "shifts attention from institutional requirements to possibilities for students' engagement in change. It highlights authority, control, participation, and resistance, issues not usually discussed in relation to target situations" (p. 108). The idea of letting multiple student voices shape the class was most significant and difficult to accomplish, but it was motivating because I had found the sense of direction and structure that I needed, and that the students were yearning for, in *backward design* (Wiggins and McTighe 1998). This curricular proposal centers around finding enduring understandings and asking essential questions that represent the place where we, as teachers, want our students to go. Furthermore, we must make sure that assessment practices show sufficient evidence of student attainment by creating activities that facilitate mastery of the enduring understandings.

Because this approach demands that one determine in advance the outcomes of learning, which, in my case, included language and content objectives, I adapted the idea of "making our own road as we walk." This was necessary for two reasons. First, because of the academic work I was trying to engage students in, it made no sense to make a road without specifically knowing where we were headed. Once students and I had a clear understanding that an enduring understanding meant a successful oral presentation based on specific preparation, practice, and delivery of academic content (content objective) involving specific language (language objective), we could engage in building roads that would take us to such a destination. This "different roads" approach meant that students were encouraged and welcomed to rely on their own backgrounds, interests, and experiences, knowing that such particularities would be instrumental in reaching the enduring understandings for the class.

Second, I realized that in pushing the issue of a single topic I would run the risk of *hypermediating*[3] the process, leading students into a terrain they did not want to explore or silencing other topics that might have been more relevant or interesting to them.

In any case, this strong sense of direction provided by the backward design curriculum worked as a pedagogical and intellectual watershed. In the fall 2003 course, I tried out new activities and authentic self-assessment as well as peer and teacher assessments that aimed at reaching both content and language objectives and fine-tuned and tailored these to the specific backgrounds of students in the spring and fall of 2004.

Making Our Own Road

In contrast to the spring 2002 course, students in the following semesters were to present three or four times. The first two or three presentations were considered practice assignments, which consisted of short speeches (usually ten minutes, including questions): one or two were presentations on books on tape, and one was on a documentary of their choice.[4] On the day of the practice presentation, a presenting student would deliver his or her topic to six students or so. On average, three students presented simultaneously using different corners or spaces of the room. This strategy served to speed up presentation time and to decrease the number of students serving as audience. In this way, the activity was instrumental in achieving my goal for the course because these first two or three presentations served as scaffolding for the last and most important presentation.

This practice mood lowered the students' anxieties in many ways. First, since each student was to report on a different book on tape, nonfiction film, or documentary, he or she was positioned as an expert in the topic, thus reducing some of the burdens of talking to a practiced audience. Second, with student-presenters and their fellow students serving as evaluators of the speech in a controlled small-group environment, the process and the feedback were privileged and the grade lost importance. I specifically stressed to evaluators that their peers needed the feedback so that they knew what they should improve and what they should keep doing. Third, presenters were talking to small groups instead of the whole group; thus, their voices could be lower and eye contact facilitated. All this contributed to create a sense of proximity and familiarity that made their speech delivery more direct. Fourth, the written

---

[3] This is a term used by Gutiérrez, Stone, and Larson (forthcoming) to describe the consequences of nonstrategic assistance (scaffolding) that are, in fact, detrimental to a student's learning.

[4] Fall 2003 students presented four times but this proved to be too much. In the following semesters, students only presented three times: one book on tape, one documentary, and their final presentation.

summary that was required to accompany the presentations was described as a personal outline of the events in the story, which helped the presenter remember important details and follow logical order. This is significant because it stood in stark contrast to the guidelines for the presentation format in spring of 2002, which required that they consult multiple and reliable sources, narrow their topic, provide a cluster of ideas, outline the entire speech, and include the feedback from the teacher on issues that needed to be further developed. It is important to highlight that these practice presentations were described as part of a process that was supposed to help prepare them for the final presentation.

The final presentation was the result of a process in which students had to periodically submit their plan. They were required (among other things) to write up

- the purpose of the speech (to inform, persuade, etc.),

- a title that was narrow enough,

- a statement explaining why the specific topic was relevant for the audience and how the presenter was going to engage the audience,

- how much time was needed and how much each section of the presentation would take,

- a semantic map of the concepts that were to be used and how they connected with each other,

- an outline for the speech,

- a statement on how the topic was going to be introduced and concluded,

- a working bibliography that included multiple and reliable sources.

I discussed and exemplified these points in class and during the practice presentations. We had specific discussions around these issues as the need arose either from my observation or from student feedback. The content guidelines outlined here were the result of a combination of resources including Byrns (1997) and Matthews (1994).

It is worth underscoring that we constantly explored language issues and content, including the use of transitions, reference, and subordinate conjunctions that add texture to the text (Eggins 1994); pronunciation training; and summary and report writing.

Pronunciation instruction included a focus on segmental (especially final -ed sounds of regular verbs) and suprasegmental (stress, rhythm, and intonation) aspects of the language and followed the principles and activities outlined by Celce-Murcia, Brinton, and Goodwin (1996) and Morley (1994). Students' needs and progress at this level (as well as in content, discourse-semantics, and grammatical levels) were evaluated through two tasks. In the first task, students were to orally describe a picture story. The second task was an oral draft of their final presentation. In both tasks, students were to produce a recording of their voices that I assessed through an oral assessment sheet (see the appendix at the end of this chapter).

First Two Presentations: Students' Selected Books on Tape

Students were assigned two books on tape. In the fall of 2003 and spring of 2004 these books on tape included *Bud, Not Buddy* (Curtis 2000) and *The House on Mango Street* (Cisneros 1998). Students were to write a 500–800-word reading response that focused on the description of the setting, the characters, the plot, their feelings about the book, and their experience with books on tape.

In addition to the assigned books on tape, students chose two other books on tape to present to the class. After students presented their selected books on tape, they completed peer evaluations and self-evaluations for their presentations. It is worth noting that none of the students enrolled in these three semesters had ever used or even thought about using books on tape to improve their language skills in English. The reaction to doing so was overwhelmingly positive.

The students' presentations on interesting and highly advanced literature exceeded my expectations. It highlighted for me the potential students bring with them that is lost when traditional curricular orientations focus on the teacher and his or her knowledge. In general, the range of topics was so diverse and numerous that it enriched our class enormously while enabling students to extensively and meaningfully work on other language aspects essential to the course such as their listening comprehension, audience analysis, summary and note-taking skills, and skills to present a coherent text. Even though students knew I was considering both the peer assessment and self-assessment in giving them a grade for their presentation, this formality was not as important as being able to convey the message to the group in a meaningful and thorough way.

There was notable improvement from the first to second presentation. For example, one student, Jana, significantly improved on the scores from the peer evaluators, especially in some of the twelve qualitative items on the rubric (e.g., recognize when it was necessary to define words and/or give an example and use visual aids as necessary). A more general improvement was evident in the qualitative comments: the student used visuals that helped her convey the message more clearly, did not look at her notes too much, and was more excited and motivated to tell the story.

Third Presentation: Film or Documentary

This time, I was present to grade the presentation. Table 1 illustrates my assessment of Jana's presentation on a documentary on Islam. The idea was to look at the things the student could improve, pinpoint them, and make sure she was still doing the same things she did well in the other two presentations.

Final Presentation

For her final assignment, Jana wrote a research paper and presented on the history of Bosnia. Jana did excellent research for this presentation, but the delivery had quite a bit of room for improvement. She seemed to have taken for granted that everyone knew the issues about the war in Bosnia. She also seemed to privilege the content over the delivery of the speech, shown by her insufficient use of visuals, which led Jana to rely almost exclusively on her notes (to which she glanced quite frequently). Nevertheless, it was an illuminating and well-prepared presentation. She maintained or improved in all the areas she had been evaluated on previously, particularly in maintaining good eye contact with all the members of the group, which had been problematic during her previous presentation.

TABLE 1. Qualitative Assessment of Sample Presentation

Speaker: Jana **Topic:** Islam	**Speech-Evaluation Form** Speaking and Listening
Content: 3 Got attention 1 Stated goal 2 Previewed main point 5 Main points clear 5 Main points logically sequenced	Delivery: 5 Natural style 2 Controlled nervousness 2 Maintained good eye contact 4 Well-prepared 5 Natural gestures 5 Didn't read 5 Good volume 5 Good rate (speed)
Language: 4 Clear and concrete 5 Appropriate	Audience Analysis: 5 Appropriate for the audience 5 Spoke at appropriate level of understanding
Comments: I especially liked . . . . The critical content. Your tone of voice. You had good notes, but you didn't read. Just used them as guide.	Some things the speaker could improve are . . . Try to control some nervous manifestations (moving one of your legs constantly). Look at all the members of your group, not only the ones in front of you.

Note. Rating scale: Excellent 5, Good 4, Average 3, Fair 2, Poor 1

At least two points about Jana's presentation and her *generic competence* (Paltridge 2001) should be underscored.[5] The first deals with Jana's sense of audience, and the second with her confusion on the expected genre. First, I interpreted her lack of sensitivity about the background on the war in Bosnia as a result of the fact that she did not analyze her audience carefully. In my feedback, I mentioned this and quoted one of the students:

> I especially liked when she explained on her own words how was Bosnia and how it is now. Also, she let us know that even in her country discrimination exists.

I asked her to think about what this comment told her about what the audience considers important. She responded in her journal:

> I myself believe that audience is very important and people who are listening are very important for presenters. For the audience, it was very important to tell them what, and how Bosnia is different from America, which I didn't consider so much in my research.

Through this communication, Jana recognized the importance of the audience, which may positively affect not only her future presentations but her written work as well.

Second, I interpreted the discrepancy between her outstanding research and her average presentation delivery as *genre confusion*. She seemed to privilege what I inadvertently had privileged over the course: the research paper. Although my instruction included many language activities that asked students to use the target language to facilitate and make content meaningful for a specific audience (e.g., delivering practice speeches about books on tape), I was never specific enough about the different types, linguistic demands, and the generic structure of oral presentation genres and ended up merging two different genres into one. My implicit assumption was that if the students were able to write the paper, they would be able to present it because they had had practice presentations. Thus, I left these intricate elements dealing with the context of culture (genre) and the context of situation (register) for the students to figure out on their own. Despite undoubted advancements, my students were still being denied access to high-stakes "available designs" (Kern 2000, 60–61; New London Group 2000, 20)—the design of research paper as opposed to the design of academic oral presentations—to advance their second language academic literacy development. This awareness, informed by genre theory (i.e., Hasan and Williams 1996), has led me to leave behind the individualistic nature implied in creative alignment. I am now writing and teaching

---

[5] Generic competence, the ability to interpret and create culturally appropriate texts, has been associated with the kind of critical literacy related to the Hallidayan school of systemic functional linguistics (Hasan and Williams 1996).

from a strategic alignment mode, which tactically aligns not only with the external thought collectives and demands but also with the rights and needs of the students themselves.

▦ PROFESSIONAL RESONANCE

As shown in this chapter, research and pedagogy that look to contest traditional thought collectives in related TESL areas need to be recursive and dynamic if they are to "make the political more pedagogical and the pedagogical more political" (Giroux 1988, 127). Once this is recognized, schools and classrooms will be seen as ideological key sites and contested terrains where teachers and students alike find space for their own voices and true potentials. This critical process of change and ideological struggle cannot be accomplished through traditional pedagogy that downplays the role of non-ESL content and treats learning as merely an apolitical training focusing on gaining skills that are practical for the real world. In the case of ESL, these neutral and "nonpolitical" tasks take the form of English vocabulary, grammar, and syntax teaching that, although important, are less than adequate if students are to critically engage the world around them. As expressed before, many theorists have recognized the impossibility of making a change through traditional pedagogy and thus feel the need to challenge it. Some have adopted the critical literacy empowerment route that focuses on raising students' awareness on issues oppressing them (e.g., Freire, Giroux, Shor, Macedo), while others have attempted to do so by making the language of schooling and its hidden curriculum explicit (Christie 2002; Hasan and Williams 1996; Schleppegrell 2004). In this chapter, I have suggested that the differences in these distinct pedagogies can be thought of as instances of creative alignment and strategic alignment, respectively.

Critical literacy advocates, however they approach it, assert that mainstream pedagogy is inadequate for English language teaching because it treats (a) learning as merely a detached cognitive activity in which modes of learning are common for all people; (b) the learner as rising above everything in the environment; and (c) knowledge as value-free, autonomous, and preconstructed (Canagarajah 1999b). Thus, one of the most tangible suggestions for challenging the traditional reproductionist orientation of schools is the advocacy and implementation of critical pedagogy despite its sometimes grand theorizing over practice, its narrow vision of inclusion and voice, and its modernist notion of change and empowerment (Pennycook 2001). I agree with Pennycook in his assessment of critical pedagogy, which is why I am proposing a postcritical approach that goes further as teachers and students engage in systematic study and authorship of texts and text production.

Following the lead of these theorists to enhance ESL pedagogy at community colleges, a more responsive pedagogy like the one exemplified here asserts that knowledge is always mediated by specific communities and, therefore, is intrinsically social. Furthermore, knowledge is always linked to power; it is precisely those in power who are the ones who have traditionally legitimized their knowledge through the institutions that they seek to control, including schools. It is in the light of these perspectives that critical approaches (including postmodern orientations) understand education and its political agenda (Canagarajah 1999b).

∷ EXTENDING THE DIALOGUE

The overarching purpose of this chapter has been to provoke dialogue around how nontraditional approaches to ESL teaching in community colleges may help students position themselves differently and attain the goals they originally sought when enrolling at these institutions. This is important because as Brint (2003) so eloquently writes: "The major contradiction remains that community college students desire higher-level attainments than the colleges are able to help them realize. Under such circumstances, the community college cannot help but play the midwife to humbler dreams" (p. 32).

Implied here is the fact that nontraditional approaches that specifically align with critical pedagogy have been attempted (as is the case here) for some time in specific contexts. This, by itself, proves that even the most powerful top-down ideology is not always totally unchallenged. However, these approaches are the exception rather than the rule. Thus, there is a need for more experimentation and implementation, which is why I have tried to be as explicit as possible about the implementation, challenges, and limitations of this project. It is done to respond to constant criticisms of critical pedagogy for being obscure, difficult to implement, and with little practical application for teachers in the real world. In fact, it not only disputes this position but further makes the case for the urgency of adopting content-based critical pedagogy models in ESL classes in community colleges in the post-9/11 United States.

Many points have been made about the importance of exploring alternative critical pedagogies at this ESL transitional level. Although the critical pedagogy of the kind I attempted during the spring of 2002 was instrumental in engaging students in meaningful activities that fostered the connection between language and content and helped develop leadership roles and academic skills that proved useful in mainstream classes, it is nevertheless limiting because it rested on a modified assumption of "White love" (Rafael 2000; Spring 1998), in which the teacher is moved by feelings of love and compassion that position her or him as possessor of that something that would empower those who do not know much.

The essential point is that alternative ESL pedagogies, such as the ones explored in this project, can indeed be implemented successfully and recursively at the community college level despite historical and structural impediments explored earlier in this chapter. A dialectic and recursive nonessentialist pedagogical approach was instrumental in my courses in helping students position themselves for academic success although, as pointed out before, gaps were always present. I call this approach *nonessentialist* or *postcritical* because it decentered the teacher, his or her privileged knowledge, and the traditional thought collectives from which he or she usually operates and favored a less certain pedagogical approach that welcomes complexity, uneven growth, and encourages local student knowledge and enduring understanding as active constructors of learning. It is an approach that accepts that even critical readings have the potential to foster alienation and, rather than imposing any reading on students (even a critical reading) or looking for the "right" reading, seeks to develop in students the ability to welcome a multiplicity of readings, meanings, and designs. This approach can help regain the democratizing and equal-access impetus that filled the rhetoric around the rise of the community college in this nation. I believe that such impetus has been eroded, in part, by the reliance of educational policy leaders on circular and technocratic discursive constructions (McKenna and Graham 2000) with authoritarian and, ultimately, antidemocratic characteristics. Current discourses prominently permeating the governance, identity, and mission of educational institutions are the ones secured by advocates of neoliberal globalization who defend the supposed natural, neutral, and beneficial effects of a market logic for education (Burbules and Torres 2000; Levin 2001; Marginson 1997; Pannu 1996; Peters, Marshall, and Fitzsimons 2000; Spring 1998; Wells et al. 1998). The approach I have adopted here sees and seeks pedagogical practice to be carried out by "transformative intellectuals" who align strategically, engage both in the "language of critique and the language of possibility," and recognize themselves as able to make changes (Giroux, 1988, 128).

Thus, I say to you, teacher (caminante): Indeed, *there are* roads that we as ESL teachers can help direct. The construction of such roads should be cooperative and dialectic and around specific locations, rights, needs, and competencies. Our role as teachers and intellectuals is to secure a space in which these roads point to essential understandings that contribute to the questioning and challenging of oppression, exploitation, and inequality while creating conditions for nonexploiting class structures.

■■ ACKNOWLEDGMENTS

Thanks to all those talented students whom I served in the years of this study. Their willingness to learn gave me the impulse to keep reflecting and transforming my own teaching. Many thanks to Marilynn Spaventa for her patience and support in editing this manuscript. The ideas and mentorship of professors Rick Wolff, Meg Gebhard, Jerri Willett, Sangeeta Kamat, Phil Graham, and Cheri Micheau are undoubtedly present in this project. Sofia, your birth in foreign lands and my beginnings as a periphery scholar concur in wondrous bliss.

⁘ CONTRIBUTOR

J. Andrés Ramírez is a native of Medellin, Colombia, and a doctoral candidate in the School of Education at University of Massachusetts Amherst in the United States. He has taught college-level ESL in Colombia and the United States. His current research uses critical discourse analysis in tracking neoliberal ideologies in educational discourses.

⁘ APPENDIX: ORAL ASSESSMENT SHEET

Student's Name:_____ Date:_____

Teacher: Jaime Andrés Ramírez

Content	Clarity of Ideas		Interest of Topic		Comments	
Pronunciation	Intonation		Rhythm		Word Stress	
	Individual Sounds					
Grammar	Structure	Syntax		Word Choice		Word Order
Other						

PART 2

PROGRAMS

CHAPTER 3

Immigration + New Literacy Studies + Digital Technologies = ESL for a New South

::

Harriett A. Allison

:: FRAMING THE ISSUE

Background

For many years community colleges in states such as California, Florida, and New York have provided English as a second language (ESL) programs for large numbers of U.S.-residing students who are English language learners. In contrast, many colleges in other areas—notably the traditional rural and suburban south—have had few, if any, matriculated immigrant and refugee students, thus having little need for classes serving this population. However, beginning in the mid-1990s, a new wave of immigration spread into these hitherto unaffected areas, bringing with it a new group of applicants who wanted to attend local community colleges. Many of this group, frequently referred to as Generation 1.5, had received a significant portion of their secondary education in U.S. schools. To serve these students appropriately, educational institutions began to provide ESL classes, developing programs that they believed best suited the needs of their students and that matched the mission of the individual institution.

This chapter tells the story of the continuing evolution of a community college ESL program in this semirural "New South," the serendipitous advantages stemming from the grassroots way it developed, and the importance of applying a theoretical perspective that recognizes and addresses the distinct characteristics and circumstances of students now living in a multimedia context. The ESL program described herein provides classes in all English language skill

47

areas, with each area undergoing assessment and revision as the program develops. This chapter concentrates on the program's advanced reading sections.

The ESL program at Gainesville College in Gainesville, Georgia, has had three different orientations:

- a traditional intensive English program (IEP) curriculum

- a content-based English for academic purposes (EAP) plan

- a new structure that is more responsive to and appropriate for Generation 1.5 learners

In 1997, when the program was established, two members of the foreign language program were given the task of setting up courses for ESL students at the college. They chose a traditional IEP format for the curricular design model. When ESL-experienced instructors began teaching most of the courses, the program and course content changed to an EAP focus. After a year with the EAP curriculum, instructors saw the need for a more relevant approach tailored to Generation 1.5 students. This chapter discusses that progression to the present program of study.

Because of an absence of ESL-specific top-down requirements from the state-level board of regents, this program, along with others in the state, was designed locally. In addition, since there was a sudden influx of students needing ESL-appropriate classes, program planning had to be carried out efficiently. After ESL-trained instructors were hired, they were given primary responsibility for responding to student learning needs as they saw fit.[1] Thus, instructors could not only innovate, design, and propose appropriate courses and syllabi but also investigate and respond to authentic student needs on a multilayered level. As program development progressed, ESL faculty perceived and responded to student characteristics and areas of concerns that might not have been addressed had the curriculum been prescribed from above. Instead of being required to structure the program along the lines of a traditional IEP or an EAP model, ESL faculty had the latitude to consider pedagogy more suitable for this particular group of ESL learners, especially for teaching and learning in the new millennium.

Considerations at macro and micro levels led to the choice of a New Literacy Studies (NLS) perspective for examining and developing pedagogy in ESL reading courses. From a macro standpoint, an NLS framework allows instructors to move away from a developmental view that regards student learning needs as deficiencies in the individual, in his or her family, or in previous schooling. In addition, from an NLS perspective, students are more easily

---

[1] All proposed courses had to meet state and regional certification requirements, and students had to make satisfactory progress toward a degree or transfer to a four-year school.

perceived as members of groups interacting to interpret and make meaning, not just as solitary individuals working alone. Finally, the lens of NLS admits the presence and significance of text, power, and identity issues in reflections on ESL reading pedagogy (Collins and Blot 2003).

From a micro position, NLS recognizes multiple literacies instead of a single, autonomous literacy model; it allows questioning the teacher's role in the classroom (authoritarian figure versus facilitator) and facilitates a reframing of learning objectives that acknowledges the prevalence and effect of digital technologies in schools and in the lives of students (King and O'Brien 2002). This theoretical framework facilitates curriculum design and instructional approaches that recognize apparent dichotomies in the ESL learning context and provides a model for apprenticing these students to academic discourse to prepare them for the world of academic literacy (Gee 1996). An NLS perspective allows the accomplishment of these goals by acknowledging, accommodating, and utilizing the range and diversity of literacies represented in each class; addressing and transforming preexisting student perceptions of teacher-student relationship possibilities; and engendering realistic student expectations concerning course tasks and learning strategies (King and O'Brien 2002).

Institutional Setting

Gainesville College, a two-year community college in the University System of Georgia in the United States, is situated in a semirural area of northeast Georgia forty-five miles north of Atlanta and just south of the city of Gainesville. During its forty-year history, it has served a population typical of the southern foothill/mountain region: white, middle and lower-middle class, and first-generation college students with a combined minority enrollment (black, Hispanic, and Asian) of less than 8 percent. However, beginning in 1997, the college's administration realized that the profile of students moving to Gainesville was changing and that some of these new undergraduates were bringing a set of learning requirements and characteristics different from those the college had traditionally served.

As a gateway institution, all first-semester students whose placement scores indicate a need for additional preparation are enrolled in learning support classes in English, reading, and/or math. Although the numbers of this new group were small—thirty-seven self-identified as Asian or Hispanic—it quickly became clear to staff and faculty that the very effective learning support instruction the college traditionally provided was inappropriate for those whose home language was not English. In response, the administration decided to establish an ESL program under the umbrella of learning support; the first semester began with an initial group of sixteen students.

When one considers that part of Gainesville's mission is to respond to the educational needs of the area served, providing ESL classes is commendable though unexceptional. However, two of the college's distinguishing characteristics have positively affected and enhanced the ESL program development. First, the college was committed to fostering a constructive, supportive, non-restrictive environment for experimentation and creation of new programs and activities. Second, it provided exceptionally up-to-date and user-friendly digital technology for all faculty, staff, and students. Both these conditions made possible the innovative and enriched quality of the ESL program.

People Involved

Instructor

Since 1998 I have developed and taught most of the advanced ESL reading courses at Gainesville, along with many of the writing and grammar and lower-level reading classes; in January 2000, I assumed responsibility for coordination of the ESL program.

Students

The ESL student population at Gainesville College is similar to that of many community colleges in the United States. However, since the school had little experience working with students who know additional languages, the particular characteristics of the group were unexpected and presented different challenges and opportunities in syllabus construction and course design.

First, most of them did not fit the profile of typical F-1 students who hold student visas and are in the United States for the sole purpose of attending school. Such students frequently attend IEPs in the United States before continuing with their major studies or returning to their home countries. An IEP curriculum assumes that participants will have received most, if not all, of their secondary education outside the United States and that, having come to the United States to study English, they are here temporarily on a student visa. For this group, U.S. culture and customs are new items and therefore worthwhile topics for instruction. Typically, these learners have studied grammar and developed an explicit understanding of English syntax. Frequently, these international students are from families familiar with academic discourse, although not necessarily its particular manifestation in the United States. With this student profile in mind, the two foreign language instructors responsible for starting the ESL program sketched out the original curriculum and selected course materials, using a combination of ESL-specific and traditional learning support texts.

It soon became evident that ESL classes at Gainesville included more graduates of U.S. high schools than graduates of schools outside the United States and that the traditional IEP model was not completely effective for them. In contrast to the assumed ESL student profile, many of these students have learned their English for the most part orally in ESL programs and mainstream classes in U.S. public schools and are not necessarily conversant with the structure of English grammar. In addition, many of them are first-generation college students and are often unfamiliar with the culture, expectations, and discourse of the academic world they are now entering. Frequently, this group is referred to as Generation 1.5 because they have experiences and characteristics common to and with U.S. students as well as those of their country of birth or heritage, yet they are still learning English (Harklau, Losey, and Siegal 1999). In the seven years since the ESL program was established, the number of Generation 1.5 students in ESL classes has steadily increased, to the point that they now constitute 75 percent of enrollees in ESL.

An additional factor that sets ESL students in community colleges apart from traditional IEP students is that they are faced with high-stakes test requirements as they are matriculated. After these students are admitted at Gainesville, they are expected to pass exit tests and progress to core curriculum studies within a specified length of time; if they do not, they face a three-year suspension. Thus, it was critical to reshape the program to assist these English language learners most effectively.

Beliefs and Assumptions

The beliefs and assumptions underlying and informing this program development evolved as ESL faculty perceived and responded to student needs and progress. In the beginning, the program worked from a developmental perspective. However, most students in ESL classes at this community college have passed through ESL programs in public schools. When they were told they must complete learning support courses in ESL-appropriate English and/or reading classes, they sometimes became discouraged or even angry. They were intuitively aware that they had accomplished a real feat in simultaneously learning a new language and earning a high school diploma in that second (or third) language. Therefore, to be told that they had more ESL classes ahead of them was sometimes unsettling. An approach and methodology that removed the stigma of a developmental perspective was essential.

At the point when ESL-specific instructors began to reshape the ESL curriculum, the focus was on the individual learner as he or she encountered academic reading tasks. However, this psycholinguistic perspective did not include or address factors that became apparent after students moved on from the ESL program. It was clear from their comments that they did not know the expectations and conventions of academia. They had developed one set of behaviors that worked in high school, but now they were finding that those assumptions did not apply to college classrooms.

While content-based reading and writing tasks, combined with real academic assignments, are essential ESL curriculum components (Kasper 2000), these activities alone proved inadequate in preparing matriculated ESL students to participate fully and effectively in an academic environment. Despite the pedagogical benefit of working with authentic content and assignments, a psycholinguistic concentration on an individual learner's skills and strategies omits recognition of social, cultural, and political environments in which learning has occurred and will continue to take place. Unloading the responsibility onto students for discovering and understanding how to operate in a new discourse community—academia—is counterproductive at best and, in reality, unprincipled. Acknowledgment of the differences between high school and college discourse communities is a more effective approach for introducing students to what they need to know. In essence, students need to be "apprenticed" to the discourse of academia to begin to acquire this knowledge and way of being (Gee 1996).

Consequently, we moved from a position of planning and providing for our students' academic success by concentrating on individual, isolated concerns to a view encompassing and building on their past pedagogical and literacy experiences and their present perceptions of how they can cope with academic literacy tasks. We had to identify and use a perspective that includes, examines, and assesses critically what our students' literacies are and how they acquired them, what they perceive as their role and agency within the teacher-student relationship, and how they can deal effectively with academic tasks. In other words, we needed to draw on a sociocultural and sociopolitical viewpoint that takes account of and incorporates the multiple literacies of our students, includes their past and present perceptions of and responses to power relationships within literacy contexts, and provides approaches enabling them to cope with the multiple literacies of today's academic environment. An NLS perspective provides such a space for reflecting on social, cultural, and political issues and concerns relevant to the lives and academic goals of ESL students. In particular, questions of what counts as a recognized, approved literacy; what power issues are inherent in academic and other literacies; and what identities can be constructed and how they may be constrained are all included in designing reading curricula. At the same time, we kept in mind that composition and comprehension of texts are not completely social events; they are simultaneously individual and collective activities (Brandt and Clinton 2002).

Impetus for Addressing the Issue

As the number of Generation 1.5 English language learners in our ESL classrooms has grown, their presence—with their distinct learner characteristics—has introduced a variety of issues, and these concerns are intertwined with the evolving milieu in which we learn and teach. Although the content-based curriculum adopted in 2000–2001 was proving very effective in preparing ESL students to pass the Compass reading test, a Web-based placement assessment used by the college to determine whether a student can satisfy the school's ESL

Learning Support Reading requirement, ESL faculty began to notice that many former students were having difficulty in core curriculum classes such as political science or psychology. The following is a sample of students' explanations:

> I thought I studied the right answers, but the teacher didn't ask those kinds of questions.

> I didn't expect to have to read so much. I don't know how to put all that stuff together.

> I expected my instructor to tell us what would be on the test so I could learn it.

> He didn't tell us to study the handouts.

> What I did worked in high school, but it didn't work in sociology.

> The stuff I found on Yahoo wasn't what the teacher said I could use in my paper.

In response to comments such as these, we took another look at who our students are and what they need to know to succeed in college. Three things became clear:

- Many of our students had expectations about their instructors that did not match the realities of college teaching.

- Students were using assumptions about content and assessment that did not apply in a college setting.

- Students were not prepared to manage the information load and multiple sources they were encountering in academia.

With these observations in mind, we considered the dynamic nature of our classes and the lives and learning contexts of our students as work began on refocusing the ESL curriculum. We also reflected on how ESL pedagogy must account for the effects of digital technologies on the academic setting.

Our learners perceive the teacher-student relationship to be one that places the teacher as the "authority" in all matters related to education and knowledge. We have found that our students not only expect us, the instructors, to have definitive answers for all their questions but also find it confusing to be told "I don't know. What do you think is an answer? How can we find out?" As has been noted previously, many of our former students depend on their instructors to tell them what and how to study, which texts to read, and the goals in doing so. If there are signals from instructors indicating how they should proceed, our students may miss them or misconstrue them. Most important, many of these students have adopted a stance that does not serve them well at all: that the teacher is the definitive authority who maintains the student in a passive, dependent role. Teachers are more effective instructors when they facilitate rather than dictate (King and O'Brien 2002).

This factor connects with another barrier to learning and presents a challenge to both student and teacher: the perception that students' primary learning task is to find and proclaim the "one, right answer," which is known by the teacher. The search for the "right answer" frequently gets in the way of real learning (King and O'Brien 2002).

When our students focus their attention and effort on quickly identifying the first thing that might be the answer, they fail to benefit from opportunities to investigate, experiment, or consider multiple possibilities. Not only are ambiguities and subtleties ignored or suppressed on the way to getting it right the first time, but those students who cannot come up with a correct response can become discouraged and disconnected. Students need the latitude to experiment and to make errors as they develop the necessary strategies for effective participation in the new millennium (King and O'Brien 2002).

A third characteristic noted was a need for students to maneuver skillfully among digital resources and to integrate print-based texts with digital ones. Learning to locate, assess, and manage information is a critical skill in a world of digital technologies (see Lanham 1994). We also have noticed that a digital divide exists among our students in ESL; this difference affects activities and learning in the classroom. Some students are very familiar with and adept at using digital technologies, whereas others have little knowledge of the Internet and are in the early stages of learning how to word process a paragraph. Some have access to a computer with online service at home, whereas others are dependent on the computers provided at school. Student differences in access to and use of digital technologies have to be considered and accommodated while working with them as they develop strategies to manage a wealth of information from multiple sources.

As noted earlier, this chapter's goal is to share the observations and reflections that informed us as ESL faculty grappling with the need to revise the ESL curriculum. It traces the evolution of our thinking about curriculum development as we worked to better equip students for their academic lives after ESL. It is also our goal to suggest a theoretical perspective that can incorporate the lives and literacies of an ever-changing Generation 1.5 population while responding to the very real academic discourse demands they will encounter. The following discussion focuses on the three previously specified conditions common to community college ESL reading classes of Generation 1.5 students and describes how we addressed them as we progressed to another, more effective point in our pedagogy. These topics include the range and diversity of literacies represented, preexisting student perceptions of teacher-student relationships, and expectations concerning course and learning objectives. Viewing these themes and concerns through the lens of NLS contributes a perspective that can expand instructor viewpoints and energize their thinking and can inform and enhance teaching efforts to address pedagogical necessities and constraints.

:: NARRATIVE

Before coming to Gainesville College, my training and education in teaching ESL consisted of working primarily with the traditional model of ESL students, that is, those whose presence in my classroom was a result of an explicit choice to learn English, not as a consequence of placement scores mandating additional English language study. The program in which I taught as a graduate student included both F-1 students and graduates of U.S. high schools, with the program orientation focused on the former. Reading syllabi typically contained topics introducing various aspects of American culture, comparisons and contrasts of types of cultures, and first-person accounts of leaving a home country. Writing topics followed a similar pattern, with the assumption that these students were new to the United States and its ways.

When I began teaching in community colleges as an adjunct, it became painfully obvious that these assumptions, practices, and literacy topics were inappropriate for an increasing number of learners in my classes. As have many ESL teachers, I heard more than once statements similar to this one: "Why do we have to keep talking about 'My Home Country'? I've been living here for X years and my life is here, not there. I don't even remember much about the town where I was born." And so I began a search for more relevant approaches, content, and methods for the students in my classes. Later, this reorientation informed choices and decisions made in the development of the program at Gainesville.

Content-based language learning held promise as an alternative to United-States-as-target-culture reading and writing topics, and we refocused the ESL curriculum toward EAP. We took readings from authentic texts found in typical freshmen and sophomore courses; worked with writing products that included essay topics, assignments, and formats students would likely encounter in core courses; and concentrated on oral/aural activities characteristic of the college classroom. Student response was immediate and positive, with many of them commenting that they now felt able to observe and respond to many of the differences between high school and college work; they were feeling more prepared for what lay ahead.

However, after a year of working with these changes in content and structure, it became clear that despite the positive effects of these curriculum alterations, we knew we were not there yet. Indeed, carrying out these modifications permitted us to notice other significant concerns that had to be addressed. The issues now in the foreground were preexisting student perceptions of teacher-student relationships, expectations concerning course and learning objectives, and the broad range and diversity of literacies represented.

In response to the increasing presence of digital technologies in academic literacy, I have, for a number of years, incorporated them in all classes, with an emphasis on Internet-based activities in the reading curriculum. This course enhancement, while pertinent to changing times and of great interest to the students, brought with it new concerns that demanded responses. My first observation was that the Internet provided an enormous array of texts on any given topic, and a very mixed array at that. As Lanham (1994) points out, when students use these new resources, instead of being required to assimilate information from one text, they have to select what is relevant for their purposes from all that is available to them not only from print but also from digital sources such as the Internet. Thus, it is not enough for instruction to concentrate on decoding and encoding skills and mastery of a single source of information; rather, learners in the new millennium also need to know how to assess and manage this flood of information. That aspect, combined with a strong tendency among my students to "look for the answer" first and perhaps question the source later, told me there were new skills and strategies that needed to be included in any use of digital technologies. With these considerations in mind, I began to make learning Internet search skills a primary component of the ESL reading classes.

Accommodating Differences in the Digital Divide

For a number of years I had arranged for as many ESL classes as possible to meet in classrooms equipped with overhead projection capabilities, individual computer terminals, and online access. When I began to work with my students on using Internet sources for academic work, I was struck by my students' expectations that I would give directions and they would follow them—completely, totally, and exhaustively, with little or no expectation that they would have to think about search terms, come up with criteria for the sites they found, and then evaluate and choose among the myriad results of their searches. Early efforts to move in that direction were frustrating for them and for me. Consequently, *scaffolding* became my watchword in lesson planning as I began to tease apart the steps and tasks involved. I found help for this project as I recognized and attempted to deal with another worrying issue: the apparent digital divide that seemed to exist in each class.

I soon realized that some students came early so they could read and send e-mail, play games, read international news reports, check on sports scores, or shop for everything from cars to music CDs, while others appeared to have difficulty logging on and using word-processing programs. After surveying the students in my classes about their online use, I learned that there was a wide range of skill, comfort, and interest represented. To provide instruction

relevant for all class members, I had to discover and accommodate these differences, both group and individual. My approach has been to devise strategies
and activities that put to use what students already know, for many skills they
have developed in the realm of digital technology are transferable to academia
and can be shared with their classmates who have less experience and facility
in this area. Doing so recognizes that cooperative learning can be as effective
and meaningful as teacher-focused instruction, and working together in peer
groups is more productive and gratifying for many of those involved (Vygotsky
1978).

I have found that one way to respond to the issue of how to structure cooperative, student-centered learning is to use surveys to create a class profile of
Internet use. I then assign three or four students to work together on a project,
placing individuals who represent the range of Internet literacies revealed in the
survey in a group. Next, I ask each student to consider how he or she makes
choices about Internet sources and to share this information with the other
members of his or her group. As a class, we develop a list of concerns or considerations that a reader needs to think about when deciding about the relative
usefulness of an Internet source. After we generate this inventory, I ask the students (in their assigned groups) to apply their criteria to selected academically
relevant Web sites. Finally, each group shares its experiences and discoveries
with the whole class, adding any additional queries they think should apply to
scholastic work. In further assignments I use authentic academic tasks involving
the Internet to refine these criteria.

Changing Perceptions of Students and Teachers

As we work together on this project, students begin to see that I sometimes act
as the class director but that, at other times, I am a learner along with the rest
of the class. The shifting of my position within the class from teacher to learner
and back again, while occasionally unsettling to a student or two, does not
present a problem for most of my students. It has required some reflection on
my part to assure myself that I am responding to the realities of the moment,
but it has been worth the effort. As I relinquish the teacher-as-authority role,
students take on more active roles in their own learning, which is one of my
primary goals in teaching. Sometimes I think of it as my getting out of their
way so that they (and we) can get on with learning.

In reviewing the thinking behind these changes, I see that I asked myself a
number of questions: Why bore them by "teaching" them what they already
know? Why not help them see that their skills are transferable? Why not create
classroom conditions that make it possible for them to share their skills with
others—including the instructor—in the class? In other words, why not let go
of a traditional version of classroom control and make room for student agency
in learning? In this complementary atmosphere, students and teachers can

exchange roles and learn from each other, to the enhancement of course objectives. In truth, learners move toward mastery of any task or skill more rapidly and completely when they are active participants in determining the rate and nature of the process (Vygotsky 1978).

Finding That Elusive "Right" Answer

The kinds of exercises previously described uncover another classroom issue that can appear when working with digital technologies: students' expectations concerning course and learning objectives. As has been experienced by anyone who has searched (and searched and searched) the Internet, the "right answer" is usually elusive and sometimes difficult to recognize. However, my experience with students fresh from high school is that their instinct is to look for one—and only one—answer to a question or assignment; they want and expect to get it right the first time. To prepare them for a different notion, I begin by asking them to talk about how they perform a task they have in common, usually something like deciding what they will wear to school. As the discussion develops, it becomes clear that every person does it differently but that we all arrive in the classroom fully clothed. From this seemingly trivial exercise we talk about more complex topics that permit multiple interpretations and solutions. Finally, we sample the myriad possibilities for answers that one finds on the Internet. Throughout this dialogue I stress that we are concentrating on *how* we can manage the information we discover on the Internet and on how we can use it most effectively.

:: PROFESSIONAL RESONANCE

As a result of these experiences, I recognized the need to acquire immediately responsive instruction models and develop the willingness and ability to take pedagogical advantage of whatever is occurring in the classroom. Classrooms open to the dynamic qualities of adolescents frequently include spontaneous and unscripted events that can and should be exploited for their "teachable moment" potential. To make this a reality, we as teachers must relinquish certain aspects of classroom control and concentrate on making these possibilities a part of our repertoire. In so doing, we can move toward a pedagogy of teacher and students as coagents in teaching and learning:

> Teachers can productively shift to thinking strategically so that they can co-construct strategic interventions on the fly, or at the point of need. . . . Like other types of scaffolded instruction, this "strategic habit of mind" . . . balances student independence, strategy acquisition, and task completion with teacher-as-mediator or scaffold. (King and O'Brien 2002, 49)

The method suggested here should not be interpreted as a form of "wing it/anything goes" teaching because, in many ways, it requires instructors to be more attentive and prepared than when working with a more structured, predetermined approach. Although this strategy may conflict with established curricula and syllabi that preclude immediate observations and responses, it is essential that ESL pedagogy recognize and include the distinct literacies and circumstances of students that can manifest at unexpected times in unpredictable ways. The task for ESL professionals is to formulate pedagogy that responds to the dynamic nature of teaching in the new millennium and adapt methods to meet the genuine needs of students.

Adopting a strategic teaching approach highlights the need for teachers to have or develop materials appropriate to this context. Instructors need to have available texts and other literacy materials flexible enough to be used in teaching "on the fly" (King and O'Brien 2002, 49). In addition, ESL materials developers need experience working in this context so they are sufficiently informed about the singular characteristics of the kind of classroom proposed in this chapter.

A further pedagogical enhancement—or necessity—is to provide for dialogue among ESL faculty. Peer observation and response can provide other sets of eyes and viewpoints that can help develop solutions for what may seem to be insoluble classroom conundrums.

∷ INSTITUTIONAL CHALLENGES

As one with some years of experience in community colleges, I am well aware of the constraints of teaching in this environment. Probably the commodity in shortest supply is time for reflection and innovation. Despite this situation, we, as ESL professionals, must continue to create ways to make our curricula and classes relevant to the educational needs and lives of our students. Setting out to establish a dialogue among ESL faculty is a first step. Via these exchanges all involved can formulate lines of reasoning to persuade school administrators of the importance of appropriate ESL pedagogy for student retention and success. Appropriate ESL pedagogy must include recognition of and response to twenty-first-century literacies, and ESL faculty need time and support to construct courses and materials that incorporate these realities.

Another challenge is acknowledging the centrality of digital technologies in education by having available online access for teachers and students to use in the learning environment. Whenever possible, instructors should arrange to teach ESL reading classes in computer-equipped classrooms. If that is not feasible, then developing lessons that coordinate traditional classroom and online environments is an alternative. However, authentic, scaffolded lessons that focus on students developing the skills to manage information must be essential components of the ESL reading curriculum. It is not enough to talk about working with Internet research sources; students have to learn to search effectively and make informed choices about the content they find. These learners need the opportunity to work with digital resources and the freedom, support, and guidance to experiment with different approaches and solutions. To prepare students for academic discourse in the context of twenty-first-century literacies, ESL professionals need to work with them in that online, digital environment.

:: EXTENDING THE DIALOGUE

While our efforts at Gainesville have been fruitful, we wish that we had had more information and greater knowledge about the academic experiences of our students before they came to us. In addition, we want to know more about how they perceive their transitions from secondary school literacies to college and university ones. Therefore, studies that contribute to the body of knowledge about Generation 1.5 students as academic readers will benefit both students and their instructors. Instructors can address these students' particular learning requirements more directly and adequately, for they will have access to more specific information that clarifies who their students really are. Generation 1.5 students will not only receive the benefits of pedagogy clearly relevant to their needs but also avoid redundant instruction in skills and topics in which they are already competent.

Our response to the English language learning needs of the Generation 1.5 students in our classes has been to go beyond concentrating on decoding skills. Rather, we have focused on preparing them, for the present, to operate independently and competently in the realm of academic discourse and, after college, in a world that will require them to be multiliterate and knowledgeable about and skilled in digital technologies.

:: CONTRIBUTOR

Harriett A. Allison is assistant professor of English as a second language (ESL) and English and is also ESL coordinator at Gainesville College in Georgia, in the United States. In 1999 she initiated and now coordinates a summer for-credit program, Steps-to-College, for more than 140 secondary school ESL students. Her teaching interests combine ESL reading, digital technologies, and multiliteracies.

CHAPTER 4

Strength in Community: Effectiveness of Community in Building College Success

::

Marcia Babbitt

:: FRAMING THE ISSUE

Background

Kingsborough Community College, a large two-year college of The City University of New York (CUNY) in an urban New York neighborhood, is home to a large number of English as a second language (ESL) students of diverse ethnicities. The challenges these students face in their new academic environment are often overwhelming: pressure to succeed in college with a new language; growing restrictions for financial aid; and the inability to enter various programs, such as nursing, without first passing CUNY reading and writing assessments. It is not surprising then that many ESL students have had to withdraw from difficult courses for which they were not linguistically ready nor offered any specific support. Worse yet, many have dropped out of college altogether.

It is with the needs of these students in mind that the Intensive ESL Program, an interdisciplinary, content-based learning community program for full-time, entering ESL students, was created. From its inception in 1995, the Intensive ESL Program, as part of the college's ESL program, has been housed in the English department. The program was designed to help students achieve success in academic English in speaking, listening, reading, and writing. Our objectives included higher pass rates in ESL classes, with the possibility of skipping an ESL level; higher persistence and pass rates in challenging content courses; and quicker entry into the academic mainstream. Our goals also included forging a strong connection between ESL learning community students and the college community and improving retention and graduation rates. To help ensure students' success in the rigorous Intensive ESL Program and to reach our goals, we provided invaluable support services in the areas of counseling, advisement, and tutoring.

Structure of the Intensive ESL Program

The shape and structure of a learning community program varies widely from institution to institution, but certain features are vital to all learning communities:

> Learning communities, as we define them, purposefully restructure the curriculum to link together courses or course work so that students find greater coherence in what they are learning as well as increased intellectual interaction with faculty and fellow students. Advocates contend that learning communities can address some of the structural features of the modern university that undermine effective teaching and learning. Built on what is known about effective educational practice, learning communities are also usually associated with collaborative and active approaches to learning, some form of team teaching, and interdisciplinary themes. (Gabelnick et al. 1990, 5)

Recent research corroborates that the formation of a strong and dynamic learning community among students, tutors, and faculty, in conjunction with collaboration among faculty in curriculum development, joint and related assignments, and shared readings, helps students gain confidence in their abilities and succeed in their first semester and beyond (see Bruffee 1993, 1995; Gabelnick et al. 1990; MacGregor et al. 2000; Smith et al. 2004; Tinto 1987, 1997; Tinto, Goodsell Love, and Russo 1994).

Students in Kingsborough's program are placed in one of three ESL levels: low intermediate (known as ESL 07), intermediate (ESL 09), and high intermediate (ESL 91). They attend class from 9:00 a.m. to 3:00 p.m. five days a week, with one hour for lunch. Students spend eight hours each week with an ESL instructor and four hours in tutorial sessions in Kingsborough's reading and writing center. ESL classes have no real credits that count toward graduation, but each class has ten equated credits; these count toward full-time status and eligibility for financial aid.

In the fall, there are six ESL learning community sections, two at each ESL level. In the spring, our entering student population supports four sections: one low intermediate, two intermediate, and one high intermediate. The maximum number of students in each cohort is 25, so that there are approximately 150 students in the fall and 100 in the spring. The total number of students enrolled in ESL classes each semester is about 375 to 400.

All students in the program take an ESL speech class for three credits and another three-credit content course such as Introduction to Psychology, Introduction to Sociology, Popular American Culture (a history course), or Health Education. Courses in these disciplines fulfill group graduation requirements at the college. Students also take two Student Development (SD) courses, taught by counselors, which provide an orientation to college life and resources at Kingsborough, study skills, and an overview of career paths. These courses are one credit each. The total number of real credits in the program is eight, with a total of eighteen combined real and equated credits, more than first-semester ESL college students generally take.

The purpose of this chapter is to explore the workings of Kingsborough's ESL learning community program. I focus on those aspects of our program that make learning in ESL and other courses so effective for our students; help them to form a community with other students in their cohort, their tutors and instructors, and the larger college community; and help them become better learners. The academic-social community that is formed in the first few days of our students' first semester gives them a foundation on which to build successful college careers.

▊▊ NARRATIVE

Student Placement

On the first day of class, ESL students at Kingsborough write a diagnostic essay to confirm placement. If, on the basis of this essay, an instructor suspects that a student may be misplaced, the ESL directors, along with other instructors who are available, read the essay. The student's entering reading score is also considered when assigning a student to an ESL level, but placement is based primarily on the student's writing level.[1]

Since fall 1998, the Intensive ESL Program has been mandated for entering ESL students because of the success rate of the self-selected students in the program during its first seven semesters (for data on the program, see Fox 1996). Most entering full-time day students are registered for the program; exceptions, however, are made for those students who work more than

---

[1] All students who apply to CUNY colleges take three university-wide assessments: the ACT Writing Assessment (an essay exam), the ACT Compass Reading Assessment (a computerized reading comprehension exam), and the ACT Mathematics Assessment. Nonpassing ESL essays that receive a score of five or lower (the passing score is seven, a combined score of two readers) are reread by ESL readers to determine placement in one of our three ESL levels. We recommend that students whose knowledge of written English falls below our lowest level attend the CUNY Language Immersion Program (CLIP). The institute, one site of which is located on Kingsborough's campus, requires that students be admitted to a CUNY college to enroll. There students can attend up to four six- to ten-week sessions, where they work on reading, writing, speaking, and listening skills for twenty-five hours each week. The cost of CLIP is low, and it also benefits the student by not using up any financial aid that the student has been awarded. At the end of CLIP sessions, the ESL directors evaluate CLIP student essays to determine placement.

thirty-five hours per week and those with demanding child-care schedules. Nevertheless, many program students work outside of the college and have family responsibilities for children or parents. Even considering their complex and often difficult lives, these Kingsborough students continue to succeed. Pass-and-skip rates in ESL courses are not as high as when the students were self-selected, but they are still quite a bit higher than those of ESL students who did not participate in a learning community program in their first semester of college. Pass rates on all three levels are 70 to 75 percent or higher, whereas non-learning-community pass rates had been between 60 and 70 percent (or lower). Pass rates in other program courses (e.g., health, history, sociology, speech, student development, psychology) remain high also. Faculty often marvel at the hard work and motivation of ESL students—often their grades and pass rates exceed those of students in their nonlinked sections.

ESL faculty meet with students individually or in small groups during the orientation period and describe the program to students. We also invite former students to talk to new students about their experiences in the program. Intensive ESL Program students, therefore, begin the semester knowing that they are part of a program that will demand that they do extensive and intensive reading and writing; that the curriculum is interdisciplinary and collaborative, with courses supporting each other; and that students will also have support from the counseling and tutoring sectors.

The Intermediate ESL, Sociology, Speech, and Student Development Learning Community

The intermediate-level ESL class that I usually teach, ESL 09, is linked with Introduction to Sociology, Speech, and two SD classes. ESL and sociology support each other, and ESL supports speech as well by encouraging student discussion, having groups report orally to the rest of the class, and requiring students to do the writing for a sociology project in ESL class. Students present their work on this project in speech class.

One such joint project is the artifact project. The sociology instructor introduces the concept of cultural artifacts to the ESL students. In the ESL class, students discuss artifacts from their own cultures in small groups, choose an artifact for the project, discuss their choice with the group, write about it on worksheets, and report to the class. Students research their artifacts on the Internet (the ESL class meets in a computer lab for two hours each week). Students organize their projects according to the speech instructor's guidelines and present their projects to their classmates in speech class. I collect a written version of the project, which I share with the sociology instructor. Students enjoy working on this project, often learning something about the history of their artifact from their research that they had not known before, and classmates gain an appreciation of each other's cultures through working on artifact projects together. Each student brings in the artifact for the oral presentation.

There is also other collaborative work completed in a learning community cohort. In sociology class, for example, students write about sociological aspects of the novels that they read for ESL. Other assignments are also constructed as joint assignments, with instructors in both classes reading and commenting on student papers.

Pedagogical Underpinnings and Practices

There is an emphasis, again through a small-group, shared-inquiry approach, on having students experience *deep learning:* the ability to read difficult and challenging material and venture below the surface in an effort to understand concepts (see Conway et al. 1997; Marton and Saljo 1976; Saljo 1984; Tagg 2003). Conway et al. (1997) conclude that "a learning schedule that repeatedly presents knowledge in different contexts in active learning exercises has a general beneficial effect in facilitating the schematization of knowledge and this effect is at least partly independent of the cognitive effort expended by the learner and of initial differences in the amount of recollection" (p. 410).

Tagg (2003) discusses strategies to promote effective student learning, that is, deep learning. In deep learning, the student concentrates on what the author is trying to say, his or her intentional content or thesis. In surface learning, on the other hand, the student focuses on learning or memorizing the text.

Tagg recommends a pedagogical shift away from the lecture mode and toward an interactive mode. He also suggests that teachers utilize different types of reading activities to get at the same concepts. He believes that students need to make personal connections with what they are reading, reflect in writing on what they have learned from their reading, and share their reflections with other students in the learning community.

At Kingsborough, we emphasize the importance of deep reading. Through a process of discovery, students work together in groups in ESL class to tease out ideas and find personal connections with abstract sociological concepts. In discussions of sociological ideas in ESL class, students attempt to explain, exemplify, and apply these concepts to concrete situations from their own experiences and from the books they are reading so that they may gain a deeper understanding of them and of their connection to the real world. Students express their understanding of these concepts in writing for ESL and sociology classes.

Our program strives to provide an integrative, interdisciplinary, whole-learning experience for the students. Putting students at the center of the learning process is central to our philosophy and pedagogy and is crucial to building strong and successful learning communities. One former student comments on her learning community experience in the following way:

> I like that all our classes are connected with each other. Now all the teachers help us with our sociology essay and this is very helpful for me. I think that without this help I could not get the idea of what I have to write about. I noticed that all the materials on ESL, Speech and Sociology are connected and it helps me to understand it better.

In our ESL learning community classes, we also emphasize talking to learn (Britton 1982) as well as reading and writing to learn. Talking to learn occurs when students connect in a personal way in a small-group setting to discuss the academic work they are doing, the concepts they are learning, application of those concepts to real situations, and activities centered on problem-solving related to course material. They also read their journals, essays, freewritings, and other written work to each other and discuss each other's work.

Talking to learn naturally leads to student gains in self-confidence: students find their own voice, they are listened to better by peers, and their suggestions and questions are valued and taken seriously. They also see other perspectives in their peers' ideas and learn to value and respect the ideas of others. We see a definite relationship between a student's feeling of self-confidence as a learner and his or her self-efficacy (see Bandura 1981, 1986; Schunk and Hanson 1985), as noted by Mlynarczyk and Babbitt (2002): "Students with a high degree of self-efficacy believe that they can succeed at school tasks if they try hard and use effective learning strategies. Such learners are more likely to persist at tasks and eventually to accomplish them" (p. 81). This is the case among Intensive ESL Program learners, as shown by samples of reflective writing found at the end of this section.

Reading to learn and writing to learn are important features of our ESL learning community program and intersect with talking to learn activities (see Babbitt 2001). All these learning community activities contribute toward preparing students to cope with difficult assignments in future college courses. In ESL class, students read extensively, about ten pages every day, from full-length books. The shorter expository prose they read is related to the books read in ESL class and to the topics studied in sociology or in their other courses. Students are expected to do in-depth analysis of reading through various writing genres, including essays, several types of reading journals, point-of-view writing, rewritten class notes, and so on.

Journaling is a valuable form of writing because it allows ESL students to focus on constructing meaning, analyzing ideas, and relating ideas in a reading to personal experience and to other ideas. Students may also express opinions about events and concepts found in the reading and explain and support these opinions in the informal and nonthreatening format of a journal entry. Here students get practice in allowing their ideas to flow freely, without having to focus on correctness. Students write journals about the novels and articles they read and about topics in their sociology texts.

When I work on sociology journals with students, I first discuss the journal questions with the class to make sure students understand specifically what they are required to do. Then students begin to work on their journals in small groups in ESL class, with all group members sharing responsibility for contributing to the journal. Students discuss questions and topics assigned in the journal, and group members take turns recording responses to journal questions assigned to their group. All groups answer some common questions, and each group is assigned its own additional questions. When groups do not finish their journal questions in a class session, each group assigns its members parts of questions to work on outside of class. In another class session or in a lab session, groups review their individual work and finish their group journals. Then the class reviews the sociology journal in a whole-class setting, with each group reporting on responses to its own questions. Group members are considered expert in the topics designated to their own group, and students from other groups ask them questions during the discussion of their topic.

I make an effort to balance groups by varying first languages in a group and by including stronger and weaker students in the same group. Groups of different students and different sizes coexist throughout the semester. For example, a student may be one of three in a group that is working on peer review of essays, one of four or five students in a reading journal group, and a member of a different group working on sociology journals. Groups are also dynamic in that students do not spend the whole semester in the same sociology, reading journal, peer response, or other group. Student membership in each type of group changes throughout the semester so that each student in a cohort has the opportunity to interact academically, socially, and on a personal level in a smaller community within the larger whole-class community. In this way, there is an intersecting and layering of smaller learning communities within the larger learning community, which facilitates the formation of stronger academic-social bonds among students in a cohort.

Of course, there may be a clash between a few individuals in a group, and this situation is often worked out by group members themselves. On the whole, however, groups are active, vibrant, hardworking, and serious yet relaxed and comfortable. The small-group setting is the ideal forum for students to interact positively, respond openly, help each other, and gain confidence in their own voices and ideas in addition to providing a safe environment for the quieter student to be heard. Another important feature of small-group work is that each student is responsible to every other member of the group community. That is, each group member must take an active role in the tasks of every group to which he or she belongs. The majority of the students take seriously the trust that their group mates place in them, and they contribute actively to the work of the group. In return, group members support and help each other with their assigned work.

Student Response

It is clear from student self-assessment in the form of reflective freewriting and from end-of-semester student evaluation (as well as from grades and pass rates) that students benefit from the strength and diversity of their academic-social learning community. They are no longer isolated in a new environment: they have friends with whom they study, collaborate, and socialize. When this is added to the collaboration of instructors, counselors, and tutors and the support network they provide for students, it is not surprising that the scaffolded, multilayered structure of the learning community environment is instrumental in helping students form positive connections and relationships on various levels within the college community.

We instructors learn much from students' written reflections on their own learning process and on their work in small groups, as well as from observing their interactions with each other. Students not only find talking, reading, and writing to learn helpful to them in learning new material and discovering new ideas but also are gratified that other students value their ideas and opinions. Through these student reflections and observations, we note students' confidence and self-efficacy vis-à-vis their own learning process. The following student comments illustrate these points:

> This group work helped me a lot. I helped my classmates and I learned from that. My classmates helped me a lot too. They explained what I needed and I connected it.

> This did help me, because I was reading others essays which helped me understand some things. Also by reading their essays I got more ideas.

> Today I solved my confusion after we discussed this chapter [in the sociology text], but I felt very tired about it. Maybe it was too much that we didn't know before, then in one time, we got all of it!

> I think that there is so good to have a group with me to do the sociology question. Because I can't do it by myself. That is too difficult to do it by myself.

> In this class, we shared the idea of other groups for the sociology journal. It help me know more about this chapter. I think it is good for me.

> In my group we helped each other to answer the questions. I enjoyed today's class.

▞ PROFESSIONAL RESONANCE

Faculty Development

A learning community program such as the one described here offers myriad innovative ways for faculty in diverse disciplines to work together to create curriculum, joint assignments and projects, and class formats. Through faculty development workshops, team meetings, lunch meetings, e-mail, and phone conversations, faculty build their intersecting course curricula. Once themes for linked courses are determined, instructors choose books and other course materials that support these themes. Faculty design at least one (and often more) joint writing project, and students benefit greatly from having assignments read by two or more instructors. Students also derive many benefits, as I have noted, from working on interdisciplinary assignments both individually and in small groups.

The mutual support and interconnection of courses in a learning community begin with collaboration on the part of instructors whose courses are linked. An important aspect of the faculty development program is having teachers from different disciplines work collaboratively to develop their linked course curriculum within an interdisciplinary framework. As I have said, the ESL curriculum requires that students do a great deal of reading and writing, and much of this work grows out of the interdisciplinary collaboration on course structure and content by faculty that share the same cohort of students. Through presentations, relevant readings, response to readings, sharing of experiences among all teams, and small-team planning sessions during faculty development workshops, faculty build an interdisciplinary curriculum and create joint team assignments, such as the artifact assignment discussed earlier.

Presemester Collaboration and Orientation Workshop

Linking faculty, in particular those linking for the first time, are expected to work together before the semester begins to choose course materials, plan curriculum, create joint assignments, and design syllabi. Faculty need to choose books well in advance so that texts, trade books, and other materials for all courses in each learning community can be ordered in time. New books are distributed at the presemester orientation workshop. A small library of books used in ESL learning communities has been created in the reading and writing center. Books are returned at the semester's end except in cases when the same books will be used in the following semester. Tutors need to have access to all books that students are reading to be optimally effective during class sessions in which they facilitate small-group work, take part in discussions, or take notes.

Before every semester, we schedule a 2- to 2½-hour faculty development orientation workshop for instructors, counselors, and tutors. These workshops begin with greetings from Kingsborough's provost and vice president and from the associate dean of academic programs. It is gratifying to faculty in ESL learning communities to be recognized by the college administration for being instrumental in creating a successful program and to know that the administration supports their initiatives and recognizes their hard work.

During our presemester workshop, we may have a discussion on an article that faculty have read before coming to the workshop. Articles we choose have relevance to learning community issues of all sorts. We attempt to focus discussions on topics suggested by faculty, which range from interdisciplinary topics about how to create shared journals and projects to how to resolve problems of students in cohorts. Generally one hour is reserved for learning community teams to work together on the curriculum, the intersection of course ideas and material, assignments, and tutors' roles in the classrooms and in tutoring sessions.

Teams also plan their own meetings throughout the semester. Ideally, teams should meet once a week to make plans, review the previous week's work, discuss problems that have occurred, and look for solutions to problems. Not all teams can do this, and some teams rely more on e-mail or other ways of staying connected. At the orientation meeting, we also schedule the faculty development workshops for the semester: three monthly workshops of 1¼ to 1½ hours for all teams in the program.

Faculty Development Workshops

The format of these workshops is similar to that of the first orientation workshop. We generally begin with a whole-group session in which we discuss topics and issues of relevance to all teams. In addition, teams often make presentations to learning community faculty about a project, assignment, or practice that worked well or about one that did not work as expected. These presentations highlight interdisciplinary learning initiatives and, consequently, have valuable practical applications for all teams. Occasionally students' problems are discussed, such as problems of assigned work or those of a behavioral or personal nature. Counselors are very helpful in dealing with many of these problems. Tutors are also very valuable to the team. They often serve as liaisons between teachers and students since they see the students for four hours each week in the reading and writing center during tutoring sessions as well as in the classroom. They may see the stresses and struggles of students in ways different from those of the instructors.

When faculty are asked to read an article for a workshop, we plan whole- and small-group activities around that article during that workshop. In the academic year of 2004–2005, we chose articles from *Crossing the Curriculum* (Zamel and Spack 2003), a volume dealing with the ESL student in college courses across all disciplines.

Reflection in Two Domains: Student Self-Reflection and Group Reflection, and Faculty Self-Reflection and Team Reflection

Student Self-Reflection and Group Reflection

By using Classroom Assessment Techniques (CATs; see Angelo and Cross 1993), students in the learning community reflect on what they learned, what problems they encountered, what they found confusing or difficult to understand, and how the group dynamics helped or hindered their progress. Reflection on various aspects of class activities on CATs serves as formative assessment for students and instructors alike. Through reflection, students develop the ability to assess for themselves what they have learned and what they have not completely grasped. Reflection enables students to heighten their awareness of how they have integrated their learning experiences into their life experiences. That is, students examine their experiences vis-à-vis the ideas they are learning about. When students make connections between concepts they are learning about and their classmates' personal experiences, they not only achieve a deeper level of learning but also gain a better metacognitive awareness of their learning process: they know about what they have learned and what they have not. Students' reflections might refer to a particular class session, project, or reading they are working on in a group or alone.

Reflections are done in writing, individually or collectively in groups, on an ongoing basis throughout the semester. Students write reflections anonymously either at the end of a class session or at the end of an activity and often voluntarily share them with classmates. Most reflections take just one to five minutes to complete. Some self- and group-reflection topics, which are examples of CATs, include the following:

- What was the most important thing you learned today? Why was it important to you?

- Was there anything that confused you during today's class/your group work? If so, explain.

- Were you finally able to clear up the confusion? If yes, how? If not, why not?

- What made the class/group work go well today?

- How could the class/group work/project have gone better today?

- Talk about how your group work went today: Positive aspects? Negative aspects? The best thing that happened? A problem or difficulty that occurred?

- Which sociological concept did you come to understand or learn about in your group today? Explain it.

- How did your group help you understand a concept or idea that was not clear before?

- How did you help your group understand a concept or idea that was not clear before?

- Give an example of a concept you talked about in your group today.

- How did peer review of your essay and the essays of the students in your group help you with your essay? Your understanding of the writing process (i.e., organization; development of your ideas; analyzing your ideas; analyzing ideas in books/articles; supporting your ideas with examples, explanations, and quotes from text)?

- What difficulties did today's reading present for you? How could you understand the reading more completely?

Self- and group-reflection topics can also be about homework assignments, journals, and other work, including the work done in tutoring sessions.

Much has been written about the benefits of CATs (see Angelo and Cross 1993; Cross and Steadman 1996; Southern Illinois University Edwardsville n.d.). As previously mentioned, reflective CATs, measures of formative assessment such as the ones described here, benefit faculty and students in many ways. They help students in a process of discovery. Students, through reflection, learn to examine their learning processes on a conscious level and to think more critically, analytically, and objectively about what they are learning, why they are learning it, and where their difficulties lie. They also begin to identify obstacles to their learning, the first step in attempting to overcome these obstacles. At the same time, students discover their strengths (e.g., what they do understand, how they can help their peers).

Reflection is an integrative learning experience for students on several levels. Students discover classmates' perspectives of concepts they are learning and the varied experiences their classmates bring to the group. They think about their own experiences in relation to the concepts and form connections among their experiences, ideas, and perspectives; their peers' experiences, ideas, and perspectives; and the more abstract subject matter. The deeper understanding of the content of the courses and their interdisciplinary nature that students gain, in part, through reflection can make what they are learning about more real and meaningful to them.

Student reflective writing also gives instructors insights into the students' needs and, in this way, helps them better plan class work and assignments and make adjustments whenever necessary.

Faculty Self-Reflection and Team Reflection

Just as reflection is an important dimension of student learning, it is also an important component in the process of faculty development. In our Intensive ESL Program, we encourage individual instructors and teams to reflect on such topics as projected outcomes of assignments and projects and whether they have been met, level of collaboration among team members, tutoring issues, student progress, student difficulties, and other aspects of the learning community experience for students and faculty.

Faculty self-reflections and team reflections are valuable to team members in ways that student reflections are to students: they make faculty more aware of the students' learning processes, their understanding and application of ideas, the role of students' experiences and perspectives in connecting with concepts in the courses, and the difficulties that students experience. Faculty also develop a greater appreciation for the interdisciplinary advantages of learning communities. For example, when students learn more about a sociological concept through reading and discussing a novel in ESL and preparing an oral presentation for speech, they come to understand the concept from multidisciplinary perspectives.

Instructors also become more metacognitively aware of their pedagogies, expectations (or lack thereof), and curriculum for learning community courses. Faculty are guided by their self-reflections and group reflections as well as their students' reflections in making constructive changes in pedagogy, curriculum, assignments (including joint assignments), and class and tutoring activities. The reflections are valuable to Intensive ESL Program directors in helping them align the focus of faculty development workshops to the needs and concerns of the faculty. From faculty and team reflection can come decisions about presentations in future workshops by counselors on particular student issues and by instructors on effective assignments and activities (or not-so-effective ones), readings to assign for workshop discussion, and other issues around which to center faculty development workshops.

As new faculty enter into the learning communities, issues of collaboration, curriculum, and pedagogy need to be addressed anew. Faculty who have been in the program help mentor new team members. Faculty development workshops are structured so that both new and experienced learning community faculty work together in ways that benefit both groups. In all workshops time is set aside for team collaboration. Weekly team meetings facilitate the integration of new faculty into the work of the team. When teams cannot meet on a weekly basis, other forms of communication are encouraged with varying degrees of success. In cases when teams do not meet regularly, collaboration does suffer. Directors intervene and attempt to resolve difficulties among team members when appropriate.

An ongoing focus of faculty development is to effect positive change in pedagogy, curriculum, and level of course integration and collaboration. An important goal is to enhance the program so that students derive the maximum benefit from participating as active members of a learning community.

Outcomes and Assessment

On their syllabi, faculty generally state course outcomes and what students are expected to do in the course to achieve these outcomes. An example of an outcome could be that students write a well-developed, drafted essay about a work they have read, with reference to the text and quotes from it to support their ideas. One series of activities that would lead students to achieving this outcome is journal writing (there are various types) about the text, including quotes from the text, explanation and analysis of quotes, connection of quotes to students' experiences, and discussion of reasons students chose a particular quote. Journals are discussed in small groups with input from peers. Then essay topics are developed, generated by either students or faculty. Students may incorporate parts of journal entries into essays. There is a peer review of first drafts; instructors review other drafts.

Assessment is built into all ESL courses as it is into developmental English courses. A portfolio system to determine progress in writing and a long-answer reading test are cross-graded by instructors. ESL and developmental English faculty have designed the assessments and continually review and refine them.

■■ INSTITUTIONAL CHALLENGES

One of the greatest challenges for any new program is to enlist the support of the administration. At Kingsborough we are very fortunate to have an outstanding level of administrative support. Eleven years ago, the former provost, with the dean of academic programs, asked the ESL director and several faculty to develop a program that would address the special needs of ESL students. The block-program structure of the Intensive ESL Program, which included two additional hours of ESL instruction, two additional hours of tutoring, and four other courses, was created. The program was more costly than having stand-alone courses for ESL students, but the payoff for the college came in terms of student success in the first college semester and beyond. Student persistence in courses was much higher in the program, particularly in content courses that have high withdrawal rates. The success of our students continued, the program was institutionalized and mandated for almost all entering full-time day students, and the extra instructional hours were also institutionalized.

In the first report I wrote as director of the program, I discussed some of the research into learning community programs, most of which were designed for the nondevelopmental college population. One way for an institution to gain administrative support to experiment with a program is to present admin-istrators with credible research into the workings and success rates of such programs. Even in these days of shrinking budgets, institutions may be likely to pilot a comprehensive program that has been found to boost the retention and graduation rates of ESL students in other institutions.

At Kingsborough, the administration has been so impressed with the program's success that it lowered the cap on content courses (e.g., sociology, psychology, history) in the program from forty-five to twenty-three students to equal the cap on ESL courses. Additionally, two years ago, Kingsborough began a new program, the Opening Doors Learning Community Program, for developmental and nondevelopmental students who were entering the college. This program was modeled after the Intensive ESL Program. At present, the learning community initiative continues to grow at our institution because of the positive results of first-semester ESL and non-ESL students who become integrated into the college community through their learning community programs.

Recruiting faculty for a learning community program requires sensitivity. Some faculty see participation in such a program as something they would not like to do. Many faculty, however, become convinced of the benefits of joining the program from colleagues who have had positive experiences in their classes with our more motivated students. After discussion with department chairs, we reach out to nonparticipating faculty who may be interested in being part of a learning community team. When faculty express their interest in the Intensive ESL Program to the program directors, we discuss the program with them and speak to the chairs of their departments before including them in the program. Occasionally faculty leave the program for various reasons, but most find the experience of collaborating with colleagues in a learning community rewarding.

▄▄ EXTENDING THE DIALOGUE

As I have illustrated in this chapter, learning communities can make a real difference in the lives of entering ESL college students. Anecdotally, students have reported in writing and orally to faculty and to prospective Intensive ESL Program students what the program has meant to them and the impact it has had on their college careers and on their lives. Quantitatively, in-house data from the college's Office of Institutional Research and from program reports indicate that students do better in their first semester and beyond in ESL as well as in other courses.

The formation of an academic-social learning community of students in a cohort provides the grounding for an integrative and successful college experi-ence. Faculty, particularly those in non-ESL disciplines, work on changing their pedagogies to emphasize writing, talking, and reading to learn within an interdisciplinary framework. In reading, the focus is on having students reach a deep level of reading, not for facts but to discern and infer the author's meaning and intentions. Through small-group, shared-inquiry learning, students hear their own voices and the voices of peers in their community. They listen to the perspectives of others in a multicultural environment. By sharing their own perspectives, they gain confidence in themselves and their ideas.

ESL learning communities can take many forms and structures. The Kingsborough model is one that can be adapted to various settings and institutional needs. ESL faculty and administrators at institutions without an ESL learning community program might consider developing a pilot program that suits their needs and the needs of their ESL population.

∷ CONTRIBUTOR

Marcia Babbitt is chair of the English department and for the past nine years has directed the Intensive ESL Program at Kingsborough Community College, in Brooklyn, New York, in the United States. She also codirects Opening Doors, a learning community program for developmental and nondevelopmental students who are entering Kingsborough.

CHAPTER 5

The Perfect Storm:
Workforce Education in the
Pacific Northwest Seafood Industry

::

Laura Lenhardt, Eileen Purcell, and Marian Tyson

In the film and book *The Perfect Storm*, fishermen battle a raging storm in their quest to bring home the riches of the sea; however, despite heroic efforts by a well-trained crew, they are overcome. The saga of Clatsop Community College's struggle to implement workforce education in the seafood industry also lacks the traditional Hollywood happy ending. Yet major barriers were crossed and many victories were achieved.

:: FRAMING THE ISSUE

Clatsop County covers 1,085 square miles in the extreme northwest portion of Oregon, in the United States, and has a population of approximately thirty-six thousand residents. The Columbia River, which empties into the Pacific Ocean from Clatsop County, forms Oregon's northern border with the state of Washington. The county encompasses twenty-six miles of coastline as well as the fir-forested Coast Range, both of which in the past supported a viable economy centered on the fishing and timber industries. With the depletion of natural resources in Clatsop County, structural unemployment has hit the county hard as resource-based industries continue to shrink. Additionally, seasonal unemployment continues to plague the county's workforce. Seasonal jobs, a restructuring of the forest industry, and a growth in nonmanufacturing jobs (many generated by growing tourism on the North Coast) have contributed to a significant gap between the per capita income in Clatsop County and the national average. In 2004 the annual average wage per job in Oregon was $35,000 and $28,137 in Clatsop County (http://www.indicators.nwaf.org).

In Clatsop County, there has been significant growth in the number of new jobs that do not provide a living wage. For example, in Astoria, cannery workers, hotel maids, housekeeping staff, and restaurant cooks are among the most frequently listed positions in the local want ads. Statewide, the unemployment rate recently dropped from the highest in the nation to third (Hunsberger 2004). Oregon also has had the highest hunger and food insecurity rate among all U.S. states for four of the past five years. Food insecurity is defined by the U.S. Department of Agriculture as "limited or uncertain access" to a regular and safe food supply (Cohen 2002, 3). Households with employed adults are at a significantly higher risk for hunger in Oregon than elsewhere in the United States; this fact is attributed to a crash in resource-based industries and the high cost of living in Oregon (Edwards and Weber 2003).

Snapshot: Impact of Literacy and Skill Gaps

Compounding changing environmental and economic factors, workplace skill levels are having a direct impact on the Clatsop County job market. Private- and public-sector companies alike are facing the problem of a local workforce with a severe deficit in basic academic and vocational skills. The 2003 National Assessment of Adult Literacy (NAAL) survey indicates that 43 percent of the nation's population scores at Below Basic and Basic prose literacy proficiency (National Assessment of Adult Literacy 2005). Adults who read at Below Basic do not read well enough to read a food label or a children's story or to fill out an application. Persons who function at the Basic level of prose proficiency can compare and contrast information but lack problem-solving skills. They also may be able to read text but have a low rate of comprehension. A deficit in basic literacy skills greatly affects job opportunities and the quality of everyday life. Low literacy skills prevent individuals from performing daily functions that many people take for granted. Fourteen percent of Clatsop County's population cannot read and write well enough to fill out a medical information form or interpret payment on utility bills. Thirty-eight percent of all county residents, including both native-language and non-English speakers, cannot cope with critical tasks such as interpreting instructions for child car restraints or Oregon voting pamphlets (Portland State University 1996).

Lacking skills to support their children's education, parents pass on a legacy of intergenerational illiteracy to their offspring. Often illiteracy is coupled with an inability to make sound decisions. The residents of Clatsop County suffer from high rates of drug and alcohol abuse, domestic violence, and child abuse. There has been a growth in single-parent families and teen pregnancy (Clatsop County Commission on Children and Families 2004). A good portion of the county's population lacks the skills to adjust to the changing demands of the new workplace as the county struggles to evolve from an agrarian and natural resource–based economy to a service and knowledge-based economy. Until about twenty years ago, people here could make a decent living with only a high school diploma or even without one. This is no longer true. These complex issues have made the integration of education, supported by a foundation of strong literacy skills, more critical than ever.

The North Coast has one small community college, Clatsop Community College, to serve not only Clatsop County but also portions of neighboring Columbia County in Oregon and Pacific County, in the state of Washington, across the Columbia River. The area is home to several diverse communities linked by limited public transportation networks. South County has a few small wealthy beach enclaves where retirees and artists reside. The town of Seaside is supported mostly through beach tourism, while the county seat, Astoria, historically has been supported by fishing and logging. There are also isolated hamlets scattered throughout the area that suffer from endemic poverty. The magnitude of the problem begins to emerge when considering the low educational levels of both the native and immigrant populations who are served by an understaffed community college adult education department.

Another important consideration must be addressed if literacy programs are to have a positive impact on the county's future—the changing cultural makeup of the county's population. A wave of new immigrants, primarily from Mexico, is influencing how Clatsop County residents work, learn, and communicate in their communities.

The Hispanic Population

During the past decade, the Hispanic population in Clatsop County has continued to rise. The 2000 Census reported that 4.5 percent of the county's population is Hispanic. It also pointed out that 7 percent of the county's population speaks a foreign language at home (U.S. Bureau of the Census 2000). We can only guess at the true number of Hispanic people living in Clatsop County. According to a member of the Lower Columbia Hispanic Council, the Mexican government recommends that any official census of the Hispanic population be multiplied by 2.5 to find a more accurate number. Using that calculation, the county's Hispanic population could rise to nearly 11 percent. Many unreported Hispanic people migrate through during periods of seasonal work; however, there is also evidence that more Hispanic families are settling here and that their numbers will continue to grow on the North Coast.

Those working with the poor in Oregon agree that undocumented migrant workers, people living in extreme poverty, are suffering in silence. Without health care or adequate benefits, these Hispanic workers struggle to feed and care for their families. At the same time, many support extended family in Mexico. In Clatsop and Pacific Counties, Hispanic people now process seafood, replant forests, and harvest holly and cranberries. They also work in large numbers at motels in housekeeping services and in restaurants as cooks and kitchen help. The U.S. Bureau of Labor Statistics found that between 1996 and 2000, one of every two new jobs created in the United States was filled by a foreign-born worker (Mosisa 2002). *The Oregonian,* Oregon's state-wide newspaper, reported that "America's middle class has come to depend on low-wage workers, 20 percent of whom are immigrants . . . two in five of the low-wage immigrant workers are undocumented" (Tilove 2004, A8).

Most of the jobs held by Hispanic workers are seasonal and pay minimum wage. Although Oregon boasts one of the highest state-mandated minimum wages in the nation ($7.50 versus the $5.15 federal level), the increasing costs of rent, food, and fuel leave minimum-wage workers in poverty. Immigrant workers are particularly vulnerable; many lead precarious lives with little social and civic support and, with poor English skills, will continue to labor in minimum wage jobs.

The short seasons, long hours, and hectic pace of many jobs contribute to poor attendance at English as a second language (ESL) classes at the local community college. Families and friends share housing and vehicles and must juggle complicated work schedules that can change daily. Workers at the fish processing plants must call in each day to know if they are working that night or the next day. Many Hispanic people work multiple jobs to support their families. Public transportation is limited, and child care is scarce and expensive. Hispanic workers often find it impossible to fit English classes into their work lives. All of these factors make language acquisition and skill upgrades extremely difficult.

A drop in literacy levels among Mexican immigrants has affected how we deliver educational services at Clatsop Community College. More of Mexico's poorest peoples are fleeing the central and southern states of Mexico. Data from intake forms for Clatsop Community College ESL classes indicate that most of our Hispanic students have between three and six years of schooling in Mexico. The U.S. Department of Labor reports that 55 percent of the foreign-born Hispanic population over twenty-five years of age has less than a high school education (Mosisa 2002). Latinos are now both the most numerous and least educated immigrants settling in the United States. We find that many Hispanic students come to ESL classes with few classroom skills. Some cannot read and write in Spanish; some speak an Indian dialect, making Spanish their second language and English their third. We must consider these challenges when we design and deliver ESL classes.

▦ NARRATIVE

Clatsop County Seafoods Bilingual Class (Laura Lenhardt)

Compounding the circumstances noted previously, Hispanics in our community face many additional barriers to attending ESL classes at Clatsop Community College. The time, transportation, child care, and energy necessary to attend evening ESL classes are often unavailable. It has been a long-term goal of the Adult Education and Family Literacy (AEFL) department at Clatsop Community to initiate workplace-based ESL classes. A class for Hispanic members of the cleaning staff had been successfully implemented for a year and half at a local beach resort. Students were able to attend class in a room where they cleaned so that they could learn English hands-on. Unfortunately, the class was discontinued when the management changed ownership. The new management was not willing to provide space for a class on-site. We feel that the development of on-site classes is crucial to overcoming some of the obstacles that prevent local Hispanic immigrants from getting to class.

Previous letter-writing campaigns to enlist local employers in hotels and restaurants to offer on-site classes had elicited little response. Only a few employers had contacted the college requesting help for their Hispanic workers. Plans to partner with local businesses rarely developed into actual classes. I went to the holly farm but could not get past a small outer office. I visited two fish processors where I encountered lukewarm responses.

We have also had to navigate within the limitations that the AEFL department faces at Clatsop Community College. We struggle with a very small staff; limited funds; and a charge to serve a large, rural county with limited support services. We decided to focus our efforts in the AEFL Volunteer Literacy Tutor program, hoping that we could staff a workplace ESL class with volunteers. We needed collaborative help to develop and deliver a class with a flexible infrastructure. Members of Clatsop's Volunteer Literacy Tutor program, the ESL department, the Lower Columbia Hispanic Council, and the management and workers of a local fish processor all contributed to the success of our bilingual class.

Description of Programs Involved

The Volunteer Literacy Tutor (VLT) program is a Title II–funded program that matches volunteers with students with low literacy skills. Usually the volunteer meets two to three hours a week with an individual or a small group. Presently we have a core tutor group of about fifteen volunteers. The program receives about eleven thousand dollars annually to pay for a coordinator to recruit and train volunteers and to supply study materials to both native and nonnative-English-speaking students.

The Lower Columbia Hispanic Council (LCHC), established in 1998, works for the equitable integration of the Hispanic community in Clatsop and Pacific Counties. The council focuses on improving access to health care, education, and social services for Hispanic residents and sponsors educational and cultural events.

Clatsop County Seafoods[1] is one of many plants that process fish on the West Coast. This plant employs about forty-five year-round permanent employees and up to two hundred temporary workers during certain seasons. It processes ground fish into fillets, cooks crab and shrimp, manufactures surimi (hake processed into a paste that is the base for artificial crab) as well as unloads and ships out sardines and other seafood products. About 45 percent of the plant's employees are Hispanic, but this percentage rises dramatically during peak work periods.

Negotiation and Development (Eileen Purcell)

Although I was skeptical, I approached the management at the seafood plant on the recommendation of a volunteer literacy tutor who is also an Oregon State fisheries biologist. At the same time, a member of the LCHC directed me to a former student who was working as the coordinator of the Spanish-speaking crews at this particular seafood processor.

Near the end of December, after several attempts to meet the manager of the plant, he and I had a hurried conversation. The first thing he said was, "I hear you're here to teach us Spanish, right? We could use some of that." "No, I'm here to teach English. We want to come at it from the other end," I replied. At our next meeting, the manager's first question was "How long will this [instruction] take?" This busy man had no interest in an English class of indeterminate length and depth for his workers. I asked what his objective would be in allowing a class at the cannery. He began to speak about communication and safety issues and about translations of important documents that did not always accomplish what was intended. He emphasized that his non-Hispanic workers needed to know some essential Spanish.

I had come with the sole objective of teaching a vocational English as a second language (VESL) curriculum (still to be developed), and I had to think fast or lose his interest. "Let's teach both English and Spanish at the same time," I offered. He asked what exactly the class would teach. I said that the employees already had a common vocabulary, be it spoken words, facial expressions, or body movements. How would I approach the issue of grammar? I replied that we would not address complicated language structures but instead would deal with a limited vocabulary unique to the floor operations in the plant.

---

[1] The company's name has been changed for confidentiality.

When asked, "How do you teach English and Spanish at the same time?" I said that essential vocabulary featuring key safety and operational words could be taught bilingually. It made sense to him, and I began to believe it was possible, too, even though there was not much precedent to support it. The manager then brought up a very pertinent point about the need to include both language groups in the class. Resentment among the English-speaking crews might fester if instruction was offered only to Hispanic workers. Accommodating this suggestion proved to be a key selling point in initiating the class.

Next, the manager questioned my ability to conduct such a class. How would I determine what vocabulary was essential? He pointed out that I did not understand the nature of the shift work and what operations the cannery routinely conducted. When I reported that I had filleted fish for many years, in fact at this very same plant, the atmosphere lightened, and we moved forward to more concrete planning for the class. Crab season was winding down, and there was a ten-week lull in operations until shrimp season began in April. If we were going to do a pilot class, we had to prepare for it quickly.

When I approached this seafood processor, I had no hopes that the cannery would be willing to pay their employees to attend a class. But when we decided to include both supervisory and floor personnel from the day shift in the class, the manager said that everyone could stay on the clock until the class was over. The night shift personnel were allowed to punch in early. This was the first time any employer in the area was willing to pay their employees to attend a language class.

To design the class, we gathered the essential vocabulary of daily operations. I worked closely with the woman who coordinates Hispanic work crews at the cannery. She arranged for me to meet with Hispanic workers; we identified and translated essential vocabulary used on the dock and on the plant floor. I took photographs on the dock, where I was spattered by airborne fish slime, and in the cold room, where a thick and opaque fog obscured my feet. I then began to prepare PowerPoint presentations for the lessons.

The quality control supervisor and other floor bosses made a list of twenty class participants with ten Spanish speakers and ten English speakers. It is important to note that they selected Hispanic workers who were being considered for a promotion from temporary to permanent employment status. They also chose English speakers from key dock and floor personnel from both day and night shifts. We held the one-hour class twice a week for ten weeks in the break room. We paired Spanish speakers with English speakers; in order to maximize short instruction time, each student was responsible for helping his or her partner learn the new vocabulary and how to pronounce it. Two evenings a week, classes began between 5:00 and 5:30 p.m., after the day shift ended and as the night shift began. Because the class started during the slower winter season, it was possible for night-shift workers to leave the plant floor. The day-shift workers stayed an extra hour. Most students paired up with people they worked with directly on the floor.

My biggest worry was that I would not be able to recruit enough volunteers. We needed at least two teachers: me, to develop and present the PowerPoint lessons, and a bilingual Spanish speaker, to communicate with the Hispanic workers and to teach the English speakers pronunciation. Both the fishery biologist and the crew coordinator committed to the class. An appeal sent out to the LCHC membership produced a bilingual volunteer who works for a nonprofit community investment bank. He had been searching for a similar project in order to bring financial education to Hispanic workers in the area.

The PowerPoint lesson plans proved simple to prepare. I chose a verb used in the cannery, translated it, and illustrated the slide with a clip art picture. I always used the singular (informal) command form of the verb to simplify the lessons. Then I paired the verb with photographs of objects in the cannery. For example, the verb to weigh and its Spanish equivalent *pesar* were paired with fish/*pescados*, ice/*hielo*, it/*lo*, bait/*carnadas*, and so on. I consistently coupled the same clip art picture with the same verb to help the students better remember. We always reviewed the previous lesson's vocabulary and then began new related words. Vocabulary was taught as spoken and not for grammatical correctness:

Weigh the fish.	*Pesa los pescados.*
Weigh the ice.	*Pesa el hielo.*
Weigh it.	*Pésalo.*
Weigh the bait.	*Pesa las carnadas.*

One good way to review was to pair a new verb with the previous lesson's nouns. For example:

Move the fish.	*Mueve los pescados.*
Move the ice.	*Mueve el hielo.*
Move it.	*Muévelo.*
Move the bait.	*Mueve las carnadas.*

Then we added directional commands:

Move the fish to the right.	*Mueve los pescados a la derecha.*
Move the ice to the left.	*Mueve el hielo a la izquierda.*

We practiced little conversations:

Weigh it.	*Pésalo.*
What?	*¿Cómo?*
Weigh the fish.	*Pesa los pescados.*

The big ones?	¿*Los grandes?*
Yes, weigh the big ones.	*Sí, pesa los grandes.*

We also addressed some elementary safety words and phrases:

Stop the machine!	¡*Para la máquina!*
Get out of the way!	¡*Quítate!*
Emergency! Let's go!	¡*Emergencia!* ¡*Vámonos!*

It is important to note that the limited safety vocabulary we covered in class in no way replaced comprehensive safety training. We had no real expectation that when an emergency occurred in the plant, the students would instinctively speak in their new vocabulary. For example, if the razor-sharp blades of a fillet skinning machine needed to be turned off quickly, an Anglo will say "turn it off!" not "¡para la máquina!" Our hope with the safety lessons was to familiarize each language group with the other's possible reactions in dangerous situations.

Successes, Problems, and Results of the Class

How did we address the limitations of our project: an unusual circumstance and setting, little class time, instruction in two languages simultaneously, and shift-change restrictions? First, we limited the scope of what we could accomplish. The final curriculum involved about fifteen verbs, seven directional prepositions, a few numbers, and about thirty nouns specific to the cannery. We presented only a few new words per class, which were then progressively integrated into larger phrases and then into small conversations.

Perhaps most important, we built the lessons on a specific vocabulary identified by the students. Students not only compiled the vocabulary but also altered words during the lesson if a better or already-used expression was available. For example, the word bucket has several equivalents in Spanish. I chose *el cajon* as the appropriate translation, but both the English and Spanish speakers working on the dock were using *la tina*. We changed the lessons more than once to accommodate the students' input. I paired the words for apron/ *mandil* with an illustration of a rather pink and feminine representation of an apron; the students protested so strongly that I replaced the illustration with a photograph of the workers' green rubber work aprons.

Pairing the students with a speaker of the opposite language intensified the instruction. It also had the effect of leveling the students; supervisors and laborers alike struggled with a foreign language. The English speakers, in particular, experienced how difficult it is to communicate in a foreign language. The resulting empathy encouraged an understanding of and a respect for the difficulties the Hispanic workers endure on a daily basis. The Hispanic workers, however, proved to be the more apt students because they had already been communicating in a foreign language. As immigrants to the United States, they are acutely aware that the onus to learn the new language rests with themselves, and not with the native English speakers.

Accommodating the shift changes proved to be more difficult than creating and presenting the curriculum. Some class days, there was no work, or it ended early. When this happened, we tried to hold class at 3:00 p.m., but we could not adapt to these hectic adjustments for long. There were too many people involved to accommodate sudden changes. We had to notify the volunteer tutors and sometimes change the call-in tape at the cannery to alert the students. We all decided the regular 5:00–5:30 p.m. time was best for everyone, even if the students had to make an extra trip to the cannery at the end of the day.

Stabilizing the time also had a weeding effect on student attendance. By the conclusion of the class, the Hispanic workers had maintained better attendance than the Anglo workers. Seven of the ten Hispanic workers and five of the original ten supervisors completed the class. The supervisors sometimes had extra paperwork after the shift ended and could not attend. If they were salaried employees, and therefore not paid to stay an extra hour, they had less incentive to stay. The Hispanic workers also understood that they had been chosen for the class because of their potential to be promoted. The company employs regular and temporary workers; regular employees are eligible for health insurance and other benefits. Regular employees also have a better chance to be called into work throughout the year, stabilizing the seasonal income that temporary workers are accustomed to earning. At least three of the Hispanic students have been promoted since that class ended.

It is important to note that the vocabulary we taught was not always the most correct, but it was the most appropriate for this particular setting. We strove to expedite verbal communication at a specific, noisy, and sometimes dangerous worksite while sacrificing the niceties of formal language structures. Our project was an experiment to see what could be done in a very short time to lower the language hurdles encountered in a bilingual workplace.

At the conclusion of the class, we took a small, informal survey of the class participants. All the participants indicated that the class had been beneficial to them in some way. The Hispanic students generally indicated that the vocabulary was relevant to their work needs, but the Anglo students felt less strongly about this. Both groups agreed that the class had increased understanding of each other's difficulties with language in the workplace. The Hispanic students said that they now felt more comfortable trying to communicate in a foreign language. All of the Hispanic students and half of the Anglo participants indicated that they would like the class to continue. Other employees at the plant, both Spanish- and English-speaking, expressed interest in attending a new session of the bilingual class.

The management at Clatsop County Seafoods decided to discontinue the bilingual class during the peak summer processing season but said they would discuss reopening the class during the fall when operations slow down. The manager also would have allowed a regular college ESL class to be held on-site, but departmental limitations precluded hiring a teacher to staff it. During lunch hours in the summer, the VLT program conducted small bilingual pronunciation workshops with a dozen or so individual workers. A few English-speaking workers signed on to practice pronunciation during breaks with their Hispanic coworkers. We also distributed grammar and pronunciation packets with a cannery theme to almost all the day and night shift even if we had no personal one-on-one time with them. None of this effort fit any criteria that conform to state and federal reporting data; outreach efforts like this, however, can and do generate awareness and interest among the students in other ESL programs available through the college.

We had also hoped that our presence at the cannery during the summer might encourage the company to take a serious look at instituting more classes in the fall. Unfortunately, this did not happen, but all hope is not yet lost; perhaps the fierce winter winds will blow in something other than million-dollar crab harvests and deep-water Dover sole—a new attitude regarding the value of workplace English instruction and a firm commitment to instituting workplace classes.

▪▪ PROFESSIONAL RESONANCE

Conflicting Cultural Perspectives of Workplace Literacy (Marian Tyson)

The dilemmas faced by the Clatsop County Seafoods workplace literacy project highlights several cultural conflicts. A look at the beliefs of these cultures can help educators better understand why workplace literacy education is so difficult to initiate, deliver, and sustain. One major cultural divide deals with the categorization of workers.

A Multinational Perspective: People as Problems

The current viewpoint reflected in the workforce reports of major industrialized nations such as Australia, Canada, the United Kingdom, and the United States is that workers with low literacy skills are problems (Darrah 1992). These workers contribute to the poor or reduced economic performance of the nation. For the nation to succeed and compete, the low literacy levels of the problem workers must be ameliorated. In one Canadian study, 70 percent of employers stated that low literacy skills were a problem in the workplace. Yet, in interviews with employers, workers who previously were considered "good employees" were now considered "poor employees" solely because of their lack of language skills (Hart 1994). Their ability to perform their jobs had not changed; however, the criteria by which they were measured had been altered. One Australian workplace literacy policy informant commented: "A lot of the time really it's probably not much about skills, some of the things could really be dealt with by better organisation of workplaces, or actually rewriting the forms or rewriting the procedures" (Castleton 2002, 2). As corporations seek to compartmentalize jobs into a list of nonvariable skill sets, more workers are found to be lacking in the skills determined to be necessary for those jobs. The skill sets may or may not accurately reflect what a worker needs to know to do the job. Literacy training is viewed as a way for workers to meet the skill set criteria and, presumably, thereby to increase their productive capacity. As Lewis (1997) states, "In the new mood engendered by global economic competition, the fundamental connection today is between literacy and productivity rather than between literacy and human empowerment" (p. 392). People who do not possess a predetermined skill set are viewed as problems. How are community colleges and other educational institutions to respond when asked to provide skill-set training in the workplace?

An Employer Perspective: People as Producers

A fundamental philosophical difference emerges when employers and educational institutions seek to educate employees in the workplace. Although most businesses have now renamed personnel offices as human resource offices, many employers still view workers solely as producers. These workers are responsible for a product or service as detailed in a job description. It is rare to find a company that views employees as valued resources who can and should participate in decisions that affect how the daily business is carried out, particularly in those businesses where the majority of the limited-English-speaking workers are employed. Businesses define the employee skill set that they believe will lead most quickly and economically to the end product. Lewis (1997) makes a key point: "But just as education was not invented to produce goods and services, businesses are ill suited to the role of producing literates" (p. 393). The employer goal in workplace education is to increase production, not to raise general education levels. Therein lies one of the greatest difficulties for sustainable workplace education. How can employees and educational institutions agree on what makes a workplace program an effective one?

An Employee Perspective: People as Pawns

Too often these days, workers in unskilled or semiskilled positions view themselves as little more than pawns that are moved and even discarded by forces with greater power. At the canneries, for example, workers are never sure if they will be working until they call in. If there is a lot of fish to be processed, they may work long hours, for several days in a row. When the catches are small, workers may work for only a few hours on each of a few days during the week. How is workplace education of any help or relevance to these workers? In this particular instance, because of the workplace classes at the Clatsop County Seafoods plant, workers have become eligible for full-time positions. Without the additional language skills, they would be limited to the jobs that provide irregular hours and pay. Many workers view workplace education as one of the few opportunities that they have to improve language and job skills. Yet workers want more than to fill out a skill set. They want to develop skills that allow them to more fully participate in their own workplaces. The Equipped for the Future (EFF) framework, developed by the National Institute for Literacy, addresses that need with broad-based objectives that workers can apply at any place of employment. The EFF framework is more fully discussed in the next section.

The Educational Perspective: People as Participants

Concern from the educational sector over the business view of workers is nothing new. Lewis (1997) voices John Dewey's concern raised in the early 1900s that education would become "a slave to industrialism" (p. 394). Dewey's philosophy set forth the roles more fully defined by EFF, that of people not only as workers but also as community and family members. The EFF worker role map states that "effective workers adapt to change and actively participate in meeting the demands of a changing workplace in a changing world" (Stein 2000, Appendix A). The EFF worker objectives translate into skills that can be transferred and applied in a variety of workplace settings. Workers are taught to be full participants in the workplace. Sample skills include taking responsibility for safety and quality, communicating with others inside and outside the organization, using technology resources, and planning ahead and being proactive to perceived changes. These concepts are taught in conjunction with, and not at the expense of, reading, computation, and English language communication. Kincheloe (1995) reasserts the idea of education for life, not limited to, but going beyond immediate workplace tasks: "A critical pedagogy of work whether in school or on the job refuses to simply adjust workers to the post-modern workplace. Such an education teaches workers to think in a way that allows them to modify values and change the future" (p. 234).

While educators attempt to facilitate holistic learning in the workplace, for example, broad-based language and computation skills, employers demand incremental, task-related, measurable progress. Curriculum developers for the community colleges struggle to develop assessments to show that workers are "making progress." Teaching an employee to understand the command "stop" is usually attainable and certainly measurable. Yet beyond the safety commands, many employers long for the nebulous goal of having their employees speak English better and be understood by their coworkers. What employers do not know, and are often unwilling to hear, however, are statistics such as "It takes from 50 to 100 hours of practice to move from the 9-year-old-level to the 10-year-old level" when referring to language improvement in vocabulary skills and automaticity (Mikulecky 1990, 306).

Part of the role of community colleges in providing workplace education is to open a dialogue among employers, employees, and educators on how going beyond skill-set training enhances worker participation both in the workplace and in the community at large. Educators need to take the lead in convincing employers that so-called "limited language" employees can make valuable contributions to the workplace if they are given a voice and allowed to be participants rather than "just" producers.

∷ INSTITUTIONAL CHALLENGES

Workplace literacy programs are crucial for both employees and employers. Yet resources for these programs continue to dwindle. What creativity can community colleges use in these times of economic crisis? The Clatsop County Seafoods literacy program shows what can be accomplished in less than optimal circumstances, reinforcing the adage "Where there's a will, there's a way." In this case, there was no ESL instructor available from Clatsop Community College to develop and teach the workplace class at Clatsop County Seafoods. The college has only one full-time faculty member who teaches not only ESL but also college preparation and GED courses. There was no funding available to hire an adjunct instructor to teach the class. The company provided release time to its employees to attend the class but did not pay to have the class taught on-site. Only through the tenacity and ingenuity of the volunteer literacy coordinator was this class made possible. Although not the ideal situation, this workplace class staffed by literacy volunteers has managed to open the door into the local canneries. As previously mentioned, the college had tried for several years to start workplace classes with little success until the cannery class. Employers should be willing to share the cost of providing workplace education; however, the burden lies with educators to convince companies that employers as well as employees will benefit.

∷ EXTENDING THE DIALOGUE

Community colleges are the institutional leaders in providing workplace education. To paraphrase the famous Star Trek line, "We go boldly, where few instructors have gone before," even into fish canneries. As Hispanic and other immigrants assume more and more vital and often dangerous industry jobs, community colleges must be on the forefront of fostering education in the workplace. An Associated Press article documented that one Mexican dies per day in the United States from job-related accidents (Pritchard 2004). Some of these deaths are directly attributable to language issues and lack of proper training in the workplace. Additionally, fatal accidents can result when workers are not participants in the workplace who can speak up and change dangerous situations. Workers should not be viewed as disposable pawns, replaceable by the next immigrant in line.

As more and more cuts are made in education, it is not easy for community colleges to find ways to bring education to those who need it most. But for workers with limited language skills, language education, particularly that including safety education, is not some frivolous fringe benefit; it can literally mean the difference between life and death. Community colleges must continue to brave the storm and work toward workplaces that foster learning and participatory processes for all.

☷ CONTRIBUTORS

Laura Lenhardt is a researcher for the Oregon Department of Community Colleges and Workforce Development in Salem, Oregon, in the United States, and has past experience in management of vocational English as a second language programs.

Eileen Purcell has taught ESL as well as English as a foreign language in Japan. She has also worked in the seafood industry. She is currently the Outreach Literacy Coordinator at Clatsop Community College in Astoria, Oregon.

Marian Tyson has taught English for academic and special purposes and ESL for migrant populations. She is currently an ESL, GED, and college preparation instructor at Clatsop Community College.

CHAPTER 6

Creating an ESL College Workforce Program: Challenges, Changes, and Solutions

::

John Thomas

:: FRAMING THE ISSUE

Introduction: The Ideal

"ESL is one of the fastest growing areas of need in the community college" (Spangenberg 2004, under "Foreword"). This statement, originally written in a report for the U.S. Council for Advancement of Adult Literacy, provides a strong indication of the importance of language instruction in community colleges. As early as 1997, the American Association of Community Colleges anticipated that "up to 75% of the workforce would require job re-training" by 2002 (Peterman 1999, 683). In 2004, the Society for Human Resource Management began tracking English as a second language (ESL) classes as a benefit because of the increased global business interest in ESL (Anderson 2004). The widespread need for effective ESL instruction and how it connects to business and academic communities is a trend that cannot be casually avoided by responsible administrators and educators in the twenty-first century. As a result, conscientious ESL program preparation in community colleges is a pressing reality. Successful preparation can provide students with appropriate learning materials according to their needs, ensure progress in language learning, and help students achieve their educational goals. This chapter considers the importance of curriculum planning, addresses the challenges of administrative-educational procedures, and proposes some essential questions for future educators to consider. These views are limited to the procedural aspects of the curriculum, yet I hope that this snapshot of one program can assist others in developing more complete programs in the future. First, a general overview of important procedures would be useful before further discussing the details of a specific community college workforce ESL program in San Antonio, Texas, in the United States.

General Procedure

Gathering information is the first step in determining the type of learners who will be taught in a program and the teaching materials that will be used. Once the relevant information has been compiled, establishing realistic goals by a policy-making authority is the next step in designing a course (Dubin and Olshtain 1986). These goals would further be supported by stating the individual program objectives. Objectives might be stated in exit-level requirements, tasks that need to be accomplished, language concepts that need to be learned or acquired, or all of the above. Productive ESL programs should formulate a well thought-out needs analysis protocol to properly ascertain language proficiency levels. As needs analysis and language proficiency are fundamental components in ESL curriculum design, brief definitions are helpful to further frame this discussion.

Needs Analysis and Language Proficiency

Needs analysis is defined by J. D. Brown (1995) as "the activities involved in gathering information that will serve as the basis for developing a curriculum that will meet the learning needs of a particular group of students" (p. 35). Simply stated, needs analysis explains what the students' needs will be. The definition of *language proficiency* depends on the perspective of how one defines language. Approaches to language can be seen as discrete linguistic points (e.g., morphemes, phonemes, syntax); the functional purposes of using a language (e.g., the language use in reading, writing, speaking, and listening); and pragmatics (the study of how language is being used in context, and in particular ways). These different approaches can be problematic, but if one frames language proficiency in terms of communication, De Avila (1997) provides a useful point of reference. He defines communication under the categories of productive skills, which involve speaking and writing, and receptive skills, which involve reading and listening. These skills are further widened into the headings of input and output skills, along with oral and literary skills. Directing these "skills" under the larger communicative heading allows for more sociological considerations when designing lessons, gathering materials, and formulating more appropriate assessment measures.

The approaches and interpretation of language proficiency will have important relevance to the role of valid and reliable assessment for program design. An academic achievement test (such as the Test of Adult Basic Education) is crucial for level placement, but additional instruments are required when considering the language needs of students. Administrators and educators, who understand language proficiency, are better equipped to properly evaluate language measures. This is important in the planning stages, as educational research groups clearly assert that "assessment, placement, and instructional decisions have to be based on a battery of measures" (Gonzales, Bauerle, and Felix-Holt 1996, 99). The assessment instruments used in the program are discussed later in the chapter.

Curriculum Goals and Objectives

Once a proper assessment of administrative and educational needs has been done, curriculum goals and objectives can be prepared more realistically. J. D. Brown (1995, 71) defines program goals as general statements about the desired aims and attainable purposes of a program, which are based on "per-ceived language" and situational needs. An example of curriculum goals and objectives for an intensive advanced ESL course could be the following:

> Students are required to integrate grammatical concepts in a communicative context and develop communicative language learning strategies by the end of the course.

Instructional objectives are based on program goals (J. D. Brown 1995); for example, by the end of this course, students will be able to

- read a menu,
- order a product on the telephone,
- give directions to a specific place.

Adult Learners

A collaborative student/teacher relationship with a prolonged student engage-ment in language learning can contribute to the success of a long-term adult ESL program. In a workforce ESL program, for example, teachers can make adult students aware of the specific purpose of an English language lesson, especially as it pertains to academic and workplace situations. Adult learners, with years of life experience, will naturally be curious (and sometimes skeptical) about the purpose and intent of lesson tasks. Although this might seem threat-ening to teachers concerned with classroom management, learners could be encouraged to express their views and objections in the second language. This encouragement helps reinforce students' individual and collective autonomy while providing them with meaningful language practice.

The Practical

In many instructional programs, incongruities will inevitably exist between the ideal design and the actual application of the curriculum. There are many

factors that can contribute to changes in the curriculum, including time constraints; budget concerns; institutional requirements; students' personal problems; changes in support; personnel changes; work overload for administrators,
educators, and learners; and different teaching styles and philosophies. As a
result, it would be useful to have a strong degree of flexibility and adaptability
incorporated into the design.

It is also important to recognize how different departmental relationships
affect performance and contribute to the overall effectiveness of the program's
goals and objectives. These entities can be seen as operating on two levels of
communication: a larger (macro) level and a more individual (micro) level.
U.S. federal government institutions communicate with state governments and
educational and business institutions on a macro level, while local caseworkers,
college administrators, counselors, teachers, and students/trainees constitute
program relationships on the micro level. Open lines of communication
between both relationship domains can either enhance or hinder the success of
an ESL program.

ESL and Job Retraining at San Antonio College

In the case of the workplace ESL program at San Antonio College, in Texas, in
the United States, the general instructional goals remained consistent while the
specific course objectives altered. This change was unintentional, yet it allowed
flexibility in teaching and administrative procedures and permitted evaluation
of learners as complete individuals, with their own needs, motives, and issues.
This approach was preferable to viewing the learners as an abstract group of
job-displaced ESL learners.

In April 2004, 152 former workers at the last remaining Levi Strauss manufacturing plant began their studies at San Antonio College (SAC) in an ongoing, two-year job retraining program. Out of that number, 107 students were
placed in a ten-month ESL course. The number of students taught at SAC was
only a small indication of the magnitude of the overall project in San Antonio.
In total, 840 workers had been permanently dislocated from their regular jobs
as a result of Levi's manufacturing relocating to a foreign country. The workers
officially came under the category of "displaced workers" and were to receive
job retraining, along with monetary support and other benefits funded from
federal and state sources, including the U.S. Labor Department's Trade Adjustment Assistance and the Workforce Investment Act (WIA).

Earlier, in December 2003, the Alamo Community College District was
called on to provide a large part of the former workers' training. Schools that
participated in this effort included SAC's Continuing Education Training
Network (CETN) and St. Phillips College. The ESL program at SAC was
scheduled for six hours a day, five days a week, for a total of twelve hundred
clock hours of ESL instruction for ten months. After students completed the

ESL instruction, they continued on to GED and job training courses for an additional ten months. A week before intensive ESL classes began, four instructors at SAC designed the appropriate curriculum for the complete duration of the program. This was quite a large undertaking to be done in such a short amount of time. I was one of the four instructors who participated in course design and instruction.

:: NARRATIVE

Background

In December 2003, workforce specialists at CETN met the Levi's manufacturing workers to provide information to the workers and gather preliminary data for future students and trainees. The same worker might fall into different categories depending on the departmental focus; the terms *trainee, learner, displaced worker,* and *student* can all refer to the same former Levi employees. Four distinct groups emerged from the data: monolingual Spanish speakers, Spanish speakers with limited English proficiency, English speakers with limited formal English language training, and students who were primarily Asian monolingual speakers (A. Luna 2005).

Some SAC trainees tested high enough in their proficiency exams to start GED training immediately: up to 61 percent were first-generation immigrants from Mexico; approximately 33 percent were second-generation immigrants from Mexico, Central America, or South America; and the remaining 6 percent were either Asian immigrants or of Anglo-American descent.

The ESL students ranged from approximately thirty to sixty years of age. Of the total 107 students, only 4 were male. Students also had been unionized, which seemed to have a noticeable influence on their behavior as the courses continued. While at Levi's, the work was repetitive, requiring students to perform continual tasks (such as sewing zippers or pockets onto blue jeans) for an extended period of time. A large number of students spent ten or more years performing the same or similar job tasks, which did not require much academic proficiency to accomplish. One worker had said that on her first day of work the hiring manager told her to "leave your brain outside." It is not clear if this was a common practice at the manufacturing plant.

Environmental Shift

The additional psychological burden of being laid off on January 1 and then having to attend retraining courses in order to receive monetary compensation must have resulted in personal difficulties for the learners. A way of life that had been steady and predictable had come to an end. Learners had to readjust to a totally new environment, become familiar with abstract concepts and skills, and were expected to complete training within a limited amount of time. Many of the learners were grandmothers, and some had dependents living at home. As a number of students were first-generation immigrants and not college students, it soon became clear that the instructors (whose prior teaching consisted of instructing primarily international students with academic experience) would have to modify the curriculum to make the course content meaningful and accessible. It was not clear at the beginning how much modification would be necessary.

Student Challenges and Concerns

Illness and personal tragedy presented real challenges. Students were middle-aged or older, and their medical problems persisted. After years of repetitive hand movements, students had nerve and bone deterioration and carpal tunnel injuries. Some students required medical attention, including surgery. These health concerns often influenced classroom attendance. Other ailments included diabetes, heart disease, arthritis, and cancer. As a result, courses such as computer training, requiring extensive writing or typing, had to be modified for shorter tasks to avoid student discomfort. Deaths in the family also occurred, and we paid special attention to slowly easing students back into instruction. In addition to administration, educational, and caseworker staff, students required additional support. For example, counseling was offered for various personal problems, such as lack of funds or other miscellaneous difficulties. Tutoring provided support to help students learn material. Additional help resulted from a constant dialogue between the students, teachers, and administration. The program's ability to change according to student needs became crucial in providing meaningful instruction to the learners.

Motivational issues were also a concern. Throughout the months of teaching and formal and informal conversations, it became apparent that there was a wide range of motivation among the students. Those who had little or no previous education generally seemed to be less motivated, compared to students who had middle school to high school experience in their native countries. Granted, the correlation between educational background and motivation was not quantified. One student told me directly that she never had the opportunity but "had been waiting" all her life to go to school. The less education one had, it seemed, the more difficulty that person faced, and the less motivated she or he became as the program progressed.

The experiences of being laid off and having to adapt to the rigors of a community college challenged some learners while it frustrated others. Although most students seemed to enjoy learning something new, others were overwhelmed and some appeared to suffer from low self-esteem. Instructors frequently heard statements such as "I can't do this" and "This is too difficult for me," often after the student had successfully completed the task. "I can't speak English" was spoken, in fluent English, more than once.

These self-esteem issues hindered learner progress. It became more important to provide an atmosphere where small successes could be built into the
curriculum. Lessons often involved tasks in which a problem could be quickly
solved (e.g., a short listening activity, student dictations, a timed reading, an
informational gap task). One instructor used drama, requiring students to
memorize and perform a dialogue. After completing the presentations, students were given positive comments from other students.

Program Scheduling

The teachers initially decided that a strong program design would be impera-
tive for student success. After meeting with the trainees and processing the
training logistics (such as office space for case management and orienting and
informing the trainees of their benefits), it was decided that the first day of class
would be April 5, 2004, and the last class would be February 4, 2005. The
students would then begin their GED and job retraining on February 7, 2005.

The content of the program was left primarily to the discretion of the
instructors and approved by the continuing education director. Instructors
understood that federal and state assistance would involve a bureaucratic component, especially concerning program accountability. Therefore, it became
crucial for the instructors to first provide clear program parameters and then
investigate other school programs in similar circumstances. It became necessary
to work from a program model and to tailor the courses to the specific needs of
the students. Teaching materials were also an important consideration. Instructors decided early on to utilize a variety of resources, including authentic (e.g.,
magazine and newspaper articles, advertisements, movies, news reports, school
maps, announcements, questionnaires, assorted realia) as well as modified
(e.g., general textbooks, ESL instructional tapes and videos), to meet the then
unknown needs of the learners.

A Plan of Action

After the first brainstorming session, the instructors formulated a plan of action
with a clear set of criteria, which included the following:

- program goals: general direction of the program

- program objectives: more specific aims of proficiency levels and course
  work; used as guidelines for instruction and assessment

- needs analysis: cyclical determination of what students required (both
  individually and collectively) to achieve the program goals and objectives

- materials: evaluation of the types of teaching materials for both content
  and language instruction

- assessment strategies: evaluation of language proficiency, student progress, and abilities in the language modes of reading, writing, speaking, and listening abilities

- teaching assignments: assignment of individual teachers to levels and specific classes

- course outlines and syllabi: classes included grammar, reading, writing, listening, and speaking components as well as computer classes and life skills classes (which were offered once a week); syllabi were mixed and were primarily functional and skills based but occasionally used theme- and task-based elements

Certain curricular criteria (such as program goals, program objectives, course outlines, and teaching assignments) had first priority and were more clearly stated at the initial stages of the program. Others, such as materials, needs analysis, and assessment strategies, were left to be fleshed out later on. The instructors knew that textbooks that had been ordered earlier in the week would not be distributed until three to four weeks into the program because of the ordering procedure. They also understood that they would not receive student-level placement information until the following week. On the first scheduled day of class, students completed an achievement assessment, which supplemented the tests given to them by WIA caseworkers in December 2003.

The lack of language proficiency measurements available to the instructors caused concern. We were not able to determine the number of students until the first day of scheduled classes. As administrators were heavily involved in managing three major programs, meeting governmental regulations, providing for student needs, and establishing a solid learning foundation, the instructors had to quickly construct an ESL program, gather and organize available teaching materials from CETN, and develop progressive levels in one week.

Review of Preexisting Models

Although the instructors developed the curriculum largely through their own experiences, they drew on existing programs and guidelines from the following sources:

- *The Arlington Adult Learning System: The Arlington Education and Employment Program (also known as REEP)*. This program, based in Virginia, in the United States, provided a reference model at SAC, where adult coordinators could link the components of adult education, vocational education, and higher education into a unified whole. Our program was primarily focused on the first two components of adult education and vocational education. At SAC, the higher education portion became emphasized in the last four months of the program, in order for students to become more prepared for the upcoming GED classes in the second half of their retraining.

- *American Council on the Teaching of Foreign Languages (ACFTL) Guidelines.* These guidelines were used mainly as a reference model for measuring speaking proficiency. Instructors ultimately used a simplified version with six levels—literacy, low beginning, high beginning, low intermediate, high intermediate, and advanced—instead of ACFTL's ten-level version, to have a clearer delineation of student assessment and progress throughout the course.

Coteaching and Class Schedule

The instructors agreed to apply a tag-team, coteaching method of instructing the classes so that all of the instructors would become familiar with each student. This rotation would also break up the monotony of routine and provide students with a variety of teaching styles as opposed to one constant approach. The first class of the day would be with the main instructor of that level, followed by the instructor rotation. In retrospect, it might have been preferable to have students first adjust to the daily routines of classroom activity and then gradually adjust to teacher rotations. As confusing as the changes may have seemed earlier on, students appeared to adapt relatively well to the changing teaching environment.

The day was divided into three major areas: grammar (with an emphasis on grammar meaning or form), reading and writing (with reading used as a support for writing), and speaking and listening (as a conversational course). In addition, there were three other courses taught once a week: life skills, computer, and media. During the week, three computer classes would rotate with the media and life skills courses. Because many students did not have computer experience, we decided that additional computer practice would prepare them for the work training courses they would later attend.

Assessment in the First Day of Class

On the first day of class, the 107 students gathered in a large auditorium after they took the Combined English Language Skills Assessment (CELSA) in the morning. The CELSA is a standardized placement exam, which measures students' reading and grammar skills, and is designed for ESL students. As this test does not expressly measure a student's cognitive language proficiency in the native language, we understood that the scores were primarily designed for initial placement and not a comprehensive assessment of overall language proficiency. During the initial days of the first term, individual, more comprehensive assessments would have to be performed in the form of quizzes, writing samples, and short interviews. As this was a ten-month program, the group consensus was to separate the course into a series of seven-week segments, so periodic assessment of each learner could be sustained throughout the course. The CELSA would also be administered at the midpoint and endpoint of the program. This drastically reduced test validity and reliability as students became familiar with different versions of the test, with some students again completing the same version.

Level Placement

As the instructors were unfamiliar with the language proficiency level of the learners, it was crucial for the instructors to receive the CELSA scores in order to place each student in the appropriate level. There were originally five proficiency levels assigned to the students, from beginning to advanced levels. At the beginning of the course, students were placed in the first four levels: low beginning, high beginning, low intermediate, and high intermediate. After seven weeks, students would be reassessed and, ideally, placed into a higher-level class. A student at the low-beginner level, who moves up a level after each seven-week session, would theoretically reach the advanced level after approximately two hundred days of continuous study. It soon became evident that this was an unrealistic goal, considering the longer amount of time required for language speakers to become fully proficient in a second language (Cummins 1980; De Avila 1997). Nevertheless, the instructors agreed to set high classroom objectives in small attainable steps. I would often tell my core students, "I will accept nothing less than excellence from you." Students understood this as the only passable quality in the latter stages of the course. If they fell short, the quality of their written and spoken projects was still within the parameters of "good" to "very good."

Once students entered the advanced level, they focused on academically demanding tasks, such as extensive reading assignments, lengthy written reports, and oral presentations. It was agreed that these tasks required an advanced level of literacy and enabled students to be better prepared for the next phase of their training: GED and job training.

In order to move students into different levels, alternate class groupings had to occur. This resulted in an extra workload for administrators because of the reassignment of entire rosters that had to be related back to the Texas Workforce Commission. It was collectively decided that although students were still placed at higher levels, the rosters remained the same. Since students had their attendance checked by a teacher in another class, it became more important for instructors to regularly meet about student performance and attendance.

Assessment

As instructors applied more specific assessments, the students were more accurately placed. We agreed to use a range of instruments during the course, as each instrument focused on different aspects of language competency and proficiency. We primarily used discrete-point tests in grammar, listening, and reading exams. Final grammar exams were originally implemented as exit-level tests but lessened to more communicative instruments (such as portfolios) as students progressed to higher levels. We used final research papers and spoken presentations for students at the high-intermediate and advanced levels during the last four-month stage. Students completed daily journals, autobiographies, science reports, and presentations for assessment in the written domain and performed individual and group presentations, oral interviews, classroom debates, and minidramatic performances for assessment in the domains of speaking and listening. We collected this body of work every seven weeks for a more complete evaluation of each student. Each instructor individually assessed exams, portfolios, and interviews and compared results with the other instructors to ensure interrater reliability.

Level Division

It became clear after the first week that the beginning level had to be separated into two courses: a literacy class and a false beginning class. Students in the false-beginner group knew a few basic greetings and could communicate in simple, frequently used words and understand these words in context. This was an issue that we anticipated, yet because of the limited number of instructors, we initially decided on a more general grouping. The literacy class required a fifth teacher, a bilingual Spanish/English specialist, to help meet the language demands of the literacy students. As the program continued, the continuing education director realized that the teaching load of six hours each day was too much for one instructor to teach; thus, two additional part-time bilingual teachers were hired to rotate teaching the morning and afternoon literacy classes. In addition, the achievement scores were so much lower in the literacy levels that we created a miniprogram for them. As this lowered expectations of their performance, the students were, unfortunately, physically distanced from the other levels. Two additional bilingual instructors were hired to teach the fluency levels; the first bilingual teacher would eventually depart to teach the higher four levels.

Changes in the Course Content

The life skills course, which featured day-to-day activities (e.g., cashing a check, calling for information, going to the doctor), was a continuing issue throughout the program. After a few weeks of informal conversations with the students, we discovered that many of the students had lived in San Antonio for more than fifteen (some more than twenty) years. It was clear that they had navigated through the day-to-day life demands with a reasonable amount of success. Most of them had functional English competency, and others could easily manage because of the bilingual environment of San Antonio. Because the life skills course was taught only once a week, we decided that the time would be better spent in a "homeroom" study situation where students could prepare for upcoming projects or work on earlier lessons reinforced by additional assignments.

:: PROFESSIONAL RESONANCE

With the luxury of retrospection, future workforce programs can benefit from the lessons learned at SAC. As mentioned earlier, most of the learners spent many years at Levi's following a regimented routine that required repetitive movements. Workers were represented by their union and, as a result, they had a voice in directing changes in the workplace. The academic environment at SAC was a lifestyle adjustment for them, requiring the learners to perform new tasks in a second language. Students had the benefit of an orientation where they were given information on how to navigate through the system, yet they would have also benefited if their instructors had more insight into the population and individual language proficiency measures.

A more focused needs analysis protocol would have resulted in better preparation during the early stages of curriculum development and allowed for a more thoughtful approach from the instructors. A detailed understanding of program challenges from administrators would have also benefited the program. An earlier timeline would have allowed for the further development of instructor-based materials.

On the positive side, students were remarkable in their ability to act as a single unit. This was evident when they organized group luncheons for more than fifty of their classmates or maintained communications with one another in times of need or distress. The instructors attributed this to their union experiences, in which leadership and delegation of responsibilities were keys to initiating progress. After observing the learners' ability to collectively complete tasks, instructors modified lessons to encourage more communicative group activities. They implemented group presentations, multiple student dictations, jigsaw readings, and participatory campus events (such as plays, lectures, and cultural festivals) to combine English instruction with authentic productive and receptive language strategies.

The life skills class could have been modified, rather than dropped, to prepare students for situational English. Students would have benefited from extended workplace role-play, such as office or pharmacy technician scenarios. Although there was productive communication between the two sections of ESL and GED and job retraining, there was not sufficient dialogue to facilitate further ESL/job retraining content learning. Pre-GED and ESL/job retraining courses could have been implemented as a supportive link between the ESL and training segments of the program.

ESL or EAP: Changes in Approach

During the initial planning of the curriculum, we thought that the program would focus on developing general ESL skills; however, it became clear that some students who had little or no previous public school experience would have to become reasonably proficient in academically demanding tasks, such as taking notes, reading faster (i.e., previewing text, skimming, and scanning), and categorizing newly learned concepts. Students would eventually have to quickly adapt to the highly literate environment of the GED courses. This required the instructors to partially modify some subjects into more of an English for academic purposes (EAP) format during the later stages of the program. They modified reading classes into content courses, in which academic content would become the focal point of learning, while English language learning would become the vehicle for understanding content. They also gradually introduced minilessons in content courses such as biology, anthropology, and U.S. literature. One instructor introduced a Hemingway short story, while another focused on cultural diversity by presenting videos and worksheets of U.S. immigrants from various countries.

As the program progressed, we anticipated that the new vocabulary introduced in the job retraining section might require extra student effort to learn well. Our intention was to first introduce general language for the job environment (e.g., hiring procedures, resume building) and then progress to the more specific vocabulary of the trades they would study (e.g., Microsoft Word, general office, pharmacy technician studies). Although we taught general vocational vocabulary, we decided to abandon the idea of teaching specialized terms and turn more to the academic modes such as learning vocabulary and identifying topics. Instructors recycled language learning strategies taught earlier in the year in the latter stages of the program.

■■ INSTITUTIONAL CHALLENGES

As mentioned before, four instructors were initially hired to design, develop, and teach the ESL course. Additional instructors were hired or transferred from other departments to teach the literacy levels. Halfway through the program, one of the original instructors was let go and one of the bilingual teachers was then transferred to take his place and become the main instructor of the low-intermediate course. The students in the low-intermediate course were ultimately subjected to a turnover of four instructors during the duration of the ESL program. These staffing challenges became problematic, as personnel changes affected classroom continuity and morale. Instructors became accustomed to fielding student questions about changes in personnel or classrooms.

The lack of a single main instructor may have been detrimental to the students' overall performance. This high instructor turnover rate was the result of inadequate screening during the hiring procedure and a lack of foresight as to the potential instructors' commitment of teaching the entire course. If community colleges are to increase the quality of ESL programs, administrators need to seriously address hiring protocols and may need to offer incentives to reduce turnover rate and to ensure a consistently high level of instruction.

In addition, instructors and administrators did not include time for weekly departmental meetings. There was no arranged schedule for instructors to check student progress, address procedural concerns, receive feedback, and further develop course design, which were primarily discussed among the instructors during their lunch hour. Teacher evaluations occurred once during the course of the program, and limited feedback was given. As the administration was generally concerned with maintaining the program, pedagogical and methodological concerns were generally left to the instructors. Because of the daunting scope of the project, I believe that administrative officials faced a task of overwhelming proportions. Time became a precious commodity. As a result, the instructors were entrusted with the responsibility to manage the progress of the ESL program and were largely left on their own. Future ESL community college programs would benefit from weekly scheduled meetings, frequent teacher evaluations, and mandatory professional and educational development courses to improve overall program quality.

■■ EXTENDING THE DIALOGUE

In light of the preceding suggestions, it is important to recognize the amount of time and energy administrative and government personnel and teachers devoted to the completion of the ESL program. In February 2005, the students completed their ESL studies with only 4 percent dropping out of the program. Since the program ended, I have seen many of the students who remarked how much they miss the courses, how much they learned, and how much fun they had.

The program was completed, but many unanswered questions persisted: Would students have benefited from a longer ESL program or prolonged ESL tutoring as they completed their GED/job retraining courses? How much did the literacy classes benefit from bilingual instruction, as compared to the English-only policy of the higher levels? Would a curriculum that gradually adjusted learning environments from previous workplace experience to a more academic setting have been more beneficial to ESL workforce learners? It is hoped that these questions will be addressed locally and in other arenas as ESL programs are created and developed for future learners in the coming years.

▝▘ ACKNOWLEDGMENTS

Special thanks to Anelia Luna, CETN Program Director for Life Studies, for her invaluable insight into the administrative goals and challenges in developing the program and SAC's Continuing Education Dean Tim Rockey for his positive influence on program objectives. Thanks also to ESL adjunct instructors J. D. Boswell and Russ Wagner for their essential contributions to this chapter. Finally, thanks to the 107 Levi's students who taught me more than can adequately be expressed.

▝▘ CONTRIBUTOR

John Thomas teaches ESL at San Antonio Community College, in Texas, in the United States; is an adjunct professor at St. Mary's University in San Antonio; and is recruiter and advisor of international programs in the Austin Community College District. He is currently editing Reading Starter, *a reading primer.*

PART 3

CURRICULA

CHAPTER 7

Curriculum Renewal in a Canadian Context: What, Why, and How

■■

Gabriel E. Ayala and Andy Curtis

■■ FRAMING THE ISSUE

This chapter narrates the experience of a curricular reform at Queen's University School of English in Kingston, Ontario, in Canada, which was carried out between the winters of 2004 and 2005. Our goal in this chapter is to provide readers with a description of the methodology used at the school so that other institutions that are engaging (or will engage) in curriculum reform can learn from our experiences. This account addresses what we did, our rationale for doing it, and how we carried it out. It is important to note that the experience of renewing the curriculum at Queen's School of English was very important for the community of individuals that work there; thus, this account represents an attempt to share this experience with the broader international community of TESOL professionals as well.

Background and Context for the Reform

Queen's School of English is an English as a second language (ESL)–intensive English program (IEP) that focuses on English for academic purposes (EAP). Every year the school receives up to a thousand students from more than thirty countries who are supported by a core of nine administrative staff members and twelve to fifteen full- and part-time teachers who work collaboratively to achieve the goals of the school. Also, every year the school hires a group of undergraduate students, called *monitors*. The monitors accompany our students on sociocultural activities, help them participate in residence life, and provide out-of-class cultural and linguistic support.

In our core twelve-week program, the students at Queen's School of English are provided with more than twenty-two hours each week of classroom instruction and extracurricular activities that help them develop their language skills in a variety of scenarios. Currently the school manages the instruction through an integrated curriculum providing students with learning opportunities in the main four productive and receptive skills: listening, reading, writing, and speaking. These skills are developed with a focus on EAP.

Throughout its sixty-four-year history (i.e., from 1942 to the present day), the school has been zero-based funded; therefore, we support our program based entirely on students' tuition. However, we have been successful in providing students in need with financial aid through scholarships and bursaries; this aid is generally used to support refugees and refuge (asylum) claimants in Canada.

The typical class size is fifteen students. The classrooms are located within the Queen's University campus and mixed with other faculties and departments, giving students the opportunity to experience university life in Canada as well the greater community. Our students have the opportunity to interact with native students at the university at the various cafeterias and residences. The students are encouraged to avoid speaking in their native languages and sign a pledge in which they promise not to. This pledge contains certain regulations, and students not honoring it may not be able to complete the program successfully.

When our students finish the program, some of them apply to undergraduate or graduate schools in North American universities, others apply for jobs in North America, and some return to their home countries to search for employment or further their studies. When the curriculum reform was initiated in the winter of 2004, the school had a skills-based curriculum that had been established in the 1970s.

∷ NARRATIVE

Rationale

In the fall of 2002, Queen's School of English appointed a new director who, from the beginning, started promoting a strong professional development practice among all administrative and teaching staff. The research and literature read, considered, and discussed by the staff as part of their professional development seemed to indicate that the school needed to move from a skills-based to an integrated language approach. Through feedback provided by teachers and administrators during several meetings, it was collaboratively decided that the school would begin a major curriculum reform for the core twelve-week EAP program.

At this stage it was clear that the implementation of the new curriculum was not going to be a top-down strategy (or even a bottom-up strategy) but rather a "middle-up strategy," as explained by McNeil (1996, 253), in which the whole school community, rather than a particular group, was engaged. Since it was this community that decided to go ahead and reform the curriculum, the confidence and trust the community placed in itself helped achieve a smooth transition of the kind not common in a large institution such as ours.

First Staff Retreat

In the early stages of the process, it was considered useful to have a retreat at the beginning of the year (January 2004) to initiate the process. The retreat was structured using Graves's (2000) model of designing language courses. Two aspects that Graves proposes as foundations for any language course are (a) articulating beliefs and (b) defining the context.

The articulation of staff beliefs was expressed in relation to four aspects: one's views of language, the sociocultural context of language, learning and learners, and teaching. Regarding the identification of the context, teaching and administrative staff were asked to identify what they believed were the opportunities and the constraints within the context of our school. For example, when asked to describe her beliefs about the language, one teacher wrote: "Language = fluid, identity, social understanding, descriptive and prescriptive, meaning-based, rules are guides, not ends." Regarding the sociocultural context, another teacher wrote: "Connection undeniable, a window, parameters to language, expectation recognized." About learning and learners another teacher wrote: "Experiential and relevant, community/classroom-based, teachers and students both responsible." Finally, talking about teachers and teaching, one teacher wrote: "Resource and authority figure, helper/facilitator and leader, 'real world stuff.'"

This retreat provided an important set of feedback and data for the reform process that represented the views of key members of the community within the school. These views became the point of departure for the rest of the process.

Project Planning

After the retreat, the management of the school decided that they needed a task force to coordinate all the activities related to the curriculum reform process. The school continued working on all its regular activities during the reform, and we needed to continue working in accordance with our teaching, learning, and administrative standards. The school hired a curriculum advisor to coordinate the activities with input from the director and the program manager. Essentially, the curriculum advisor would review the research literature and create a schedule for completion, along with training and coordinating the teachers and administrative staff. The curriculum advisor had previously been a student at the school, which gave him essential firsthand knowledge of what it meant to be an international ESL student (he was from Venezuela) at Queen's School of English.

The project was planned to be completed in one year and included the following steps:

- creation of foundational documents and presentation of these documents to the rest of the Queen's School of English community

- needs assessment

- review of literature

- determination of goals and objectives

- organization of content

- selection of materials

- presentation and training

Different deadlines and indicators of completion were agreed on with teachers and administrators.

Foundational Documents (Values)

In the early stages of the project the director, program manager, and curriculum advisor suggested that in order to have a solid community-based curriculum, it was necessary to have a document that reflected our beliefs as an institution and as educators with respect to second language education and pedagogy. We believed that this document was crucial for our curriculum because it would determine the framework within which all of our activities would be performed. There were some limitations to this document, but it represented an understanding or agreement about the spirit of the curriculum and that of the school.

The values for the new curriculum came from the retreat that was held in January 2004 and also from further input from the curriculum advisor and the management of the school. We produced a list of values that enabled the school to set the pedagogical parameters for our reform:

- spirit of cooperation

- student-centered pedagogy

- shared responsibility and participation

- respect for diversity

- inclusion of every person

- excellence and professionalism

- error as an opportunity for learning

- promotion of academic attitudes

- respect for the physical environment

The last value, respect for the environment, appears to be relatively unusual, as we did not find it in any of the literature we reviewed; we believe it reflects the Canadian commitment to a sustainable environment, which many of the school's teachers include in their materials and in their lessons.

The document was revised based on input from the teachers and administrators, who were encouraged to make suggestions. After reaching general agreement, the director signed the document to make it a contract among the community. From that point on, any activity or product of the reform process would be aligned with these values.

Literature Review

After the completion of the values document, the curriculum advisor started a process of searching in the literature for articles and books on integrated content-based second language education. We collected and analyzed several papers with the intention of identifying seminal work cited in those papers. During several meetings, we agreed that in order to have a coherent and solid document, it was necessary to avoid combining too many different models. Thus, the task was to identify two or three major models that would challenge us but also conform to the general practices and beliefs of the school.

A Methodological Framework

The first model was Graves's (2000), which worked for us as a methodological framework. Our interpretation of the steps proposed by Graves in order to design a language course revealed the following:

- needs assessment

- formulation of goals and objectives

- organization of the content

- organization of the course

- evaluation plan

115

These were the steps that we followed when implementing the curriculum change, but, as Graves explains, this model is not linear; the process overlaps with different subprocesses, and we were able to go back and correct or revise the different stages.

Conceptual Background for the Curriculum

In addition to Graves's model, we used for the conceptual background of the curriculum the work by Brinton, Snow, and Wesche (1989), which explains that organizing the language learning process around structures and functions is not enough. The goal is to contextualize the language within a meaningful approach: "In a content-based approach, the activities of the language class are specific to the subject matter being taught, and are geared to stimulate students to think and learn through the use of the target language" (p. 2). The teacher sets the target language in context by using content as a point of departure. In addition, Brinton, Snow, and Wesche identified several elements of content-based second language education:

- an English for specific purposes (ESP) perspective: different uses that the learner will make of the target language

- use of informational content to increase motivation

- pedagogical principles: any teaching should build on the previous experience of the learner

- pragmatic- and experience-based instruction that prepares learners for a variety of student life demands

- language used in university and occupational settings

- outcomes suitable for people with identifiable objectives

- use of academic language

- content-based instruction that can serve all age groups well

- instruction appropriate for learners who have specific functional needs regarding the target language

- more of a focus on the meaning rather than on the language structures

- a functional approach

Brinton, Snow, and Wesche (1989) also describe three different models for content-based language education in universities:

Theme-based language instruction. This kind of instruction might be organized around several unrelated topics or one major topic. It includes ways to increase the use of subject matter content in language classes, applies the same topic in a variety of activities (different skills), ensures the inclusion of context and significance of the target language, and uses teacher-generated materials or materials adapted from outside sources. This model is the most widespread of the content-based models.

Sheltered content instruction. Sheltered content instruction consists of content courses taught in the target language to a segregated group of learners. The students are exposed to the second language by means of the regular lectures, readings, and discussions that take place in the content course. The difference between theme-based models and this model is that sheltered language courses assume an institutional framework, such as a high school, community college, or university, in which there is access to content courses and content teaching staff proficient in the target language.

Adjunct language instruction. In adjunct language instruction, students are concurrently enrolled in two linked courses: a language course and a content course. The two courses share the content base and complement each other in terms of mutually coordinated assignments. This kind of instruction requires a large amount of coordination, and the materials used in the language course differ significantly from a more traditional ESL course.

Taking into account the context of Queen's School of English and the nature of our program, the theme-based model of implementation was the most appropriate for our school. This is because our students are in an immersion program and do not attend class in the regular university classroom; institutionally, the school was designed to work separately from undergraduate or graduate studies.

Additional Curriculum Options

Another conceptual model included in the curriculum reform and proposed by D. M. Campbell and Harris (2001) was not specifically designed for language courses but for general education; however, it has some aspects that were useful for our project. We make a distinction between *traditional curriculum options, integrated curriculum options,* and the *integrated thematic curriculum option.*

The traditional curriculum "has its roots in the behaviourist school of thought" (D. M. Campbell and Harris 2001, 3), a leading proponent of which was B. F. Skinner. According to this school of thought, knowledge should be "broken down" into pieces. For example, "reading skills are developed during a block of time called reading; math skills are developed during a block of time called math; and science is taught independently from social studies. . . . Then the curriculum specialist builds logically from the simplest sub-skill up to the complex skill" (p. 3). In short, this is the traditional skills-based curriculum.

The integrated curriculum is based on constructivism as a school of thought, "principally on the ideas of by Piaget (1954, 1963), Vygotsky (1962, 1978), and Dewey (1916, 1938)," which posited that "learners are always actively constructing their own knowledge by striving to make sense of their world. Primarily, students make sense by making connections among ideas as they integrate new experiences into their prior knowledge. The constructivist views the learner as competent and capable of dealing with complexities" (D. M. Campbell and Harris 2001, 3).

According to Campbell and Harris, the integrated thematic curriculum option allows the curriculum to be organized around a central focus, linking content from a number of disciplines and enabling students to study the material in-depth while building a knowledge base and developing learning strategies that can be transferred.

In their model, D. M. Campbell and Harris (2001) suggest different types of roles for curriculum reform: the curriculum team, the teachers that will implement the curriculum, and the students. According to this proposal, we divided the curriculum team into two subteams: the curriculum working group (some volunteer teachers chaired by the curriculum advisor and the program manager) and the curriculum management team (director, program manager, and curriculum advisor). This team had to "understand the full range of theme studies undertaken in the past and currently being planned in the school" (p. 13). Also, the curriculum working group had to have knowledge of institutional requirements, values, and initiatives to maintain a wide perspective and to be sure that the institutional needs and the teachers' and students' needs are addressed in the integrated curriculum. The curriculum management team selected possible themes in line with the values of the school, the goals and objectives of the curriculum, and the needs assessment findings.

Another role for this team was to design guidelines for the assessment of the achievement of the objectives. Also, if possible, the team should coordinate the creation and collection of resources. Finally, according to D. M. Campbell and Harris (2001), "the final responsibility of the school-based team is to evaluate the curriculum. . . . This evaluation should include significant input from the implementing teacher" (p. 14).

The implementation teachers would tailor teaching units to particular students while accommodating some or all of the concepts generated by the team, including additional objectives identified by the individual teacher as being important to specific groups. The plans would be based on a combination of the teacher's judgment and input from the students.

The students would share ideas, ask questions, and express preferences. "They can expect support from their teachers but will realize that they are accountable for reaching certain decisions in collaboration with their classmates" (D. M. Campbell and Harris 2001, 15). This suggestion highlights the importance of the students being included in the unit plans.

As well as developing our theoretical understanding through reviewing and discussing the research literature, we conducted a benchmarking process through which we selected some schools of English in Canada that we identi-fied as similar to ours and analyzed their approaches to content-based English language education. This research helped us visualize what the structure of the curriculum and the course organization might look like during the implemen-tation phase.

Needs Assessment

Graves (2000) also proposes a series of steps in order to proceed with the needs assessment: (a) decide what information to gather and why; (b) decide when, from whom, and how to gather it; (c) gather the information; (d) interpret it; (e) act on it; and (f) evaluate the effect of the action. In addition, J. D. Brown (1995) describes the type of decision regarding needs assessment, including (a) who will be involved, (b) what types of information should be gathered, and (c) whose points of view should be taken into account. Following the authors' advice and because of our community-based approach, we decided to include all three stakeholder groups: students, teachers, and administrators.

To select the information to be gathered, we adapted what Nunan and Lamb (1996) suggested:

- biographic information

- motivation, goals, and objectives—resources

- language proficiency and subjective needs

- attitudes toward error correction

- preferred themes

- attitudes toward the curriculum reform

- challenges faced

- support needed from the administration

We analyzed the data obtained for themes and presented the results to the community for further discussion. The actual information-gathering process was carried out at the middle of the twelve-week summer session using written questionnaires with voluntary participation. The majority of the students, all the teachers, and all the administrators participated (though the administrators gave input in more informal ways). Also, while conducting the written needs assessment, the program manager and the curriculum advisor performed a series of classroom observations to contextualize the data collected.

:: INSTITUTIONAL CHALLENGES

Developing Goals and Objectives

The process of writing the goals and objectives for the whole program and each of our five levels of instruction proved to be an important and considerable undertaking. The curriculum advisor suggested the methodology proposed by Mager (1962) since it is considered very useful for different types of training programs because of its clarity and specificity. Even though Mager's model was developed more than forty years ago, it continues to be relevant in adult skills development. Also, it is an approach to classical models of objective writing that enabled members of the school to develop strong objectives with observable outcomes and well-defined performance criteria. Mager defined objectives as an "intent communicated by a statement describing a proposed change in a learner—a statement of what the learner is to be like when he[/she] has successfully completed a learning experience" (p. 3). Goals and objectives also provide an essential role for our students in that they communicate expectations and help students understand what success means in our program. These objectives formed the framework around which course organization, activities, and evaluation methodologies are planned throughout the curriculum renewal process: "Basically, a meaningfully stated objective is one that succeeds in communicating to the reader the writer's instructional intent. It is meaningful to the extent it conveys to others a picture (of what a successful learner will be like) identical to the picture the writer has in mind" (p. 10).

In adapting this approach, we developed objectives that described what the students will be doing when demonstrating the acquisition of the skills beyond the classroom and after completion of the course, rather than only what the students will accomplish in the classroom. According to Mager (1962), an objective must have three constitutive elements: a description of the *terminal behavior*—what the student will be doing when demonstrating that he or she has achieved the objective; a description of the *conditions* under which the learner will be asked to perform the behavior; and the *criteria* for performance.

The curriculum working group was trained in this methodology by the curriculum advisor, the program manager, and the director, and the group was given the task of collaboratively writing the goals and objectives for the whole program and the new curriculum. At this stage, the main problem was that it was difficult for the teachers to change from a *classroom* perspective to a *beyond the classroom* perspective. This emerged as an area needing more input when the teachers began by writing activities rather than objectives, and the issue was solved by further training and discussion. The completion of this task made the rest of the process run more smoothly since we had, at this stage, a "map" of our pedagogical intent.

Selecting Content and Materials

After much discussion among teachers and administrators, including drawing information from the old curriculum at the school, we selected the content. As a result of our discussion, we were able to design a content matrix, which contains the skills to be taught regarding reading, writing, listening, and speaking.

Regarding the selection of materials, the school invited several publishers to showcase their products and materials at Queen's School of English. We analyzed books and audiovisual materials according to the values of the curriculum and to our goals and objectives. The main aspects considered were physical and practical elements, language pedagogy elements, alignment with our values, and alignment with the levels at the school. The curriculum working group members and other volunteer teachers selected the materials.

Drafting the Document

The curriculum advisor had the task of writing the curriculum document, but he also received regular input from the program manager and the director. In a brief explanation of the document, we can say that it contains the values, a brief rationale, goals and objectives, organization of the course, evaluation guidelines, and content matrices (see the appendix at the end of this chapter). It is important to note that this document is not prescriptive about activities in the classroom. We strongly believe that this document provides a framework for the teacher to negotiate the microcurriculum with the students in the classroom. To achieve this, the document does not have any sort of prescription about lesson plans or teaching methods.

As part of the implementation process, the curriculum was presented to the teachers and administrators. For several weeks, they discussed the draft, and their suggestions were taken into account. By December 2004 the document was ready, and in the first twelve-week session of winter 2005, the curriculum was implemented.

Evaluating the Curriculum

At the end of the first session (April 2005), another schoolwide survey was conducted to gather feedback on the new curriculum and the attitudes of students, teachers, and administrators toward it. One significant problem emerged at this stage: a mandatory ethics review of the survey by Queen's University. In Canada, institutions need to pass through an ethics review process when conducting research with human subjects. It was the first time that the school (not being a research unit or a regular academic department) faced the ethics review board. The board performed the review in an accelerated manner, and the school satisfactorily completed the process. However, by the time the survey could be distributed among the students and teachers, they were completing the semester and involved in final assignments, exams, and so forth. Because the surveys were distributed so late in the session, we had a low student participation rate (all the teachers participated), but we were able to identify different themes and positive aspects and elements to be revised and improved.

▪▪ PROFESSIONAL RESONANCE

The curriculum reform at Queen's School of English entailed a shift in the way we conceived our teaching and pedagogical framework. As practitioners, the teachers felt that they were constrained by the boundaries of the skills-based curriculum since the teaching was somehow isolated from the "real world."

The main successes of this process included the communitarian approach that we chose to adopt throughout the process and the many hours of paid professional development that the school and teachers invested in the process. At the beginning of the curriculum renewal process, almost none of the teachers had any experience in curriculum design. With the guidance of the director and the curriculum advisor, they learned how to bring about a significant curricular change. The teachers stated that they felt their voices were heard and that their ideas, comments, and suggestions were taken into account by the curriculum working group and the management of the school. Also, professionally speaking, the teaching seems to have more resonance in the lives of the students; they are more engaged since the language learning is now articulated within a content-based and combined skills framework instead of the more traditional approach formerly used at the school (i.e., separate lessons with different teachers for each of the four language modalities).

▪▪ EXTENDING THE DIALOGUE

In this chapter we have described the experiences of different groups and individuals at the Queen's University School of English in response to engaging in a major curricular reform. We hope that this account can help other institutions that are starting their own curriculum reform process (or are thinking about doing so).

Ayala, Thornton, and St. Amand (2005) make some recommendations for those engaging in a curriculum reform:

- Plan ahead for the assessment phase.

- Have a person dedicated exclusively to the task of coordinating the project.

- Examine your context (opportunities and constraints).

- Be prepared for a long but rewarding path.

Also, McNeil (1996) suggests that staff professional development plays a key role in successful curriculum implementation: "Intensive staff development rather than single one-day workshops is an important strategy" (p. 254), which proved to be an essential part of a successful process for us. By linking curriculum reform and renewal with professional development, we helped all parties see a range of potential benefits in working collaboratively and cooperatively to effect such a desired series of changes.

▋▋ CONTRIBUTORS

Gabriel E. Ayala is a master of education candidate majoring in curriculum and instruction at Queen's University in Kingston, Ontario, in Canada. Until recently, he was the curriculum advisor and cochair of the curriculum working group at Queen's School of English. His area of research is curriculum development for workplace learning and ESL and EAP programs.

Until recently, Andy Curtis was the executive director of the Queen's University School of English. He received his MA in applied linguistics and his PhD in international education from the University of York, in England. He has coedited two books, coauthored one, and published thirty book chapters and scholarly papers.

▋▋ APPENDIX: OUTLINE OF INTEGRATED CURRICULUM DOCUMENT

Queen's University School of English 2005

1. Rationale
   - Reference to participants
   - Goals
   - Nature of the document
   - Explanation of the curricular model
   - Values (with brief descriptions)
   - Collaborative work and the curriculum working group (brief description)
   - Description of our conception of student-learner centeredness
2. Structure of the curriculum
   - Description of the levels
   - General goals of the twelve-week integrated curriculum
   - Instructional objectives per level and description of the courses
3. Evaluation guidelines
   - Brief description of the school's conception of assessment
   - Grades distribution
4. Skills matrices per level

CHAPTER 8

Whose Technology
Is It Anyway?

⊞

Carol J. Brutza and Martha Hayes

⠶ FRAMING THE ISSUE

> I've got two pieces of bad news about the experimental English composition
> course where students used computer conferencing. The first bad news is that,
> over the course of the semester, the experimental group showed no progress in
> their ability to compose an essay. The second piece of bad news is that the control
> group, taught by traditional methods, showed no progress either.
>
> —Dr. Stephen Erhmann, director of Flashlight of the
> American Association of Higher Education

Given this somewhat perplexing observation, what are we, as writing instructors for at-risk populations, to do *about* and *with* technology in our classrooms?
How should we engage the enabling power of information technology?

For five years, we, the authors of this chapter, have conducted classroom
research to answer for ourselves what to do about and with technology by
examining our own and then our students' reactions to the hardware and
software, tracking student retention and success rates, and ultimately refining
our composition pedagogies. In doing so we have synthesized an evolving
technological approach with the techniques and skills that all effective writing
teachers, with or without those pesky computers, use to engage learners.

College Background

We teach at Gateway Community College in Connecticut, in the United
States, which has an urban campus in New Haven and a suburban site in North

Haven. In the 2003–4 academic year, 5,527 students were enrolled: 13 percent were Latino, 3 percent were Asian, 20 percent were African American, and 64 percent were Caucasian and other (nonspecified). More than half of the total population are women, with an average age of twenty-eight.

The native-English-speaking population is composed of inner-city students graduating from area high schools and students returning to school after a period of time in the workforce or at home with children. Many are considered at-risk because of low retention rates in required first-year credit classes of developmental writing, reading, and math classes.

We define the English as a second language (ESL) population as students enrolled in the ESL academic credit program. These students are from all over the world, but in recent years more prominently from the west coast of Africa, Brazil, Bosnia, the Dominican Republic, Ecuador, Japan, Korea, Mexico, Peru, Poland, and Vietnam. Also, we have growing numbers of students graduating from area high schools without proficiency in English or in their native language spoken at home.

All new students applying for Gateway's certificate and degree programs must take an untimed computerized Accuplacer test (a College Board product) in reading, grammar, and math. ESL students take the Accuplacer language and math proficiency tests. Almost 95 percent of new students identified as second language learners place in the ESL courses of integrated skills, reading, writing, and pronunciation. Students enrolled in developmental and ESL courses often overlap, especially in math and advanced writing courses. The ESL program includes four integrated skill levels: low intermediate through advanced. In addition, the program offers two levels of writing, ESL 159 and ESL 169; pronunciation; reading; and technical English. All of the ESL courses are worth three academic credits. The developmental writing program is designed around two basic courses: English 043: Paragraph to Essay and English 063: Introduction to the Essay. Over 70 percent of new students place in one or more developmental classes.

At Gateway, we have no separate developmental and ESL departments. Since the late 1990s, both units have been a part of the humanities department. After this merger, we began an informal collaboration among the ESL, developmental, and college-level instructors, hoping to create a seamless transition for students into college-level composition. For this particular study, one full-time English instructor and one full-time ESL instructor collaborated. We evaluated our course goals, outcomes, and assessment measures and, when possible, designed our classes synthesizing assignments, mostly for the higher-level writing classes (i.e., English 063: Introduction to the Essay and ESL 169: ESL Writing II). At the semester's end, we assessed our collaborative project for these two populations.

Although writing classes, especially ESL, had been using computer-assisted instruction for more than ten years, it was mostly as a word-processing tool. The developmental classes were using this technology less. Neither program was using online technology. Statewide initiatives, modeling a nationwide trend that had been occurring at the university level, prompted administrators to encourage the development and implementation of online courses at community colleges.

Program reviews indicated that little classroom research and software development addressing the developmental and ESL populations were taking place. Clearly, they were not part of this online phenomenon. Surely, the advantage of learning how to navigate online courses would benefit community college students, especially at-risk populations, in their future college careers. Experience with technology would make them more competitive at school and in the work place. In addition, their writing skills would grow in direct proportion to their computer skills because, we projected, as their computer skills improved, their confidence would grow. This new confidence in their ability to succeed would have a direct impact on their writing process, we reasoned, resulting in a more enthusiastic and directed approach to the writing process, including thoughtful composing, revising, and editing. Furthermore, federal and state monies were available to fund initiatives that had the technology tag on them. We wanted a piece of that initiative pie for our special populations.

▪▪ NARRATIVE

Six years ago, in an effort to integrate online technology into our writing classrooms, we developed an online version of our advanced Introduction to the Essay and ESL courses. The curriculum in these courses is similar. The structure of the English essay is taught, emphasizing rhetorical modes and the usual lectures on grammar structure in problem areas such as run-ons, comma splices, and fragments. The ESL classes focus on differences in second language logic and second language errors such as tense usage, word forms, and articles. Using the online class management program Blackboard, we intended to run a hybrid model whereby students worked online in a computer classroom. We planned to teach them how to navigate the technology so that, by midsemester, we would no longer have to meet on campus; instead, we would be participating in a distance learning writing class.

By the fourth week of the semester, we realized that we were never leaving the classroom.

What Classroom Research Revealed

Some students did indeed succeed in this online environment; their writing processes and products improved as their confidence grew. They prepared themselves for entry into English 101, our college-level composition course.

Students who may have needed another developmental course were instead prepared to move into this composition course. These successful students in this online course, however, typified successful students in traditionally structured classrooms. They were motivated, anxious to succeed; they asked questions and approached the instructors for extra help. They were skilled enough to navigate the technology, adaptable enough to adjust to this kind of learning environment, smart enough to recognize their responsibility for their own learning, and independent enough to carry it all off.

However, a good percentage of our developmental students disappeared into the distance learning universe. They forgot to show up for class, did not send work to us, or came to class but produced writing that was no stronger than that of the students in the control group. We concluded that our students, especially the developmental writing students who were often experiencing their first college course, were tackling two learning curves: learning to write *and* learning the self-discipline and independence expected of college studies. They needed the support and direction that in-class instruction provides. They needed us *live*.

The ESL students needed us too, but in a different way. These students came to us from area high schools, from intensive language programs, or with no formal college language training in their native country. The culture of the U.S. college classroom was new and often frightening. This hybrid writing course was the last class they took in order to matriculate into the college composition courses needed for graduation. At many community colleges, academic ESL programs are restricted in their course offerings because of space, budget, and philosophical concerns. Frequently, our advanced students were not so advanced. The ESL students, like their developmental peers, depended on the classroom culture to successfully use the technology designed to take them out of the classroom.

Our ambition to synthesize our composition pedagogy with a technical classroom was not thwarted, but our online course, while providing students with the means to work and communicate with the instructor from outside of the classroom, did not provide students with enough resources to learn independently. They could communicate with us, even send drafts via a drop box, but did not have adequate access to computers outside the classroom to reinforce the skills they learned in class.

Six years ago, most of the developmental and ESL students did not own home computers. This lack of resources still remains a challenge for some of the developmental students. Now, however, one of the first investments an ESL student frequently makes upon arriving in the United States is a computer with Internet capabilities because the cost of contacting his or her family and friends in other parts of the world is much cheaper with e-mail than with regular mail. Also, phoning via computers has become a cheap and efficient way to communicate. Still, these students must often compete with other family members for time on their home computers. Therefore, the majority of our students needed to come to the open computer labs at the college to complete their work. Also, the majority of our students work either full- or part-time. They simply could not arrange their time to come to labs, work, take care of families, and answer the teacher's latest e-mail or participate in chat room discussions.

Finding the Right Solution

Two years into using Blackboard and "perfecting" our hybrid courses, the state of Connecticut decided to eliminate the use of Blackboard and crossover to WebCT, another online class management system. Because of our resistance to the changeover after spending so much time using Blackboard and the perceived unfriendly format of at least the earlier version of WebCT, we decided to look for other instructional technology that would benefit our students.

A promising solution emerged from our college president's request that we pilot a structured, computer-mediated writing course called Academic Systems. Academic Systems is published by Plato and is designed around writing modules that include prereading and postreading exercises, selected readings, and writing assignments. In addition, the software provides students with a structure for essay writing that includes the key elements of process writing: brainstorming, focusing, freewriting, drafting, revising, and editing. The online program also serves as a tutorial with links to Web sites that provide language and grammar instruction and exercises as well as clear and helpful instructions on the site's writing pages. After reviewing its focus, content, and structure to confirm that it aligned with our pedagogy, we decided that this interactive writing program complemented our approach to teaching writing. Although it was created for native speakers, we decided its content and approach were flexible enough to accommodate the ESL curriculum.

▋▋ PROFESSIONAL RESONANCE

Our classroom experience has raised pedagogical questions about the synthesis of teaching writing with the growing use of technology in higher education. Will the increasing dependency on technology determine our pedagogy? In spring 2004, we shared our research in a presentation for colleagues at the TESOL convention in Long Beach, California, in the United States. After our presentation, we led a roundtable discussion about technology in the writing classroom and the pedagogical concerns and adjustments that we must make as we meet more students who have experienced education in a technological environment.

We also pondered the exception—students who, in the midst of a technological world, have no technological skills whatsoever. What, we asked, is the affect of this phenomenon on our classroom teaching? Finally, we shared our professional challenges and successes in the computer-aided writing classroom. We continue, at our own institution, to study our students, refine our pedagogy as needed, and share with our colleagues our developing professional analysis of technology in the classroom for this specialized population.

▓ INSTITUTIONAL CHALLENGES

Several years (and many technical ups and downs) later, our research has convinced us that programs like Academic Systems, not online courses, merit consideration for a diverse population of at-risk writers at community colleges in the twenty-first century.

Student Retention

Student retention, sadly enough, cannot be guaranteed with the use of such programs. For the most part, problems outside the classroom door, not skill deficiencies or limited intellectual ability, are the more serious attrition culprits. Even in a world as technologically advanced as ours, cars still break down, babies still get sick, and love still tangles the stillest heart. A small percentage of students who would have failed in the traditional classroom, however, managed to overcome the obstacles of their personal lives and the challenges of learning a new skill because planned writing programs support the writing process, explaining and allowing practice at each stage. Links to grammar exercises and external support sites supply further explanation and opportunity to hone English skills. Just as significant as process and grammar to student success is access, and these programs allow students tutorial support where and when they need it, even if that means three o'clock on a Sunday morning from a computer three thousand miles from campus. Given the added benefit of cultivating computer skills (an important goal for most students), many students remain on course and put forth added effort not always forthcoming from those in a traditional writing class.

Student Reactions

Student evaluations have been mixed, but most students (especially by the end of the semester) are very satisfied with the program. Even students who enter the classroom lacking strong computer skills become comfortable working in the program. And, unlike a computer classroom (which is what our online courses turned out to be), students appreciate live class lectures such as "What is an essay?" "How do I begin a paper?" "How do I avoid writer's block?" and "The absolute necessity of revision, re-envisioning, and careful proofreading," which teach them, as one student put it, "how to write an essay the proper way before you print your information." This deliberate and readily available reinforcement promises a more intimate relationship between students and their writing. As another student explained, the system "not only helps you fix your mistakes, but it tells you why you made that mistake." This immersion in the writing process allows students to review key points, giving them time out of class to review and learn at their own pace.

Confident computer users are more receptive to writing because they can easily navigate the program, taking pleasure in their ability to do so. One such student liked the way she could "work on parts of [her] paper in steps, a process that makes writing the paper easier and results in a more well rounded final copy." Those less skilled or more hesitant about computer use struggled at first, but many of the students in our survey reflected the sentiments of a student who said that she "learned more about typing on a computer."

The technical skills gained satisfied the majority of our students, even if their writing skills lagged a bit. One student came into class with little, if any, computer knowledge. In fact, she did not own a computer. Her writing skills were also very weak. By the end of the semester, she had mastered the computer, the structure and development of an essay, and the language of writing. Although she was not quite ready to move on to a college-level writing class, she was not discouraged; she was proud of the progress she had made, determined to strengthen her writing skills, and confident in her ability to remain in college.

Student Success

Student success is usually measured by the product produced: that final draft/ portfolio or, for some institutions, an exit exam. But why students are success-ful is harder to determine. Having revised and refined these classes, we found that student success is tantamount to providing in-class writing time, so our classrooms now resemble a very busy workplace where students actively write their essays, collaborate with their peers, and consult with us. The teacher/ student relationship is enhanced in such a classroom, as is the students' sense of a vibrant writing community. This technological classroom setting provides teachers immediate access to student writing and process for in-class review and quick commenting on work in progress, reminding students individually of areas that need work and encouraging their best skills so that they can use their own writing as a model. They do not have to wait for a graded paper to receive feedback, feedback they often ignore since a grade can dampen the desire to act on suggestions and make improvement. Because many at-risk students have lives that do not provide the time and quiet necessary for writing, this class-room time—though short—is used wisely, and the writing is consistently better than traditional out-of-class papers.

When students leave, they take the classroom with them in a system that supports their process. They can send work, review tips for developing their essays, and practice sentence-level skills at their own pace and in their own time. They are never severed from the course as they would be in a traditional learning environment. And we are never far from them. We can track the time they spend in each part of the writing process, enabling us to make suggestions about their process that will improve their product. This kind of intervention prevents the disappointment students often experience when they submit a final draft that results in a discouraging grade. It also cuts down on last-minute acts of plagiarism.

The stronger students quickly excel in this environment, often moving at their own pace through the paper assignments to complete the course work before the semester's end. This mobility promises a chance to reconfigure the structure of these developmental and ESL writing programs, providing a means of self-paced skill-building modules that give students more opportunity to complete these courses quickly while allowing others to take their time without feeling left behind.

The students who struggle with writing skills, on the other hand, are not necessarily saved by the technology. They still struggle, especially with sentence construction. But their papers, while often littered with errors, are much more organized, developed, and detailed than their control-group counterparts. They are able to order their ideas, create coherent paragraphs, and expand their content more quickly and easily with the technical support. Moreover, since the programs support in-class lectures, we can spend more class time responding to students' essays and less time repeating and reinforcing writing skills. For students who straddle family, work, and many other responsibilities and who often lack any quiet space for themselves, in-class writing produces the best work. They are more focused and get more done in this three-hour class than they can in an entire weekend at home. When they do leave the classroom, they take the language of composing with them. Perhaps soon, Dr. Erhmann will be able to revise his comments if the use of technology, coupled with strong composition pedagogy, is implemented long before students show up in his college composition classes.

▪▪ EXTENDING THE DIALOGUE

To conclude, when considering computer writing programs for special populations, we recommend the following:

- Do not choose distance learning programs that take place entirely online for this population. Look for "distance close" or hybrid programs.

- Use technology in the classroom as an added and invaluable asset.

- Use effective computer writing programs that immerse students in the language of composing, not grammar.

- Embed an abundance of in-class writing to create improvement in the quality of students' writing.

- Provide consistent informal feedback to enhance formal feedback. This also cuts down on plagiarism.

- Make an institutional commitment to providing upgraded computer classrooms and comfortable work environments for students and faculty.

- Provide strong institutional support both in the classroom and in the computer labs. This is crucial for student success. Labs need to be staffed and open to accommodate student needs, including those students who need nights and weekends to complete their work.

- Offer the necessary and sufficient training opportunities to faculty who choose these computer programs for their classrooms.

So, whose technology is it? It is all of ours: administrators whom we trust to make logical technology decisions for the institution, teachers who commit to experimenting with and implementing innovative learning for students, and students who are motivated to learn an old art in a new way.

∷ CONTRIBUTORS

Carol J. Brutza is a professor in humanities and an ESL coordinator at Gateway Community College in New Haven, Connecticut, in the United States. She conducts teacher training courses and workshops in Connecticut and in many foreign countries, most recently the Kyrgyz Republic and Kazakhstan. She was a senior Fulbright lecturer in Mozambique in 1998.

Martha Hayes is an associate professor in humanities at Gateway Community College. She teaches college composition, literature, and creative writing. She is the campus's Center for Teaching learning consultant and an accomplished published poet.

CHAPTER 9

Writing for an Audience: Interviews of Working New Yorkers

::

Melinda Thomsen

:: FRAMING THE ISSUE

In this chapter, I describe how the students in our vocational intensive English program (IEP) at the Center for Immigrant Education and Training completed a booklet called *Interviews of Working New Yorkers*. It was a project conceived during a writing-to-learn seminar led by Gayle Cooper-Shpirt and Hilary Sideris of the City University of New York, Division of Adult and Continuing Education.

The students who participated in this project were in a multilevel intermediate class; skills of students ranged from those who spoke and wrote quite fluently to students who had difficulty expressing themselves clearly because of lack of vocabulary or poor pronunciation. Each student had different strengths and weaknesses; a poor speaker might be a good writer or vice versa. In vocational English as a second language (ESL) classes, I have found that a thematic project-based curriculum works best because it lets students work at their own pace, which is why I chose to do an interview booklet for this multilevel class. The students also had to use computer skills for this project. The eleven students in this class, who were from Colombia, the Dominican Republic, Ecuador, and Peru, were learning English to either continue their education or enter new fields of work. Writing about work was fine, but they needed to find work themselves. Thus, the students conducted interviews to address their verbal skills as well as their writing skills by publishing a booklet.

The purpose of this project was to improve students' writing and conversation skills within the context of discovering how different New Yorkers found work. The project also addressed the Equipped for the Future standards, developed by the National Institute for Literacy as a coherent vision of the skills and knowledge that adult learners need to be considered literate. (More information is at http://eff.cls.utk.edu.)

These employability skills underline our vocational IEP at the Center for Immigrant Education and Training, which is part of adult continuing education at LaGuardia Community College in Long Island City, New York, in the United States. We teach students English and prepare them to reenter the workforce or go into training programs. I conducted this writing-to-learn project during the winter session of 2004. Most of the students in this course were displaced factory workers affected by the downturn in New York City's economy after September 11. Absenteeism was another issue I needed to confront when selecting a project. The reality was that these students had other pressing concerns besides learning English, and during the winter months I noticed that the absenteeism rate was higher. Some said they missed class because they were looking for work because their unemployment checks were late. One woman fell and broke her wrist, and another student's daughter was very sick for a week. In this project, I made sure that students could still participate even if they missed classes. The tasks were designed to reinforce skills that were learned over several weeks. The project began with a focus on group work and, as the project progressed, the focus changed to more independent student work. I formulated lessons to include group work so if a student was absent one day, he or she could still participate in the class and learn from the others.

Many of the papers I had received in the past were first drafts, scratched out the night before they were due. I realized that the students did not see me as an "audience" but more as a "doctor" who would fix their writing. When we decided to publish an interview booklet, it was obvious that I needed to implement different writing strategies to change my position from doctor to audience. This would help the students take responsibility for their own learning and see themselves and their classmates as legitimate audiences as well.

For the booklet, students interviewed New Yorkers they were curious about, met at school, or knew as friends or family members. The main questions the students addressed were the following:

- How did the person find work?

- What skills or education did he or she need?

- What were the person's reasons for getting into this particular career?

- How did the person's English skills affect his or her work?

- What cultural differences did he or she have to address?

- What did this person want to do in the future?

This curriculum addressed writing and communication skills equally. I integrated classroom activities to flow between students' writing and speaking. The students wanted to write stories of workers but needed to develop their questioning and conversational skills to speak to people they did not know in an appropriate manner. Many of the students were starting to look for work, and it was absolutely necessary that this project develop their communication skills and give them confidence to go out on job interviews.

Goals

Interviewing is one way of conducting research. Students conducted these interviews to learn the steps used to collect information and organize it into a written piece to be shared with others. Interviews required the students to be responsible for a project that reflected issues they wanted to investigate. For example, one student wanted to know how the secretary in our office got her job, so she interviewed her. Interviewing also addresses many of the Equipped for the Future (EFF) standards. The EFF standards the students worked on included the following:

- Speak so others understand. (Tasks 2 and 11)[1]

- Listen actively. (Tasks 2, 5, and 11)

- Learn through research. (Tasks 1, 5, and 9)

- Take responsibility for learning. (Tasks 7 and 14)

- Reflect and evaluate. (Tasks 3, 4, 8, 10, and 12)

- Observe critically. (Tasks 2 and 5)

- Convey ideas through writing. (Tasks 6, 7, 8, 11, and 13)

Furthermore, this project helped the students to

- build confidence when speaking to people outside of class;

- prepare for situations, such as job interviews, where they would have to converse with someone on a topic in-depth;

- practice interpersonal skills needed for the workplace;

- learn the basics of networking by asking people how they found their jobs;

---

[1] The tasks for this project are described later in the chapter.

- share information through speaking and writing;

- understand how to conduct research and analyze information;

- evaluate written and spoken interview procedures;

- be active listeners and pose appropriate follow-up questions;

- summarize information from notes and retell clearly;

- learn how to write first and second drafts and how to revise and edit.

:: NARRATIVE

I used writing-to-learn strategies drawn from readings by Atwell (1998) and Mayher, Lester, and Pradl (1983). Writing-to-learn strategies are ways of teaching writing that encourage independent learning; the teacher is not the only one to assign topics or provide feedback. One of the strategies is to publish the writing so that the students put more effort into their work. The ESL classroom is usually a comfortable place because students must practice their English and not feel afraid to make mistakes, but this comfort zone can sometimes work against teachers. Publishing the writing makes the students take their work more seriously, and their work becomes more than an exercise. Another writing-to-learn strategy is the conferencing technique used by Murray, Garrison, and Harris (see "Lessons from the Masters" in McAndrew and Reigstad 2001, 103–112). Students read their papers out loud to classmates and identified areas that were unclear. Tierney's (1999) *How to Write to Learn Science* was helpful in developing rubrics. Students evaluated their own work on the basis of a checklist. This project helped the students develop other audiences as they relied on themselves and their peers for feedback.

Students wanted examples and reinforcement because it gave them a clear idea of what they were to do. My colleagues and I not only modeled the tasks but also developed criteria of what was acceptable for interviews or written work. This procedure of modeling the task and evaluating it was repeated after each step of the project. We modeled interviews in class, and the students watched television interviews on videotape and on Web sites such as Inside the Actors Studio (Lipton n.d.). They also read worker stories from their class texts and the newspapers. Afterward, they developed two rubrics, one for the interview procedure and one for the human interest story. The final tasks included feedback on their drafts. By the time they started writing, they had seen so many examples that they knew what to do—even from my briefest comments.

From past experience, I knew students would cringe when they heard that they had to interview someone. To calm students' fears, I modeled the procedures from the very beginning. I wanted them to see the classroom as our space to practice before they conducted their interviews. This made the students much more excited about the project. Interviewing someone in class is critical because the students would know what to expect. They also noticed how much speaking practice the interviewer received and felt more confident about their own ability to conduct an interview. The students started to attend class more regularly because they saw that interviewing was helping their speaking. I told them that their interviews would be published in a booklet. As Atwell (1998) notes, "publication is crucial: writers most often write to be read" (p. 98). The students needed to know that this was serious, and I instilled a sense of professionalism from the start. If it had been just a classroom exercise, they would not have given it their full attention.

Task 1: Developing Interview Questions

In small groups, the students read two articles: "Dangerous Work" and "The Washroom Technician" (Caesar 1987a, 1987b). The students had to analyze the readings and come up with the questions that they thought the interviewer had asked to write these pieces. I told them to think of these stories as a page of answers and to write the questions. It was a good exercise for them to practice past-tense questions. When they had come up with as many questions as possible, we wrote them on the blackboard. These two articles were the models that I presented as a "written interview." I envisioned the interview booklet to be a series of personal profiles or human interest stories similar to those found in the newspaper.

Task 2: Developing the Interview Procedure from a Practice Interview

After writing the questions on the board, one student volunteered to be the class interviewer. She had good verbal skills but was weak in writing and eager to practice in front of the class. I invited a colleague, Wilman Navarreto, to class. He was going to be interviewed about his work, but he did not know what we were doing. I did not tell Wilman about being interviewed to see if the interviewer could explain the project to him so he would understand and feel comfortable during the interview. Also, I wanted to see what the student already knew about interviewing techniques. We had already practiced opening and closing conversations in the class from our *Speaking Naturally* textbook (Tillett and Bruder 1985). I was paying special attention to see if the student would do this well. Wilman is legally blind, so we left the questions on the board. This made it easy for the interviewer, who could look up to ask any question she wanted.

The interview went fairly well. The student made Wilman feel at ease and asked good follow-up questions while we took notes. I typed up my notes so that students who were absent that day could have a copy of what Wilman said. It is good for the students to see the teacher participate in class writing activities.

Task 3: Evaluating the Interview

After the interview, we discussed what had gone well and what needed work for the next interview. The students said that the interviewer had made Wilman feel comfortable because of her warm personality and politeness. As a result, he had been able to tell some interesting stories about work. Wilman had talked for a while, and the interviewer had asked good follow-up questions; she had listened to his answers and thought of other questions accordingly. The class noticed that Wilman had been confused about why he was there. I believe this happened because the student knew him well and was a little too casual in the interview. The purpose of the interview needed to be made clear, and a rubric is a good reminder of the steps that sometimes can be forgotten. Also, we noticed that while Wilman was talking we had stopped taking notes because his story had become very interesting, but the interviewer had not asked permission for a follow-up interview. The session concluded with students looking at a list of interview questions from *Interviews—A Low-Level ESOL Curriculum about Work* (Casey 2000) to see if there were other questions that might be interesting to ask at future interviews.

Task 4: Developing Interview Criteria

We put our observations on the board to develop criteria for the interview procedure. The idea for developing a rubric came from Tierney (1999), who discusses having the students develop their own rubrics so they have a stake in the results of the class. In his example, the rubric gives the criteria to answer the questions, "What makes a good teacher?" and "What makes a good student?" I was very careful to make sure the students in my class contributed their ideas about what was appropriate interview procedure. We brainstormed names of people who were excellent interviewers: Barbara Walters, Charlie Rose, Christina Saralegui, Oprah Winfrey, and so forth. A week later, I modeled another interview with Alecia D'Angelo, the assistant director of the Center for Immigrant Education and Training, and the rubric was finalized (see Figure 1).

Task 5: Revising and Evaluating Interview Standards

The interview I conducted with Alecia was used to revise our interview procedure. One example of an interview (e.g., the one with Wilman Navarreto) was not enough because some of the students had been absent that day. Interviewing a person with a different goal (to evaluate the process itself) made it interesting and new for everybody. I decided that it would be best to model two interviews so the students could grade me twice on my interview

Interview Procedure

Purpose: To ask questions in order to get enough information to tell an interesting story about work.

✔	**Excellent Interview Procedure**
☐	Welcome—introduction. Tell the person about yourself and what you intend to do with this interview.
☐	Ask questions in order to get complete information. Examples of questions: What is your name? Where are you from? Where do you work?
☐	Ask questions that get background information, experience, present job, and future plans.
☐	Ask permission to do follow-up questions or to have the person read what you wrote.
☐	Ask direct and clear questions.
☐	Be serious, not sarcastic—and respectful.
☐	Listen well.
☐	Be specific; get details.
☐	Use a tape recorder.
☐	Enjoy the interview—both of you!
☐	Say thank you!

Figure 1. Rubric for Interview Procedure

procedure. The first interview I did intentionally badly. I wanted the students to use their rubric and then tell me what I needed to work on. After watching the demonstration, I asked for a grade for my first attempt—the students gave me an F. They said that I was not very respectful, did not make the purpose of the interview clear, was not prepared with a paper and pen, did not listen to Alecia's answers and ask appropriate follow-up questions, and said thank you but did not ask for permission for a follow-up interview. After this interview, we added the lines "Use a tape recorder" and "Enjoy the interview—both of you!" to the rubric (see Figure 1). Enjoying the interview makes it more like a conversation between friends. If the purpose is to have a good interview, then the result will be an interesting story about someone's life.

The second time I interviewed Alecia they gave me an A–. They said I forgot to ask about her future plans, which would have given a good ending to her work story since it was a combination of her past and present working life. Afterward we used the rubric again and watched an interview clip of Joseph Campbell and Bill Moyers (1988). Students felt that Moyers fulfilled the criteria of enjoying the interview, showing interest, and asking good follow-up questions.

By this time, the students had observed and evaluated four interviews in class: Wilman's interview, my two interviews of Alecia, and one videotape of Bill Moyers. They also were assigned a follow-up task in the computer lab to analyze interviews at Inside the Actors Studio (Lipton n.d.), which gave them many more interviews and videos to review.

Task 6: Writing Up a Draft from Notes

Now the class was ready to write up a first draft from the notes that we took during the interview with Wilman. I placed the students in groups of three, with the students who were absent the day of Wilman's interview distributed among the groups. One person served as scribe while the other two dictated the story. Then they edited the paper together.

We discussed the writing steps they completed and what they needed to do next. The writing process described in Mayher, Lester, and Pradl (1983) is characterized by "percolating, drafting, revising, editing, and publishing" (p. 5). The students brainstormed and wrote a first draft from their notes. They finished the first draft in the computer lab and brought it back to discuss with their classmates. Writing is a process that develops over time, with several revisions required. I wanted to be clear about that and not let the students think that a paper was finished just because it was typed.

Task 7: Editing a First Draft

The following is the first draft from one group:

Wilman Navarreto

Wilman is a man with strong beliefs. When he came to the United States he started to work in a computer place, and mass production factory. He found this job reading adds in the newspaper, but we think that he did not know what to do on his free time and he decided to find and other job. A night shift job, that was when he made the decision and went to El Centro Español Hospital in 1988, in Tampa Florida. When he was interviewed, the interviewer did not ask him if he could understand or speak English, and he got the job. On his first day of work the boss told him that he had to answer the phone, but he did not speak or understand a word of English and that was a problem for Wilman, that's why he got sick everyday and he prayed that the phone did not ring. And then he said to himself I need to find a way to learn English, and a wonderful idea came to his mind. He started to carry a dictionary and that helped him to feel more positive with his job. He worked in the Hospital for about a year and then he decided to quit the job and go back to school so he can improve his English and find a better job. But in that process something unexpected happen to his vision. For an undefined amount of time he could not see anything and that affected him and his plans. But not even that stopped Wilman. At that time his goal was to become a professional, so he went to college and got a degree as a counselor. By that time he could speak English well and he was very proud of himself. Wilman is a good example for us so we can follow in his steps and be whatever we want it to be in life

By Ana C., Ana L. and Esperanza E.

The students used their peer-editing worksheets to give feedback on their papers. This worksheet included three questions:

1. What is interesting in this paper?

2. What do you want to know more about?

3. What didn't you understand?

Students read their papers aloud to each other. From this draft, students wanted to know more about Wilman's present education plans. They also wanted to know his plans for the future. In my comments, I suggested more background information on Wilman for people who do not know who he is.

I found that Murray's conferencing technique of reading the paper aloud (see McAndrew and Reigstad 2001, 105) was useful to develop another audience. Murray has the students read from their papers aloud to readily identify inconsistencies. This technique puts the ball back in the students' court as they are the first to identify problems just from the sense that something does not sound right. The teacher becomes more of a coach than a doctor. The students read their papers and located errors that they had missed. Many students heard mistakes better. They stopped themselves as they read and then reworked those parts. The students responded to each other as what Harris refers to as a "middle person"—someone between the teacher and the writer (see McAndrew and Reigstad 2001, 112). It was satisfying for me as the students corrected mistakes that were basically content-based or low-level ESL "boo-boos," as I call them.

Task 8: Revising a First Draft

After the feedback from the groups, the students invited Wilman back to class for follow-up questions in order to revise their first drafts. During this interview, Wilman took questions from anyone in the class. It was not as formal as the first time when one student was responsible for asking questions. Students added more background information to the paper. We now knew where he worked and what his future plans were. As the following extract from the second draft shows, it was the content that primarily changed (the changes are underlined). The mistakes in usage, for example, "But in that process" (see the first draft) remained because the students did not know this expression in English. In their final draft, after talking to me, they changed it to "During that time." Also, their spelling mistakes were not corrected because the purpose of peer feedback is to work on content.

Wilman Navarreto

Wilman is a man with strong beliefs. When he came to the United States <u>in 1988; he is now working at LaGuardia Community College as a counselor.</u>

...

By that time he could speak English well and he was very proud of himself. Wilman is a good example for us so we can follow in his steps and be whatever we want it to be in life. <u>At the present time, Wilman is attending school. He is now studying a new career in psychology. We wish him luck on his new decision.</u>

Task 9: Presenting an Example of Someone to Interview

After having practiced in class, the students were ready to select someone to interview. We read a human interest story about Napoleon Barragan, the founder of the company 1-800-MATRESS, in the Immigrant Success section of the *Queens Tribune* (Paybarah and Lin 2003). The students discussed Barragan's story and compared it to their own lives. They were inspired by his success and kept this story in mind as they thought about people they wanted to interview. All of the people they interviewed for the booklet were successful in their work. I had selected this article to read and analyze because it was about an immigrant with a story similar to many of their stories.

Task 10: Analyzing a Human Interest Story

The students analyzed this article and used it to develop a rubric for writing their interviews or human interest stories (see Figure 2). The students came up with the criteria from our discussion of Barragan. First, they summarized the article and highlighted what points they thought were important. They most appreciated the information about Barragan's education, his past life in Colombia, and his wife's career; his story of starting a business; and the fact that he was the owner of such a famous company. I then asked them to look at the article and come up with the questions that the interviewer had used to get the information. This was the same technique we used in Task 1. The students found this exercise very enjoyable because they loved grammar. They needed to practice past-tense questions, and this provided an excellent opportunity to review. This was the second time they had done this same activity, so if a student had missed the earlier class, he or she had the opportunity to practice. Students who had attended the previous class also benefited from the repetition.

Standards for a Human Interest Story

Purpose: To tell an interesting story about work.

✓	Excellent Human Interest Story
☐	Interesting
☐	Informative
☐	Specific
☐	Clear
☐	Beginning—Introduction
☐	Middle—Journey/experience
☐	End—Current job
☐	Future plans
☐	Education
☐	Title—Give a title so the reader knows what to expect

Figure 2. Rubric for Human Interest Story

NOTE: Students used this rubric to check their drafts to see if they included all the components they had identified by reading the Barragan piece.

Task 11: Interviewing

Now that the students had practiced interviews in class, written an interview with their partners, analyzed it, and developed a rubric or criteria for evaluating it, it was time for them to interview someone outside of class. Many of the students were interested in how people found work when they did not speak English fluently. Others were interested in their teachers' backgrounds. Still others wanted to interview a son or daughter. All of the students conducted their interviews in English and had two weeks to complete their interviews. Their interviewees included a restaurant manager, a doctor, a medical secretary, an elementary school teacher, a lawyer, a secretary, and English teachers. After the interviews were completed, we sat in a circle while the students summarized their interviews. I wanted to know the following:

- Whom did you interview?

- What did you learn?

- How did the interview go?

- What problems did you have?

- What corrections do you need to make for the next interview?

Each student spoke for about fifteen minutes. The other students and I asked questions and gave feedback on what was interesting and inspiring about their colleagues' interviews. As the students spoke, I noticed that they did not look at their notes much but spoke from memory.

Task 12: Conferencing on First Drafts

After Celia, a student from Ecuador, spoke about her interview with Jirawat Arjariyawat from Thailand, I was surprised to read her first draft and had a brief conference with her. These conferences with students, which occurred after they presented their interviews to the class, were similar in form to Garrison's "quick conference approach" technique (see McAndrew and Reigstad 2001, 107). I gave Celia verbal feedback by simply saying, "You left out some very important information that you told us today." (We were all interested in one part of Jirawat's story that had turned into a lengthy conversation for us that day.) I suggested she insert it into her story after the sentence, "However sometimes she comes back from work with her parents in their car." Notice that the underlined part in her second draft was what she had left out of the first.

JIRAWAT

Jirawat was born in Thailand; she's 24 years old. She came to the U.S on August 10, 1998 with her family. She entered 3rd grade in September in the school P.S.89. In school she met my daughter Grace and other friend's from other countries. She was 13 years old when she started to work. Her first job was as a waitress in the restaurant <u>that</u> her mom owned. Thai Pavilion is were she worked after school, its located at 37–10 30Ave Astoria, NY 11103. Jirawat is now one of the managers of the restaurant. She works Monday, Wednesday, Friday and Sunday from 11am-to-12am. She controls all of the employees and takes care of the customer bills. Jirawat <u>has accumulated</u> 11 years of experience in this field. She gets to work sometimes by train and other times by car. However, sometimes she comes back from work with her parents in their car. <u>She has a boyfriend that her parents do not like because he is from Mexico and he has different costumes, religious and race. Her father was worry because of difficulties with daughter. He had a lot of stress at work. That he fell on the floor and had a heart attack. He was in the Elmhurst hospital. Now he is better</u>

but still under care but the family much happier. Her upcoming plans are to visit her grandparents in Thailand. In the future she wants to graduate as a Marketing Mayor in St. John's College. She wants to have a successful life and travel around the world. Jirawat later wants to have a family, her own house and move to a different state.

By Celia V.

This piece is an example of what we were aiming for—a personal work interview that was not just a chronological work interview. Celia reworked it with just brief verbal directions from me.

The following extract is an example of the question-answer interview format. Initially, I intended the students to write human interest stories because those were the models that we had studied from our texts (see Tasks 1 and 9). This interview by Elvia was included in the booklet because it conveyed the experience of the interview itself. The reader gets a sense of the politeness and the atmosphere that the interviewer created for the conversation. If you read this and critique it using the standards for the interview procedure mentioned earlier, you will see that the interviewer followed the procedure.

> My name is Elvia Ruiz, I am interviewing my friend Maria, a famous Lawyer.
>
> *An Interesting Life.*
>
> ELVIA: Well, Maria, Let's begin with some information about your childhood. When were you born?
>
> MARIA: I was born in 1946. I was born on August 1st in 1946.
>
> ELVIA: And where were you born?
>
> MARIA: I was born in Peru in a little village. The houses were small and simple. My village was peaceful and the people were very friendly.
>
> ELVIA: And when did you come to New York, Maria?
>
> MARIA: I come to New York 15 years ago. I wasn't a Lawyer then. I was a Flight Attendant; I worked for a Big Airline.
>
> ELVIA: How was it?
>
> MARIA: Well, it was exciting at first. I stayed in very fancy hotels. I went sightseeing everywhere. I was never bored. I spent a lot money, but I was never broke.
>
> ELVIA: What happened?
>
> MARIA: After a while, it wasn't exciting anymore. I knew many people but I didn't have any close friends because I always had to leave. And my co-workers were selfish. So I quit my job and I come to New York. I took a course called "Changing Your Life." and I went back to school and became a Lawyer at the age of 55.
>
> ELVIA: What do you want to do in the future?

MARIA: Well, I would like to help people that can't resolve their legal problems.

ELVIA: What a beautiful story! Thanks for you time and good luck.

Task 13: Editing for Sentence-Level Errors

On the students' second or third drafts, I edited for sentence-level mistakes. I used an underlining and verbal feedback approach, defined in *Writing Clearly* (Bates, Lane, and Lange 1993). I had a brief conference with Elvia about the verb tense errors in her paper (see the two underlined errors in her interview) and, instead of fixing them, I showed them to her. We talked about tense and how that was something to recheck when writing a paper.

Task 14: Compiling the Stories into the Booklet

When the students finished their interviews, they sent me their papers as e-mail attachments. I looked over their finished pieces, made some last-minute edits, and then sent them to be duplicated into a booklet. The modeling and class examples were well worth it as the students took more responsibility for their papers and did not ask me to look at everything they wrote. In the next session, I would need to do modeling for their papers. It is an ongoing process; teachers cannot assume that the habits students learn during one project will automatically stick.

∷ PROFESSIONAL RESONANCE

I was pleased that this writing project not only improved the students' writing abilities but also addressed the EFF standards. These employability skills drive our vocational English courses at the Center for Immigrant Education and Training. Writing is one of the main problem areas for the advanced students, but if we do not address confidence levels at the same time, the students become dependent on us. That is especially true with writing as it is usually the last skill addressed when teaching language. Writing needs to be taught as a form of communication that is as valuable as speaking. It is one way to improve critical thinking skills because students must reflect on and evaluate their work. Students in retraining programs need to learn English, yet if they are displaced workers, they also need to adapt to a changing workplace. We found that students enjoy our classes so much that they do not want to leave us. This is why it is important that projects like this encourage independent learning. This is also what I meant by feeling like a "doctor" when I introduced this chapter. This project frees teachers from the doctor role and recasts them as coaches, until they finally become the audience. The classroom becomes more like the real world, where there are many audiences. The audiences addressed in this project were classmates, teachers, administrators, acquaintances or family members, and the readers of the booklet.

∷ INSTITUTIONAL CHALLENGES

Training the ESL instructors is one of the main challenges facing institutions that are using a curriculum based on EFF standards. The sixteen EFF standards pose a difficulty in that the instructors are faced with criteria that are fairly new in ESL curriculum. At this point there is not an ESL/EFF publication for instructors to share curriculum. At our center, we received the standards in the form of a large book that took me about six months to digest. At first, I looked at my lesson plans to identify inherent standards. One of the first was "Speak so others can understand." If teachers are conducting classes with a student-centered curriculum already, they will find that incorporating the standards flows along those lines. In one session, we focused on the EFF standard "Observe critically." The students used that standard as a way to generate language—specifically information questions—to describe pictures and paintings.

∷ EXTENDING THE DIALOGUE

How do instructors teach writing to ESL students that makes their experience in the classroom as realistic as possible? Many writing books address writing in forms such as argument, comparison/contrast, persuasion, description, or summary, but, in daily life, when do people write in such overtly rhetorical ways? Writing clearly and for a purpose is a combination, such as in letter writing. Writing interviews incorporates speaking with writing and reinforces the language that the students need to communicate in a more formal way. It also addresses basic interview skills that they need for the job search. Treating writing as an integral part of ESL learning would be beneficial at all levels, instead of relegating it as a separate skill reserved only for advanced students.

∷ CONTRIBUTOR

Melinda Thomsen is a vocational English instructor at the Center for Immigrant Education and Training, LaGuardia Community College, in Long Island City, New York, in the United States. She has taught ESL in New York since 1997. She has a master's degree in English from the City College of New York and a Cambridge Certificate in English Language Teaching to Adults.

CHAPTER 10

Variety Is the Spice of Life— and English Classes

::

Carmella Lieske

:: FRAMING THE ISSUE

Setting

This chapter discusses materials development at a Japanese two-year community college for a program focused on vocational training, specifically for the health and medical welfare industry. After graduating from this program, students work in hospitals; for companies that send trained home health care workers to individuals' homes; in government and nongovernmental organizations; and at health care facilities including those for the elderly, for persons with physical disabilities, and for those with mental challenges. The students, therefore, enter college with similar academic goals, and, to this end, the building was designed so that the students are taught in their classrooms and the instructors go to those rooms to teach. As a result, the fundamental courses (e.g., English, sociology, physical education) as well as the core medical and health care courses (e.g., rehabilitation, welfare, nursing techniques) are taught to the same groups of forty to forty-five students in each classroom. The only exception is the few elective courses that are offered. This unity of students is further maintained by the expectation that nearly all of the students—historically approximately 95 percent—will graduate after two years. This policy is effectively enforced by an administration that asks instructors to give second, third, and even fourth examinations to students who initially fail so that they can pass each course.

In addition to structured course work and common academic goals, the students in this Japanese community college differ in several aspects from those in English as a second language (ESL) classrooms in the United States. First, there is relative outward uniformity among the students. All of the students are Japanese, rather than being from different ethnic and linguistic backgrounds. In addition, with approximately 80 percent of the students entering college directly from high school, there is less deviation in the age of the students than in many ESL community colleges. Second, there is more consistency in the previous educational experiences of these students. All of the students have studied English as a foreign language (EFL) for at least six years before graduating from high school; in spite of this, there is great variation among the students in their English skills. In this respect, the challenge of meeting the needs of a broad range of student abilities and levels of confidence in one classroom is similar to that in many ESL classrooms. Although there are exceptions, the students generally have a low level of English competency.

Attitudes and Beliefs

Unlike their ESL counterparts who attend community college to overcome vocational and academic restrictions because of limited English proficiency, there is a high probability that Japanese health and medical welfare students will not use their English outside of the classroom. They are aware of this and, as a result, often lack intrinsic motivation to use English as a living language; it is simply an academic subject for them to take during their first year at the college. They do not, however, have negative attitudes toward native English speakers, so this is not a limitation to their language learning (H. D. Brown 1994).

To better understand the students' abilities, needs, and attitudes toward English and their English skills (i.e., reading, writing, speaking, listening), a needs analysis survey, in the form of a simple questionnaire, was administered to both classes (eighty-two students) in April 2003, at the beginning of the first semester of the 2003–2004 year. The questionnaire was also deemed necessary to reduce classroom conflict that can result from differences in expectations between students and the instructor. Thirty-two percent of the students said they either disliked or hated English while only 4 percent noted they loved English. Correspondingly, 40 percent of the students said they wanted to study English. Even though 50 percent of the students felt least proficient in speaking English—as opposed to one of the other three skills—53 percent said it was the skill they wanted to study the most. Equally important, 82 percent of the students believed speaking would be the most useful English skill for them in the future.

Impetus for Change

In Japanese high schools, English education focuses on grammatical competence (e.g., translation, lexis, grammar) to prepare students for college and
university entrance exams. At this vocational college, however, only the few
students who applied for scholarships had an English section on their entrance
examination. In spite of the focus on grammar during high school, most of the
students lacked confidence in their English grammar. During the first semester,
they sought reassurance during pair practice, even when they actually knew the
answer. The students could spontaneously produce only basic utterances; many
first sought confirmation with a peer, the teacher, or the textbook because of
an almost obsessive concern to produce grammatically correct utterances at the
expense of communicative ability. Many textbooks that would be appropriate
for the overall level of the classes, including the one used first semester, utilize
only short dialogues. After six years of English studies, these textbook conversations not only seemed insulting because of their brevity but also were boring
to the students and did not match the learners' interests or meet the needs of
their vocational studies.

On a questionnaire at the end of the first semester in 2003, students
were asked to write English words concerning health and welfare and were
instructed to disregard possible spelling mistakes. Sixteen percent of the students knew the word *welfare,* but only one or two of the eighty-two students
knew the English equivalent for the other ten words that students listed (e.g.,
doctor, hospital, health, barrier free). The questionnaire further revealed the
students' lack of knowledge about health and welfare in eight other countries.
For each country named on the questionnaire, between 68 and 100 percent of
the students responded that they had no knowledge of that country's health
care system. Furthermore, all of the students noted that they had not previously studied the health and welfare systems of other countries.

An informal query of students at the end of the first semester also showed
that although more than half of the students had never used the Internet
in their first language (L1) of Japanese and only one student had used it in
English, they were interested in studying with it. Additionally, when an oral
examination for the second semester was mentioned, the students seemed
nervous but excited because they were interested in speaking and this form of
assessment appealed to them. It was also a challenge they had not previously
undertaken.

In addition to the lack of an appropriate textbook that addressed the language needs of health and welfare students, the disinterest of 60 percent of
the students in studying English was the primary reason for designing material
for the second semester in 2003 that would allow the students to expect and
experience success, to find pleasure in the tasks, and to value the material as

useful for the future. These factors are all associated with second language (L2) motivation and, therefore, contribute to conditions that increase the likelihood of successful learning (Strevens 1987). Based on the student feedback at the end of the first semester, a theme-based course focusing on health and welfare with seven interrelated components and integrating the Internet seemed most appropriate. The general goals of the new curriculum were to

- motivate students so they would become excited about using English,

- help learners view English as a living language,

- convince students that they already had sufficient English skills to communicate in English,

- increase students' confidence in their English abilities and decrease students' anxiety.

:: NARRATIVE

The new material had seven components; material studied earlier in the semester aided students with later tasks. For example, by studying "How to Use the Internet," students were equipped with the skills for "Presentation Preparation." The study of "Nonnative Speakers" allowed students to overcome their fears of incorrect utterances when they gave their presentations and when they studied "Dialogues." During the presentations, "Active Listening" encouraged students to interact with those presenting. "Dialogues" further reinforced students' speaking skills with conversations related to their field of study, and the "Final Assessment and Application" component required students to actively apply their new skills.

1. How to Use the Internet

Perhaps surprising to anyone living outside of Japan, computer use and the Internet had not been incorporated into elementary or secondary education until recently; many schools still do not address this need. As a result, many students lack computer skills. Because of this, it was necessary to use one class period to explain the presentation and teach these skills. To prepare for their presentations, students had to find information about the country they had been assigned. During later classes, the five students who had studied the same country gave their presentations together. To enable the students to research countries, during the first class the students were given a handout on using the Internet that demonstrated how to

- choose key words,

- use search engines,

- use a translation Web site to understand unknown words,

- open two or more windows at the same time,

- use the cut and paste functions,

- search for and evaluate information for their presentations later in the semester.

Only two of the eighty-two students did not use the Internet to find at least one answer for their presentation material. Some students told me that they spent several hours searching for the answers to their assigned questions as well as for additional information about their country. Because there is a learning curve to successfully finding data quickly, it is not surprising that students who were new to the Internet took a great deal of time to find their information. Many students also used the translation site, a second skill that will be helpful in the future. Because many students had not used the Internet before, I had, in fact, expected many more students to use the books in the library to do their research so I had made certain that all of the answers could be found in the school's small library. The process of learning how to search the Internet was a huge success.

2. Nonnative Speakers

Five nonnative speakers (NNSs) of English from four different countries recorded short introductions in English. They were chosen because of their potential to help students overcome their fears about incorrect utterances; if native speakers (NSs) had been chosen, students might have continued to unrealistically compare themselves to a "perfect" speaker. To increase comparability, each speaker gave his or her name, stated how long he or she had been in Japan (without saying his or her home country), and said something about Japanese food and something in the past tense. Listening to the tape, the students had to listen for each speaker's name, guess where he or she was from, and then focus on how each speaker expressed the same idea using different words. This final task was designed to help students develop sociolinguistic and discourse competence by understanding the cohesion found in various expressions with the same meaning as well as the appropriateness of various forms.

Class participation and discussion indicated that students benefited from listening to these nonnative speakers in three important ways. First, this class allowed the students to perceptually understand that pronunciation and lexical choice alone are not the only factors for intelligibility. For example, one speaker referred to food as "he," and most of the students heard and were interested in this use of "he" rather than "it." This also demonstrated nonnative speakers' ability to communicate in spite of grammatical and lexical errors. Because students found it difficult to understand people's names, they now had a better understanding of why foreigners sometimes do not immediately comprehend Japanese names. As a result, they realized that they should say their own names slowly and clearly.

Second, this activity reinforced the fact that there is not one correct accent and that the students can understand various accents. This is important because they are more likely to participate in NNS-to-NNS conversations in English rather than in NS-to-NNS conversations using English (Jenkins 2002). Because the accents of the two Chinese speakers were so different, the students were surprised that they were both from the same country. A Chinese woman speaking English was the most difficult for them to identify; in one class, only three students guessed that she was from China. The answer most often given was Peru. When the class heard nonnative speakers use English with varying degrees of comprehensibility, their fears about communication began to diminish. This in itself was an important learning process in the students' development of their speaking skills. It also increased their confidence to give presentations and perform dialogues.

Third, students indicated that they moved beyond a theoretical understanding that there are many ways to express the same idea. While, for example, one speaker said, "I like Japanese food," another said, "Japanese food, I think, is very good." Realizing that English is a living language and that there is not just one "correct answer" relieved concerns that their utterances could be wrong.

3. Presentation Preparation

To encourage learner autonomy, students prepared for the presentations primarily outside of class using previously studied Internet skills. For comparative purposes, Japan was included as one of the nine countries. Although Denmark was selected because of its progressive health care, most of the other countries were chosen to increase students' awareness of the use of English in countries that they normally do not associate with English (e.g., Cameroon, Hong Kong, Nigeria, South Africa). Care was also given to include countries from Africa, Asia, Europe, and North America. In addition, the countries were selected based on the results of the questionnaire administered at the end of the first semester in 2003 that queried students' knowledge of health and welfare in Japan and other countries.

Students were randomly assigned and were required to answer two questions about their country. In addition, the students had to present at least one additional fact about that country. Writing for an audience other than the teacher creates a more natural situation (White 1987) and is an important aspect of both face value and authenticity.

I have to admit that even I was surprised and excited to find that almost all of the students had prepared their material for the first day of presentations. Unconsciously, I had expected some of them to say they could not find the answers or have other excuses for not completing the assignment and then ask for an extension, but this was not the case. The students learned to take responsibility. None of the students lost their handouts during the entire semester; the few students who forgot their materials when they were chosen to present did not argue but instead acknowledged that they would receive a zero. They seemed to be truly motivated by the new material. This was a lesson not only for the instructors of other subjects but also for me. Even when students continue to let us down, we cannot give up. When they are motivated, they will break out of their usual patterns (e.g., of not preparing, as sometimes happened during the first semester), perhaps surprising themselves as well as the instructors.

4. Presentations

To decrease performance anxiety, five students gave their presentations together on one of the nine countries. The presentations included general background information (e.g., population, projected elderly population, life expectancy) as well as health care issues in those countries (e.g., leading cause of death, national health insurance, wheelchair accessibility). To avoid problems with students being unprepared and to increase enthusiasm, the country that would be presented was randomly chosen at the beginning of each class period; the presentations were given during nine classes, one for each country. The presenters wrote difficult English words that class members would not know (e.g., diseases) on the whiteboard and translated them into Japanese.

As a result of the presentations, there was a great amount of nonlinguistic learning. The new material increased awareness about the location of countries. Before each presentation, I asked students to locate the country on a map, but many in the classroom audience were often unable to do this. For example, only two students knew the location of the Philippines. More important, learning was enhanced through a series of questions comparing countries. For instance, while discussing Cameroon and previously presented countries (e.g., Hong Kong, Singapore, Canada), one student deduced that the reason for the small elderly population in Cameroon is because many do not live to the age where they can be classified as elderly. With prompting, this led to a discussion of how AIDS is ravishing the country. The young woman who had researched the leading cause of death provided additional information during this discussion. An additional benefit was that the presentations served to dispel some myths students unconsciously held about various countries.

5. Active Listening

The students in the audience were required to fill in a chart with the information their classmates presented; each week, I graded the chart for accuracy and completion. I required note-taking, a cognitive strategy (H. D. Brown 1994), so the students would have an incentive to actively listen as well as write in English. After the presentations, the students in the audience could ask the five presenters to repeat any information they had not written down, but there was a limit of three questions from the audience. This encouraged every student to listen closely from the beginning. When the audience asked questions, those presenting also received feedback about how their material was received (e.g., they spoke too softly) so they could improve in the future.

After the first presentation, students in the audience were reluctant to ask presenters to repeat their information. Instead, they conferred with their friends sitting nearby, but with encouragement and enforcement of a rule to ask presenters rather than friends, they began to use the example questions as a model for repetition. By the fifth week's presentations, the students had become more comfortable in asking for information and were asking the maximum three questions. They also had become more fluent in asking the questions and had to refer to the model questions less often. Using the communication strategy of direct appeal for help allowed the students to develop the ability to compensate for and overcome imperfect knowledge and other limiting factors, thus sustaining communication (see H. D. Brown 1994, 228). This is an important skill, and the progress the students made in using it would prove valuable when they talk to foreigners in Japan and other countries.

After the audience finished their clarification questions, I asked questions to aid in the development of the cognitive strategies of inference and elaboration, both of which have been shown to aid learners in the development of effective listening skills (J. D. Brown 1995). Asking the students to draw conclusions from the material also provided purposefulness for the listening. Additionally, without these questions most of the students would not have taken the time to compare the countries.

The students were interested in the comparison questions after each presentation and were pleased when they could use their completed listening chart to understand everything I asked. Although neighboring students assisted those students who lacked confidence about whether they had understood the question, the students had usually grasped the concepts and looked happy when they were able to answer. This proved to be a good method for increasing students' confidence that they can both understand and use English.

6. Dialogues—Life at a Retirement Village

After the first few weeks, approximately half of each lesson was devoted to the presentation while the other half was spent studying dialogues. The English conversations, which I created, were both longer and more substantial than those studied with the textbook during the first semester. Although based on life in a retirement village in Sydney, Australia, there were realistic applications to everyday conversations. For example, while studying "Talking to a Patient as

You Get Them Ready to Go Somewhere," students learned how to make small talk. They also learned the important skill of redirecting a conversation. Each conversation also had a cultural point that emphasized how language is used in other countries. For instance, students were interested in learning about the custom of many people in the service industry who say "Have a nice day" when the conversation is ending.

Because the conversations were interesting and applicable to their field of study, the students practiced the dialogues with a zest they had lacked in the first semester. The students also enjoyed the realistic features. For one dialogue, students had to shake hands when they were meeting someone for the first time, but they found this difficult to do. Also adding to the authenticity, they found it fun to practice "howrya doin," "kainna," "gonna," and other commonly used blends to which they had previously been unexposed and, in fact, did not recognize.

The dialogues allowed the lower-level students to practice speaking more smoothly and naturally rather than haltingly reading the text. At the same time, the higher-level students were able to practice the provided substitutions before creating more original conversations. During this process, the students made discoveries about the language that was used. For instance, in one of the dialogues, when asked, "How're you doing today?" the resident responds, "Good, but my back kind of hurts." One of the higher-level students asked what he should say instead of *good* if he really hurt.

7. Final Assessment and Application

During the last two classes of the semester, students applied their learning. First, a short written test required them to use their listening charts to answer questions about various countries. Then, after randomly selecting a number corresponding to one of the dialogues, pairs role-played that situation. During this time, the students not involved in the role-playing applied their new Internet skills by finding the answers to a quiz about Christmas.

Although the assessment took a disproportionate amount of time, the students were pleased to find they could practically apply both their presentations and their dialogue study. After completing the role-play, the students appeared thrilled to have been able to use English in a more natural manner. The combination of review for this oral test and the actual role-play not only reinforced their learning but also increased their confidence.

⠃ PROFESSIONAL RESONANCE

The combination of Internet usage, analysis of nonnative speakers' English, presentations that focus on the students' major, and applicable dialogue study provided the students with variety that is often missing when ESL/EFL textbooks are used. In addition to naturally integrating the four language skills of speaking, listening, writing, and reading into the second term's curriculum, we also used English for interpersonal and informational purposes. The pace and perspectives of the presentations and the dialogues, as well as the speaking styles (i.e., formal to very casual) and venues, differed enough so the students sustained their high motivation throughout each class period. In addition, the presentations allowed for individual and group activities while the dialogues involved pair work. Most important, communicative competence and transferable skills became the focus of the semester. Communicative competence is "both knowledge and skill in using knowledge" (Yalden 1987, 21); it is not only grammatical competence but also sociolinguistic competence, discourse competence, and strategic competence. Transferable skills include those used in self-learning and self-management, information technology, communication, presentation, and organization. By combining the Internet, nonnative speakers, presentations, and dialogues, the curriculum allowed for the integration and achievement of the following:

- communication goals, including enabling learners to discuss topics of interest, to share information in spoken form, and to obtain information by searching for specific details in a spoken text and by using communication strategies (e.g., seeking repetition)

- sociocultural goals, including enabling learners to not only grasp geographical concepts but also develop knowledge and understanding of the target language community as broadly defined to include countries where English has official status and to examine the countries' political and social institutions associated with health and welfare

- learning-how-to-learn goals, including enabling students to take responsibility for their own learning

- language and cultural awareness goals, including increasing awareness of the many ways to say the same idea in English and enabling learners to develop an understanding of forms of linguistic variety in English

- general knowledge goals, including learning how to access and search the Internet and use online dictionaries as well as the cognitive-processing skill of drawing conclusions from given information

End-of-Semester Evaluation

In addition to the noticeable change in attitudes toward English class, the students' responses to an end-of-semester questionnaire in December 2003 revealed the overwhelming success of the new material. When asked whether they preferred studying with a textbook (as in the first semester) or without (similar to second semester), 90 percent of the students selected the content-based material. Several students preferred the first semester because of the ease with which material can be comprehended using a textbook, but other reasons were also given. One student believed that it was wasteful to have purchased the textbook and then not use it but also noted that the second semester was enjoyable. Another student said using the Internet was bad for her eyes so she wanted to use the textbook. On the other hand, students who preferred the content-based material gave reasons such as the "fresh" atmosphere without a textbook, the opportunity to study things they never could have studied using a textbook, and freedom from textbook conversations that do not vary from those studied in junior and senior high school.

At the end of the semester, the students also ranked the seven components of the curriculum using several variables. When asked about how helpful the studies would be in the future, nearly three-fourths (74 percent) believed "How to Use the Internet" would be the first, second, or third most helpful. Similarly, 60 percent thought "Dialogues" would be helpful in the future. Students ranked "Presentation Preparation" as the most educational (57 percent) and indicated they were glad it was incorporated into the curriculum (64 percent), in spite of the fact that they also rated it the most difficult (64 percent). Students felt their English ability increased the most by studying "Dialogues" (60 percent) and "Nonnative Speakers" (59 percent). "Presentations" and "Active Listening" were viewed as the third and fourth best elements for increasing English ability.

Although this suggests that the presentations and corresponding listening were less positively received than I had hoped, the reasons for preferring the second semester as well as the free comments on the end-of-semester questionnaire were primarily related to the presentations and associated listening and preparation. These comments show the positive impact of these components of the curriculum, even though the students' ratings were not as high. One student, for instance, noted that the course made her think rather than just listen, memorize, and repeat, and 15 percent of the students mentioned positive aspects of learning about other countries. Three students reflected on how, at the beginning of the semester, the preparation for and giving of the presentations seemed daunting, but they found the semester to be enjoyable and felt they had benefited from these activities. Similarly, 22 percent of the students mentioned autonomous learning and putting forth more effort than for classes during the first semester. One student's comment summarizes the overall atmosphere of the second semester classes and demonstrates the fulfillment of the goal to help students become excited about using English: "I always came to class with anticipation and excitement, wondering what was going to happen that day."

The "Final Assessment and Application" was the only portion of the material that was consistently rated poorly. This may seem natural for assessment, but the students were asked to only evaluate the Christmas quiz, which applied their Internet skills. The negative evaluation may reflect the fact that it was the last day before winter vacation. It may also be the result of the students leaving the room to perform their role-plays one pair at a time while the rest of the students worked on the computers. In the future, however, I would prefer to give the final role-play evaluation outside of class time, allowing for the elimination of the quiz about Christmas.

Wider Application

Taylor (1987) discusses the importance of having "engaging content" and "activities in the target language which focus on issues that are relevant and meaningful to students" (p. 49). The free-comment section on the end-of-semester questionnaire allowed students to write additional impressions of the semester, and these remarks demonstrate both the variety of perceived success and the students' perceptions that the content was engaging, relevant, and meaningful. To begin with, 43 percent of the students demonstrated their engagement when they wrote about their enjoyment or interest in the new curriculum. Several students expounded on their newly found interest in English, noting that before they either did not like or were not good at English. In the free-comment section of the questionnaire, 23 percent of the students noted that they felt they had learned something or had accomplished something, and seven students attributed engagement in the learning process to variety. In addition, several students mentioned the practical nature of the studies and the ability to use English more naturally. Although statistically the comments would not be significant, it was inspiring to find many students had written similar positive opinions of the material. The students' perceived success, as demonstrated by their statements in the free-comment section, is the result of creating material that motivated them while matching their needs.

The success can also be attributed to clearly defining my expectations for the second semester with a four-page handout that detailed the class procedure and assessment criteria. Because the semester only has fifteen 50-minute classes, including assessment, and since the explanation of the presentations and assessment was complex, the handout was written in both English and Japanese. In an ESL classroom with students from multiple L1s, this would not be possible.

Foreign language instructors with students in other fields of study can effectively use this same combination of the Internet, analysis of nonnative speakers, presentations, and dialogues. For instance, science and engineering majors could present material in their specific field while studying dialogues between researchers in the laboratory and conversations at international conferences. Business students could present their concepts for a new business venture, perhaps in coordination with a business course they were presently taking or had previously taken. The applications of this curriculum are endless, limited only by imagination, time restrictions, or administrative restraints.

Because my Japanese students were unfamiliar with the Internet, giving the Internet demonstration during the first class strongly contributed to the motivation, excitement, and positive response of the students. In fact, in the free-comment section of the questionnaire more than one-third of the students mentioned using the computer and the Internet as one of the reasons for preferring the content-based material. For instructors with students who are more computer savvy, a different source for this burst of initial energy would be necessary to spur the students beyond their preconceived notions of what they can and cannot do in their L2. In other schools, I have created enthusiasm for the material by first having the students brainstorm about what they would like to study.

The assigned questions and examples of the answer forms were provided for the vocational college presentations so the students in the audience would be better able to understand the content in spite of lexically advanced sentences. Providing the questions to be addressed in the presentations also ensured different information from each of the five students presenting on the same country. Furthermore, because these students had never given presentations in either Japanese or English, guidance was necessary. Whereas this modeling was appropriate for these students, with more advanced students I have been able to give more latitude from the beginning. Students can either brainstorm in class or as homework, thinking about not only their presentation topic and specific content but also the steps they must take before the presentation. To extend this material to two semesters, I would retain this new curriculum for the first semester but use these brainstorming techniques for the second semester's presentation. Beginning with the brainstorming phase allows the students to focus on both the process of developing presentations and the end product, but for students who have done little brainstorming—as is the case with most Japanese tertiary students—initial guidance is necessary until they discover the joy of "thinking outside the box."

By using the computer room for each class that had presentations, I was able to project images from the Internet onto a large screen in the front of the classroom. When viewing the pictures from Canada, for example, one student commented in English to his friend, "Canada is beautiful." It was exciting to hear him use English in a natural way without thinking about it. Although it took three to five minutes to show a variety of pictures for each country (e.g., scenery, people, food), this time was well spent. It made the students more interested in the countries, the presentations, and English; it also indirectly demonstrated the value of and the resources available on the Internet.

Although it is logistically difficult in the college discussed, for instructors where it is feasible, it would be preferable for students to prepare the slide presentations or find the Web pages from which to show pictures.

■■ INSTITUTIONAL CHALLENGES

The Japanese Ministry of Education, Culture, Sports, Science, and Technology (*Monbukagakusho*) requires the inclusion of English in the curriculum, and, as such, the course described in this chapter is credit bearing. The community college provided few guidelines or restrictions on class content, although there was a general assumption that there would be an academic orientation. This provided me with the independence to create an appropriate curriculum, a freedom many colleagues may not share. As with many Japanese educational institutions, the full-time instructors, all of whom teach health- and welfare-related courses rather than the fundamental courses, perform many of the administrative roles at the college. Like the students, before beginning this curriculum the full-time instructors did not recognize the value of the English course or the nonlinguistic learning that could be accomplished within a well-designed EFL program.

During the development phase, the first-year homeroom teachers expressed concern that many of the students did not know anything about computers and did not know how to do research using books, even in Japanese. Although this may seem surprising, it must be considered when teaching EFL and ESL students because secondary education in other countries may not always emphasize presentations, reports, research, or independent study to the extent the college instructor assumes. Students may simply not have been taught the skills needed to prepare a presentation before entering tertiary education. Several times the homeroom teachers at the community college emphasized the students' general inability to perform these functions and suggested I keep this in mind when grading the students. During the second semester, however, the homeroom teachers expressed amazement; they were impressed at the diligence of the students as they worked to prepare their presentations. They noted, for example, that one young man who was always late for first period was in the library an hour before school began trying to find his answers. I, too, noticed a marked change in the students, whose apathy was replaced by a new zeal and excitement to use English for a real purpose. During the lunch period before class, students eagerly asked how to pronounce words, confirmed sentence construction, and asked how to express ideas clearly. Through this curriculum, the students learned that they were capable of doing much more than they formerly thought. Equally valuable, the other instructors discovered the importance of not discounting the students' potential and began to recognize the value of an EFL curriculum that integrates general knowledge, linguistic studies, and autonomy. In spite of these new discoveries, this style of class must continue or the students and other instructors may return to their status-quo assumptions.

Even after the curriculum revision, this course does not have equal status with the health and welfare courses. In all fairness, neither do the other fundamental courses, and perhaps this is natural since each is one of the thirty-five courses that are taught during the first year at the community college. Furthermore, part-time instructors, whose roles are further marginalized by their inability to meet students more than once a week, teach the fundamental courses, which are not required for licensing in the health and medical welfare industry in Japan. Even so, the new English material began to challenge the full-time instructors' assumptions. It also proved that when the students are motivated, the policy of giving students repeated chances to pass the course is no longer needed. This, alone, was a personal victory.

:: EXTENDING THE DIALOGUE

The two most important factors in the success of the new material were the appeal of the Internet and the variety within the curriculum, both of which were in response to the students' needs, abilities, and interests. The synthesis of nonlinguistic and linguistic learning not only provided variety but also made the class less theoretical and demonstrated practical applications for using English. Furthermore, the seven-point curriculum encouraged learner autonomy to which the students positively responded; the material also enabled students with different learning styles and intelligences (e.g., intrapersonal, interpersonal, logical-mathematical) to succeed. The importance of each component of the curriculum was obvious from the students' perceptions of educational worth, difficulty, helpfulness in the future, and increased English language ability.

Because of the union of these factors, the students became more enthusiastic about and interested in English. They actively participated in class as they began to view English as a living language rather than simply as an academic subject in school. Through the learning processes, the students' desire to communicate increased. Self-discovery, such as one student's discernment of the pleasure as well as the difficulty in speaking English, provided the momentum for students to gain confidence and believe that they already had adequate English skills to communicate. This resulted in a corresponding decrease in students' language anxiety. The results demonstrate that the adage "variety is the spice of life" is also true in English classes.

▪▪ ACKNOWLEDGMENTS

Portions of the dialogue element of this curriculum were presented at the Seventh Annual Scientific Conference of the Japan Academic Society on Health and Welfare Policy on November 29, 2003, in Izumo, Japan.

▪▪ CONTRIBUTOR

Carmella Lieske has been teaching English as a foreign language in Japan since 1993. She teaches not only on the tertiary level at universities, junior colleges, and vocational colleges but also in junior and senior high schools. In the community setting, she has taught students of all ages, ranging from preschool to adult.

PART 4

ASSESSMENT

CHAPTER 11

Thelma and Louise on the Road to Student Learning Outcomes

::

Margaret Connell and Ann O'Leary

:: FRAMING THE ISSUE

The Community College of Rhode Island (CCRI) is distinct in that it is the state's only community college with four campuses. These campuses are located in Warwick, Lincoln (both suburban settings), Providence (where the authors work), and a newly opened campus in the seaside setting of Newport. CCRI offers English as a second language (ESL) courses at all of these campuses; however, the majority of ESL students attend the Liston campus in Providence, the urban setting where many recent immigrants live. The Liston campus was founded in 1990, although there was a smaller building in Providence that was utilized for a few CCRI courses before that time. Liston grew from approximately 460 students to more than 4,900 students in the 2004–2005 academic year.

Historical Overview

To detail some history of CCRI's academic ESL courses, we look back to the late 1960s. In 1969, CCRI created its first ESL course. At that time, there were a number of second language learners enrolled in the regular Freshman Composition I course. The college thought that it would be a benefit to both the second language students and the English department faculty to create what was essentially a section of Composition I that clustered the second language speakers. The administration felt this was prudent in that the students exhibited errors in writing that were at times significantly different from those of the native English speakers and that the second language students deserved instruction from faculty trained and experienced in teaching this population. The curriculum committee created the course and titled it Composition I for Speakers of ESL and, in that it paralleled Composition I, the committee awarded students who successfully completed it three graduation credits.

English professors Gerry Richard and Arthur Mossberg could be called the "founding fathers" of academic ESL at CCRI. To meet the increasing demand from second language learners in the late 1970s, these two tenacious leaders advocated for the addition of two other ESL courses: ESL I and ESL II, which were considered developmental and received three in-house (i.e., not counted toward a degree) credits each. In the mid-1980s, the department discussed a proposal that ESL I and ESL II be expanded to six credits each and given graduation credit, which was in line with a growing trend at community colleges throughout the country. One of the arguments for credit was that the college was already awarding credit to entry-level and advanced foreign language instruction.

The proposal also included new courses: a six-credit course titled Paragraph Writing in ESL (ENGL 1090), a three-credit course titled Speech and Articulation in ESL (SPCH 1120), and a three-credit course titled ESL: Reading I (ENGL 0312). Since the writing and speech courses paralleled English department offerings that received credit, it was argued that they should also be granted credit. Similarly, since the reading course paralleled a noncredit course, it was deemed to earn three in-house credits as well.

All of these ideas, proposals, and initiatives indicate the beliefs and assumptions held by the principal individuals in our institution. The department debated the changes in ESL courses and eventually supported the initiative. The curriculum committee then voted to accept the program as presented. These courses have remained in place without alteration since that time (see Appendix A).

A New Chapter

In the past at CCRI, each academic department completed a program assessment every five years. During the assessment of 2003, it became obvious that the English department had too many branches on its "tree." The chair was in charge of approximately forty-five faculty who taught reading, writing, speech, theater, literature, and ESL. Shortly after the 2003 assessment, coordinators were elected or assigned for the separate branches of the English tree. Each coordinator's responsibility was to hold meetings for the related faculty and bring issues or concerns to the campus coordinator or the chairperson of the department. The desire to enhance the academic status of the ESL courses resulted in the revision of the catalog course descriptions and updated sample syllabi.

After completing these tasks, the mission to create student learning outcome statements was recommended by the visiting New England Association of Schools and Colleges (NEASC) accreditation team in 2004. Our adventure began when the newly formed ESL committee set out to write the outcome statements at a time when no one was sure how this would be done.

The aim of this chapter, therefore, is not only to provide background for the ESL sequence of courses at CCRI but moreover to describe how the outcomes for these courses were written.

▪▪ NARRATIVE

Developing Student Learning Outcomes

In the summer of 2004, members of the newly formed ESL committee (composed of volunteer faculty) decided to begin the task of developing the student learning outcomes for the ESL sequence of courses. Our beginning course, ESL I (ENGL 1070), was our starting point. During the summer, the writing committee completed the extended course description for several of their courses, so we followed the model they created. It contained the following categories: course description, class profile, overview, introduction and/or reinforcement of course-specific skills, ending competencies, and course measurements (see Appendix B for a model of ESL II [ENGL 1080]).

At the August 2004 ESL meeting, the members focused on the question, "What needs to be learned in ESL I?" Everyone decided to bring copies of ESL I final exams and some Test of English as a Foreign Language (TOEFL) practice tests to the following meeting to help determine a unified and consistent course content and outcomes expected from an ESL I class and then move on to ESL II (ENGL 1080). At this time, the members viewed outcomes as common goals for the students that should be covered in each ESL course. After discussion at the October meeting, members chose to focus on ESL I solely, which would be the only topic covered at the subsequent meeting to which all ESL faculty, adjunct and full-time, were invited to attend.

In November 2004, the group brainstormed and listed the necessary skills that need to be taught in ESL I and formulated a list of outcomes based on the model from the writing committee. These outcomes were reviewed and edited at the December committee meeting. It was at this gathering that the adage, "How many ESL teachers does it take to create one outcome statement?" was born. However, at the end of that session, we did feel that we had developed a draft for ESL I. Now we only had five more courses to go. After the holidays, we were scheduled to progress to ESL II.

In January 2005 several committee members attended the Assessing for Learning Workshop given by Dr. Peggy Maki, who studied our outcomes for ESL I and suggested identifying an assessment of each skill by using listening, speaking, reading, and writing measurement tools. She also advised obtaining the outcomes that TESOL recommends and comparing them to ours. We read *ESL Standards for Pre-K–12 Students* (TESOL 1997), which was not geared to higher education, and *Standards for Adult Education ESL Programs* (TESOL 2003), which did not address credit-bearing courses.

Committee members also attended the Massachusetts Association for Teachers of Speakers of Other Languages (MATSOL) workshop at Rhode Island College in February 2005, where we were made aware of the WIDA (acronym for an original consortium of states—Wisconsin, Delaware, and Arkansas—that created new proficiency standards for ESL) English Language Proficiency Standards (see http://www.wida.us/ for a downloadable version). According to Bernstein (2005), this set of standards was created as a response to the No Child Left Behind Act. However, we felt these standards were also not suitable for higher education ESL students. At the February committee meeting, which should have focused on ESL II outcomes, the committee was updated on the assessment workshops, and confusion set in as to which model to follow.

With no direct signposts as to which road we should take in creating all six outcomes, we decided that representatives of the ESL committee would meet with the chair and dean to agree on a template for our mission and a time frame for its completion. The completion of the outcomes during committee meetings was put on hold and now became "the outcomes saga."

Moving in a New Direction

At the March 2005 meeting with the English chair and academic dean, we explained that we had three different models that we could follow: TESOL's standards for pre-K–12, WIDA standards, and the English department model. When asked which one to implement, the dean stated, "There is no magic template to follow." He suggested that we look at the six-course ESL sequence as a whole first; incorporate the terminology of "introduce-reinforce-emphasize"; and connect assessment to listening, speaking, reading, and writing skills for the grammar courses. He did not set an implementation deadline.

At the March ESL meeting, members realized that the outcomes project would be postponed because there were other vital issues that had more priority, such as the revision of Composition I for Speakers of ESL (ENGL 1300).

At the end of March, Margaret Connell, one of the authors of this chapter, attended the TESOL convention in San Antonio, Texas, in the United States, where she met Craig Machado from Norwalk Community College in Connecticut. When asked if he had a template from which we could design our student learning outcome statements, Machado said, "We currently do not have higher education standards for ESL, other than those that were drawn up by TESOL for Adult Ed" (C. Machado, pers. comm.). Additionally, he acknowledged that there is a need for an interest section within TESOL for community college ESL (apart from the existing Adult Education and Higher Education Interest Sections).

Connell also contacted other TESOL participants who sent her lists of Web sites where we found further community college information and syllabi. Still, no community college that we know of has been charged with exactly the same mission for creating student learning outcomes.

As our priority changed in April 2005, the two of us sat down with our chair to write a proposal for ENGL 1300—changing it from a three-credit course to a six-credit course. For this paperwork, the curriculum review committee required a list of the major learning outcomes for the proposed course, a list of the techniques/methods used to achieve the outcomes, and a list of the assessment tools. We later presented this proposal to the statewide articulation meeting of the three Rhode Island sister colleges. As we were completing this proposal, we realized that the same information could serve as the foundation for the student learning outcomes, which invigorated us to proceed.

Putting It All Together

Once classes were over in May, and grades were submitted, we settled into the idea of meeting at the Liston campus, our base, for the next few weeks to draft the outcomes and have them ready to present to the ESL committee in the fall.

"Why on our own time?" the reader may ask. We recognized that in the fall we would be busy with beginning courses, placement problems, and schedule adjustments, along with the curriculum revision process, so we decided to utilize this precious summer time. We had a five-week window of opportunity to formulate drafts of outcomes and new course descriptions.

Thus, we collected all our resources for developing outcomes and asked English faculty member Barbara Legg to meet with us about her success in writing course outcomes for the writing committee. We filled one folder with outcomes from various colleges and some workshop papers and another folder with Barbara's models, and we took over a conference room. ENGL 1010, the regular freshman writing course, was similar to our ENGL 1300, so we used these as we revised and adjusted our information and outcomes to follow the same pattern as the writing committee. We also consulted with Peggy Maki, the consultant for the Office of Higher Education in Rhode Island, to make sure we were on the right path. As we entered our information, we were delighted to realize that we could also update our course description sheets for adjuncts simultaneously.

Initially, we thought that we would formulate the outcomes for the most advanced course first, Composition I for Speakers of ESL (ENGL 1300), and then the entry-level course, ESL I (ENGL 1070), figuring that we would look at the sequence of courses deductively (as suggested earlier by our dean). However, once we started on ESL I, we realized that it would be easier to evaluate the entire sequence inductively after each course was done.

ESL I (ENGL 1070) and ESL II (ENGL 1080) are similar but for different levels and follow the same format. We determined that these two grammar courses must specify the four language domains of listening, speaking, reading, and writing. Our writing courses, Paragraph Writing in ESL (ENGL 1090) and Composition I for Speakers of ESL (ENGL 1300), specified the writing process, rhetorical modes, and computer writing. Finally, our complimentary courses, ESL: Reading I (ENGL 0312) and Speech and Articulation in ESL (SPCH 1120), followed a reading/writing focus and a listening/speaking focus, respectively.

For inserting information, our approach became one of focusing on one course and completing the course description sheet for it first. After that, it was easier to transfer those outcomes to our draft, which included the outcome, the standards, the techniques/methods, and the types of assessment used (see Appendix C).

This process worked for us, and we believe that the information provided for each course fits the content and requirements so that each successful student can make a smooth transition from one level of ESL to another. This project will also provide pertinent information for adjunct faculty who sometimes receive a course assignment only a few days before the semester begins.

:: PROFESSIONAL RESONANCE

As experienced educators in the fields of English and ESL in higher education, we must note our concerns before, during, and after completion of this somewhat daunting task. Before the process really began, we and the ESL committee believed we had a general idea of what we were being asked to do. Most of us considered these outcome statements to be very close to what had been called "course objectives" in the past. During the compilation of student learning outcomes, however, we realized all too often that we had to either reevaluate what we had written or scrap it completely and begin again. After completion, we felt a greater sense of clarity and pride in what we had accomplished. Creating student learning outcomes proved effective in terms of instruction, professionalism, and practicality.

In the pedagogical sense, we have always considered ourselves to be classroom teachers in a "teaching" college. Other than action research, we teach through active learning and immersion into academic English in the second language classroom; we do not conduct research, publish articles, or perform many administrative duties. From a curricular standpoint, we strongly believe that CCRI's academic ESL courses should remain part of the English department because our courses parallel and articulate smoothly into the mainstream English courses.

Another issue is that of credit-bearing versus noncredit-bearing ESL courses. Although CCRI does offer its own set of noncredit ESL classes through its lifelong learning program, *our* role is as educators in the faculty of the English department. Nevertheless, many students move from noncredit to credit courses, sometimes placing into ESL II (ENGL 1080) when testing into the academic ESL division of the institution. The credit ESL courses are college level, academic, and rigorous, as explained earlier, and intended for students who are pursuing an associate's degree.

Professionally, we discovered that these outcome statements provided an opportunity to review the four language domains—listening, speaking, reading, and writing—and how each of our ESL courses concentrates on them. The outcome statements clearly delineate what students will accomplish upon successful completion; this is critical information to faculty members, students, support staff, administration, and the NEASC and CCRI's Board of Governors.

The results of this work are also important in keeping with our ongoing resolve to uphold as much consistency as possible regarding placement and evaluation of ESL students from campus to campus and instructor to instructor. This experience has also validated the academic standards to which ESL faculty must hold the students. Additionally, we were able to update our adjunct ESL manual and provide adjunct faculty with substantive information.

Because of the trial-and-error method we used until a clear target—student learning outcomes—emerged, others may now benefit if they find themselves with the same or similar charge. When we wrote the outcomes, we not only satisfied the NEASC team and Rhode Island's Board of Governors for Higher Education but also discovered practical and professional rewards for ourselves and others in the field—something that does not always transpire when an administrative task is assigned.

∷ INSTITUTIONAL CHALLENGES

Every institution must address the needs of the students. As student enrollment increased at CCRI, so did the level of change within the English department, which comprises fifty full-time faculty and seventy-three adjunct faculty who cover approximately 436 sections of courses in speech, writing, literature, ESL, reading, and theater at four campuses.

The first change occurred recently in response to the amplified number of faculty and campuses; there is now a coordinator for each discipline and a campus coordinator at each location. This sharing of responsibilities across the campuses has been supported by the administration.

Specifically, the ESL coordinator calls and chairs committee meetings, examines and develops curricula, reports to the whole department, researches curricula of other institutions, presents to the curriculum committee, develops learning outcomes, interfaces with other departments, participates in the placement process, and meets regularly with the chair. The Liston campus coordinator serves as a liaison between the department chair and all English faculty at the Liston campus, in addition to performing many coordinator duties.

The sequence of ESL courses at CCRI is distinct in that the courses are a secure component of the English department. ESL is not isolated or freestanding but embraced and considered a vital discipline taught by many faculty. Perhaps unique to CCRI, professors can choose to teach a schedule that includes a literature course, a speech course, and an ESL course. All teachers of ESL are supported and guided by our chair, who consults with the dean of arts and sciences who, in turn, confers with the vice president of academic affairs.

When revising ESL curriculum, the procedure begins with a majority decision from the ESL committee members and approval from the English chair. This revision requires representatives to present a proposal to the curriculum review committee at CCRI. ESL issues, concerns, or suggestions from any faculty member can be explored at ESL committee meetings or discussed directly with the chair. Open communication and dialogue remain crucial and valued: everyone has a voice. Opportunities for field-related workshops are extended to all teachers of ESL from the chair and dean; however, reimbursements are dictated by the travel budget. In addition, the administration sponsors a professional development day each year.

As the mission to develop student learning outcomes was charged to the different departments, the dean publicized assessment workshops for all interested faculty. Departments then set time frames for completion of student learning outcomes.

Unfortunately, we realize that an aura of mystery still surrounds the ESL sequence, fostered by some who are not comfortable with the mission of educating students whose native language is not English. Misinformation can be disseminated by well-meaning staff and instructors because of their confusion over ESL placement procedures and course enrollment. This is a challenge that our institution should meet to improve ESL student success.

In our roles of campus coordinator and ESL coordinator, we endeavor to be advocates for the ESL students at our campus. As our chair boasts of CCRI as the "port of entry" for nonnative speakers, we appreciate his willingness to explore ESL/English revisions and to provide proper networking.

■■ EXTENDING THE DIALOGUE

Undoubtedly, there are still unanswered questions. Some of these answers should come from a broader audience, specifically ESL faculty at other community colleges nationwide. Perhaps those readers will be able to address the issue of student learning outcomes with a more directed focus on their own circumstances and institutions. The following questions remain:

- What is the "ladder of power" with regard to ESL at community colleges?

- Should ESL courses be credit bearing, noncredit bearing, or both?

- Who should teach academic ESL and noncredit ESL courses? Are different credentials and training required for each?

- Do administrators or faculty have responsibility for determining course content, credits, and standards, or is this a shared responsibility?

- Depending on whether one teaches a credit or noncredit ESL course, who supervises the instructor?

- Should there be national ESL student learning outcomes? What about objectives or goals?

- Have other community colleges based their student learning outcomes on the *Standards for Adult Education ESL Programs* (TESOL 2003) or perhaps revised them to suit their particular case?

- Who should be asked to create learning outcomes? Administration? Faculty? Private consultants? All of these? Should student learning outcomes follow any explicit format?

Through our own experience of forming student learning outcomes, we discovered a successful strategic approach. These may be summarized within the three major chronological steps, or stages, that we followed. First, we gathered much advice and knowledge from colleagues, the administration, and workshops or conferences. In our case, this meant the writing coordinator, the dean of arts and sciences, and the Assessing for Learning Workshop. At other community colleges, there may be similar players or other paths to follow in the beginning stages.

The next step was, of course, the most involved because it meant the actual structuring of our own learning outcomes for each of the academic ESL courses in the sequence. The first two courses took an inordinate amount of time, energy, and patience since we were unsure of the process itself. The other four courses and their outcomes were much less demanding because of our familiarity with the first two courses.

Eventually, it became clear to us that we had unearthed three jobs instead of one. The outcomes were our primary responsibility, and those were carried out. Meanwhile, we completed the extended course description pages for each ESL course in the sequence. It was extremely advantageous to do this at the same time as the outcomes, for there was a great deal of overlap. The final task was evident after we had contemplated submitting a piece of writing to Craig Machado for this volume. This was an "aha" moment—we could describe our recent bumpy road trip toward the creation of student learning outcomes.

We hope that our journey will be constructive and informative to other educators who are faced with similar challenges in the field of teaching English to speakers of other languages at the community college level.

■■ CONTRIBUTORS

Margaret Connell is an associate professor at the Community College of Rhode Island (CCRI) in the United States. She began teaching as an adjunct instructor at CCRI in 1985 and became a full-time ESL instructor in 1991. A graduate of Rhode Island College with a master's degree in English/ESL, she has served as CCRI's Liston campus coordinator for several years.

Ann O'Leary is an associate professor at CCRI and has taught English and ESL classes at the Liston campus since 1993. She became a full-time faculty member in 1998. A graduate of Rhode Island College with a master's degree in education, she was elected ESL coordinator by her peers in 2004.

■■ APPENDIX A: CATALOG COURSE DESCRIPTIONS FOR ACADEMIC ESL COURSES AT THE COMMUNITY COLLEGE OF RHODE ISLAND

ESL I (ENGL 1070) is the first course in the sequence of academic ESL offerings at the Community College of Rhode Island (CCRI). This course is designed for students who are pursuing academic studies at the college level. Prior knowledge of the English language is necessary. Students study grammar and sentence building in English, with sequential emphasis placed on listening, speaking, reading, and writing. Outcomes of this course include the ability to form several complete sentences regarding one topic. Students who successfully complete ENGL 1070 take ENGL 1080.

ESL II (ENGL 1080) is a continuation of ESL I and is also designed for students pursuing academic studies at the college level. Listening and speaking continue to be areas of second language practice, with more emphasis placed on reading and writing skills. As an outcome, students are able to form a coherent paragraph of eight to ten sentences. Students who have successfully completed ENGL 1080 take ENGL 1090.

Paragraph Writing in ESL (ENGL 1090) is designed to increase the writing performance of ESL students. It emphasizes the writing process and advanced grammar as students progress from generating acceptable sentences to combining sentences to form paragraphs in all rhetorical modes. In addition, students will be able to form a multiparagraph essay as an outcome of the course. Students who have successfully completed ENGL 1090 take ENGL 1300.

Composition I for Speakers of ESL (ENGL 1300) has the same purpose as ENGL 1010 (the regular freshman writing course). Composition I students sharpen their academic writing skills through a sequence of essay assignments, including a research project, with emphasis and grammatical issues particular to ESL. Students successfully completing ENGL 1300 may take ENGL 1010 as a follow-up course for elective credit.

ESL: Reading I (ENGL 0312) is designed to improve the vocabulary knowledge and reading comprehension of students speaking English as a second language. The content includes such college reading skills as developing word knowledge, identifying main ideas, locating important details, and applying basic study strategies. Students should be enrolled in, or have already completed, ENGL 1090 or ENGL 1300 as a corequisite.

Speech and Articulation in ESL (SPCH 1120) emphasizes correct pronunciation of the English language, particularly through practice of the International Phonetic Alphabet. In addition, course content includes syllable stress and intonation. Perhaps equally important, ESL students refine their listening skills in rapid American English speech.

▪▪ APPENDIX B: EXTENDED COURSE DESCRIPTION FOR ESL II (ENGL 1080) AS A MODEL

Course Description: ESL II is the second course in the sequence of academic ESL offerings at the Community College of Rhode Island (CCRI). This course is designed for students who are planning to pursue academic studies at the college level. Grammar, compound/complex sentence structure, and some short paragraph construction will be studied with sequential emphasis on listening, speaking, reading, and writing. Outcomes of this course include the ability to form short paragraphs on one topic. This is a six-credit course with a class maximum of eighteen students.

Class Profile: Students in ENGL 1080 have scored at least 50 percent on two-thirds of the in-house ESL placement test. Students should also exhibit competency in intermediate English communication skills. They should be able to demonstrate the four language components. Students are motivated to improve their skills for success in this endeavor.

Overview: The goal of ENGL 1080 is to improve students' chances of collegiate success in the subsequent courses of CCRI's academic ESL program. The competencies developed in ENGL 1080 are essential to advance to the levels demanded in Paragraph Writing in ESL (ENGL 1090).

Your course should introduce or reinforce the following understanding and skills to the students:

I. Listening Domain

Students will

1. recognize and distinguish among simple present, present progressive, and present perfect verb forms;
2. recognize and distinguish among simple past, past progressive, and past perfect verb forms;
3. recognize and distinguish between the use of "will" and "be going to";
4. recognize question formations;
5. understand the contextualized meaning of phrasal verbs, modals, and modal expressions;
6. process time clauses;
7. distinguish between comparatives and superlatives;
8. identify measure words and quantifiers;
9. interpret the combining of sentences;
10. perceive a group of sentences focusing on one topic.

II. Speaking Domain

Students will

1. produce and distinguish among simple present, present progressive, and present verb forms;
2. produce and distinguish among simple past, past progressive, and past perfect verb forms;
3. produce and distinguish between the use of "will" and "be going to";
4. utilize question formations;

5. engage in the appropriate contextualized meaning of phrasal verbs, modals, and modal expressions;

6. process time clauses;

7. distinguish between comparatives and superlatives;

8. integrate measure words and quantifiers;

9. construct sentence combinations;

10. vocalize a group of sentences focusing on one topic.

III. Reading Domain

Students will

1. recognize and distinguish among simple present, present progressive, and present perfect verb forms;

2. recognize and distinguish among simple past, past progressive, and past perfect verb forms;

3. recognize and distinguish between the use of "will" and "be going to";

4. recognize question formations;

5. process the contextualized meaning of phrasal verbs, modals, and modal expressions;

6. process time clauses;

7. distinguish between comparatives and superlatives;

8. identify measure words and quantifiers;

9. interpret the combining of sentences;

10. comprehend a group of sentences focusing on one topic as a short paragraph.

IV. Writing Domain

Students will

1. construct simple present, present progressive, and present perfect verb forms;

2. construct simple past, past progressive, and past perfect verb forms;

3. construct sentences with "will" and "be going to";

4. apply question formations;

5. employ the contextualized meaning of phrasal verbs, modals, and modal expressions;

6. integrate time clauses;

7. make use of comparatives and superlatives;

8. vary measure words and quantifiers;

9. write sentence combinations;

10. write short paragraphs focusing on one topic.

At the end of the semester, students should have the following competencies:

1. Identify and employ simple present, present progressive, and present perfect verb forms in the four language domains.

2. Identify and employ simple past, past progressive, and past perfect verb forms in the four language domains.

3. Identify and employ "will" and "be going to" in the four language domains.

4. Interpret and develop question formations in the four language domains.

5. Understand the contextualized meaning of the phrasal verbs, modals, and modal expressions in the four language domains.

6. Process time clauses in the four language domains.

7. Distinguish between and produce comparatives and superlatives in the four language domains.

8. Integrate measure words and quantifiers in the four language domains.

9. Interpret and develop sentences in combinations in the four language domains.

10. Conceptualize and construct a group of sentences focusing on one topic in a paragraph in the four language domains.

Course Measurements

- Quizzes
- Tests
- Midterm
- Final
- Homework
- Role-play
- Pair and group work
- Sentence creation
- Sentence combinations
- Construction of short paragraphs
- Dictation
- Recitation

Texts

Sadlier, M., H. Riggenbach, and V. Samuda. 2000. *Grammar dimensions 2.* Boston: Heinle & Heinle.

Benz, C., and A. Roemer. 2000. *Grammar dimensions 2 workbook.* Boston: Heinle & Heinle.

⠃⠃ APPENDIX C: LEARNING OUTCOMES FOR ESL II (ENGL 1080)

I. Students Should Employ Listening Strategies in Academic English Standards

Students will

1. recognize and distinguish among simple present, present progressive, and present perfect verb forms;
2. recognize and distinguish among simple past, past progressive, and past perfect verb forms;
3. recognize and distinguish between the use of "will" and "be going to";
4. recognize question formations;
5. understand the contextualized meaning of phrasal verbs, modals, and modal expressions;
6. process time clauses;
7. distinguish between comparatives and superlatives;
8. identify measure words and quantifiers;
9. interpret the combining of sentences;
10. perceive a group of sentences focusing on one topic.

II. Students Should Employ Speaking Strategies in Academic English Standards

Students will

1. produce and distinguish among simple present, present progressive, and present perfect verb forms;
2. produce and distinguish among simple past, past progressive, and past perfect verb forms;
3. produce and distinguish between the use of "will" and "be going to";
4. utilize question formations;
5. engage in the appropriate contextualized meaning of phrasal verbs, modals, and modal expressions;

6. process time clauses;

7. distinguish between comparatives and superlatives;

8. integrate measure words and quantifiers;

9. construct sentence combinations;

10. vocalize a group of sentences focusing on one topic.

III. *Students Should Employ* Reading *Strategies in Academic English Standards*

Students will

1. recognize and distinguish among simple present, present progressive, and present perfect verb forms;

2. recognize and distinguish among simple past, past progressive, and past perfect verb forms;

3. recognize and distinguish between the use of "will" and "be going to";

4. recognize question formations;

5. process the contextualized meaning of phrasal verbs, modals, and modal expressions;

6. process time clauses;

7. distinguish between comparatives and superlatives;

8. identify measure words and quantifiers;

9. interpret the combining of sentences;

10. comprehend a group of sentences focusing on one topic as a short paragraph.

IV. *Students Should Employ* Writing *Strategies in Academic English Standards*

Students will

1. construct simple present, present progressive, and present perfect verb forms;

2. construct simple past, past progressive, and past perfect verb forms;

3. construct sentences with "will" and "be going to";

4. apply question formations;

5. employ the contextualized meaning of phrasal verbs, modals, and modal expressions;

6. integrate time clauses;

7. make use of comparatives and superlatives;

8. vary measure words and quantifiers;

9. write sentence combinations;
10. write short paragraphs focusing on one topic.

Techniques/Methods Used to Achieve Outcomes

- Lectures
- Exercises, quizzes, tests, and exams
- In-class writing
- Role-playing
- Pair and group work
- Dictation
- Recitation
- Private conferences
- Meaningful class contribution
- Attendance within department mandate

Types of Assessment for Student Learning Outcomes

- Exercises, quizzes, tests, and exams
- Homework—sentence creation/combining sentences into paragraphs
- Student progress via conference
- Class participation

CHAPTER 12

From Marginalized to Integrated: ESL Placement Testing Goes Mainstream

▪▪

Craig Machado and Suzanne Solensky

▪▪ FRAMING THE ISSUE

When Craig Machado assumed responsibility for the credit English as a second language (ESL) program at Norwalk Community College (NCC) in Connecticut, in the United States, in the fall of 1999, ESL placement testing was solely the responsibility of the ESL department. This meant, among other things, that he was responsible for hiring testing proctors who administered the placement instrument, the English Placement Test, originally developed by the Testing and Certification Division of the English Language Institute (ELI) at the University of Michigan. Known by many as the EPT, this test has been widely used since 1978 and consists of one hundred multiple-choice items, which are divided into twenty listening, thirty grammar, thirty vocabulary, and twenty reading questions and are given in the same order to all test takers. Each of the three different forms—A, B, and C—is administered with paper and pencil and cannot be scored immediately. According to ELI's Web site, "the EPT is used to group students into homogeneous ability levels as they enter an intensive English course. Alternate forms of the EPT can be used for pre-testing and post-testing. The EPT is designed for optimal discrimination at the intermediate proficiency level" (Test Publications n.d.).

Since NCC has two distinct programs, noncredit and credit, both with five levels, the EPT could theoretically place students into these ten combined levels. Students move from the noncredit program when they write an essay placing them into an intermediate academic ESL writing class. However, a

187

written essay of forty-five minutes was also administered, and this was, as Machado learned soon enough, the chief determinant of level placement. EPT test scores were considered, but the writing assessment prevailed. Because the college tests well over one thousand ESL-identified students a year, oral interviews and listening comprehension assessments, more common in intensive (university-based) ESL programs, were not considered feasible.

While the credit and noncredit ESL programs shared the cost of testing proctors, the credit program alone was responsible for sorting the placement tests into the appropriate program and maintaining a master placement test list. In contrast, NCC was using the College Board's computerized Accuplacer to test and place non-ESL students into English composition or developmental courses. The scores of non-ESL students were regularly uploaded to the college's academic computing system, Banner, where they were available to counselors. In addition, the non-ESL testing was conducted by part-time proctors who were supervised by the admissions office, which also made all appointments for testing—ESL and non-ESL. One of the components of Accuplacer, ironically, was Levels of English Proficiency (LOEP), intended for ESL student placement.

Like the other sections of Accuplacer, LOEP tests adapt to the proficiency level of the individual student. As the *Accuplacer OnLine Technical Manual* (2003) explains, "Unlike many traditional tests where all examinees take a single form of an exam, the computer adapts or 'tailors' the exam to each examinee. This tailoring is done by keeping track of an examinee's performance on each test item and then using this information to select the next item to be administered" (p. 3). As a result, each student not only sees a different set of multiple-choice questions but also has to answer fewer questions for his or her skill level to be determined. Finally, the calculation of scores can be done instantaneously by the testing software.

When he inquired why LOEP was not used for ESL testing, Machado received several differing responses:

- The EPT test, while not perfect, seemed to do the job, so why switch?

- A very small cohort of ESL students had been part of a pilot to try LOEP. The pilot showed a weak correlation between EPT and LOEP, especially at very low levels (problematic for the noncredit program).

- The college was not in a position to handle ESL placement testing through admissions because it did not have enough personnel.

Never mind that the Connecticut Community College System had adopted Accuplacer statewide and that its Basic Skills Council recommended in 1996 that the LOEP portion be used to test ESL students!

Machado was particularly concerned that the college had not wanted to take on the responsibility of ESL placement testing. While he understood that the arrangement in place for ESL testing was working adequately, nonetheless, it seemed to him that the college was, in effect, marginalizing ESL students. It was also putting an additional burden on the ESL department to take care of "those students." Why couldn't admissions handle ESL placement testing? Why did ESL have to find its own test proctors every semester? Why did ESL students have to be crammed, sixty to seventy students at a time, into mass test sessions, when non-ESL students were tested in small groups, in settings in which the security of the test questions could be maintained and proctors could attend more effectively to students' needs?

In meetings held with the dean of students and admissions personnel, Machado's concerns about marginalizing ESL testing were aired and acknowledged as was the growing feeling that the college needed to revamp its entire testing process. This chapter, cowritten by Craig Machado, ESL program director, and Suzanne Solensky, associate director of admissions, describes the efforts to bring ESL testing under the umbrella of college-wide testing, the necessary personnel changes (i.e., hiring a new full-time testing coordinator), and an evaluation of replacing the EPT with the Accuplacer LOEP.

∷ NARRATIVE

When Solensky was hired as the full-time testing coordinator in February 2002, her top priority was to oversee a major change in basic skills testing (in reading, writing, and math) for native English speakers. The college switched from using the Windows-based version of Accuplacer to the Web-based version (called Accuplacer OnLine). Throughout the months of that transition, plans were also being made to bring ESL placement testing under the control of the testing center and to conduct the tests using LOEP. Two goals had to be met: (1) finding and equipping another location for testing (a room with the necessary computers) and (2) determining the accuracy of LOEP in placing students into the college's ESL program. The dean of students and the directors of admissions and ESL met and decided to pilot LOEP during the summer of 2002; the pilot would prove to be the first of three stages in mainstreaming ESL testing.

Stage 1: Piloting LOEP (Summer 2002)
Design
Although a number of people, including deans and professional staff, participated in initial discussions about the transition to LOEP, the responsibility for designing and conducting the pilot fell on three people: Machado, Solensky, and the part-time ESL coordinator in the noncredit division, who also proctored ESL placement tests.

The first question to be answered concerned the format of the test. The ESL department decided that only two of the four LOEP sections would be helpful: Language Usage, which indicates fluency with English grammar and syntax, and Reading Skills, which measures reading comprehension. Sentence Meaning and Listening were not administered, primarily because of time constraints. In addition, students would, as before, write an essay based on in-house prompts.

The decisions became more difficult as planning continued, even though Solensky consulted a vice president at Accuplacer for advice on designing a test pilot. For two reasons the pilot team seriously considered the vice president's suggestion to administer LOEP to new students, who were applying for the fall semester. First, by observing students in actual sessions with LOEP, Solensky could develop appropriate training materials for proctors to use in the future. Second, if such students were also given the EPT (as they would have to be, so that they could be placed accurately), the college could correlate EPT scores with LOEP scores. The ESL department would then be able to match LOEP scores with the fluency and skills needed for each ESL level in the curriculum. Unfortunately, scheduling such dual testing for a large enough number of students proved to be too difficult, and the idea was soon dropped.

The planning team decided instead to limit the pilot to matriculated students, who had already been given the EPT and placed into classes. These students would be tested at the end of their summer courses; their scores could, it was hoped, determine the minimum level of competence students would need to move to the next ESL level. For example, average scores for students testing at the end of the sixth-level course could become the cutoffs for placement into the seventh-level course.

It was therefore essential to test students at all levels—or at least at each of the nine levels offered that summer. In planning the details of such an extensive pilot, the team dealt with a number of potential obstacles:

- Money: Unlike the EPT (which was given without cost) and the in-house essays, each Accuplacer test unit or section carries a fee. The deans approved funding for the several hundred units that would be used in the pilot.

- Space and equipment: Computers would not be installed in the designated ESL testing center until the fall. Solensky had to arrange for up to twenty-five laptops to be configured, set up, and reserved for the length of the pilot.

- Student data: Because the students to be tested were enrolled at NCC, they had college identification numbers. If they used those numbers for the test, however, their scores, which were for research purposes only, would be uploaded to Banner just as actual scores for incoming students would be. Dummy identification numbers, therefore, had to be assigned to test takers.

- Scheduling: Students would test during the final week of their classes, in August, and those class times were already in place. Furthermore, many of them conflicted with actual placement sessions, which had been scheduled and could not be canceled since August is always the college's heaviest month of testing. Solensky blocked out potential times for pilot tests, and the ESL department chose the instructors and classes that would participate.

The pilot sessions would not mimic a true placement situation. First, because the students were already enrolled, they did not need to hear the usual orientation to the college. Also, class sessions lasted only two hours, while the LOEP test (like all Accuplacer tests) is supposed to be untimed. There was a chance that some students would not finish both LOEP sections before class was over. Finally, students were not being asked to write an essay.

Solensky intended to proctor all the pilot tests herself, because no one else on campus had her experience with Accuplacer OnLine (she had been proctoring three to four basic skills tests a week for several months) and because she wanted to closely monitor students as they worked with LOEP. Over a two-week period, she conducted nine ESL pilot tests (for both morning and evening classes) while also overseeing the basic skills testing. The schedule was difficult to maintain, but when the pilot was over, the college had scores from about 150 students—not to mention a wealth of valuable qualitative data, such as comments students made about the test.

Analysis

Once placement testing was completed for the fall 2002 semester, representatives from the ESL department and student services (the division responsible for placement testing) met to discuss the results of the pilot. Solensky shared several observations with her colleagues:

- The laptops were intimidating for many students, even those who seemed to have used computers before.

- Many students misunderstood the purpose of the pilot; because the LOEP test came at the end of their course (the last or second-to-last class session), they frequently thought they were taking their final exam. That perception may have caused them needless anxiety.

- Classroom dynamics played a major role. Instructors stayed in the room throughout the test, and their assistance was vital, especially with large groups (eighteen students or more) and beginning classes. Yet the presence of instructors meant that students took their cue more from them than from the proctor. At the same time, the students often sought help and encouragement from classmates before the test began.

On top of these difficulties, the data obtained were of little help in establishing cut scores. A crucial set of scores was lacking: those for students in the final noncredit level, which might have been used to set a cutoff between noncredit and credit classes. During the test of those students, the college lost its Internet connection, and students could not complete the two LOEP sections before their class time ended.

In addition, the ranges for the other four levels of noncredit students varied widely, even when the results for both Language Usage and Reading Skills were added together. At the upper noncredit levels, some students scored near the maximum—in other words, where advanced credit-level students would be expected to score. Dr. Jean Kelley, then the director of student services, thoroughly analyzed the credit-level data and found no significant differences in test scores, even when she compared them to final grades in the summer classes.

Several possible explanations (besides a small sample size) could account for the inconclusiveness of the data:

- The 120-point range for each LOEP section cannot possibly differentiate among ten course levels.

- The pilot used only two sections of LOEP, not three; perhaps a combined score of three or more sections would better indicate a student's abilities.

- Students may not have been placed correctly in the classes to begin with.

Whatever the reasons, the pilot had failed in its main goal: determining cut scores.

It would be wrong, though, to say that the pilot had accomplished nothing at all. Solensky realized that many students would need instruction (often one-on-one) in using computers and that computer facility seemed directly correlated with fluency in English. Once students were oriented to the nature of the test and to the computers, most were able to complete both sections of LOEP in forty-five to ninety minutes. With those findings, she could estimate the time to allot for actual placement tests as well as a limit on the number of students who could be tested at one session.

Solensky also discovered several strategies to overcome students' unfamiliarity and anxiety, strategies that differed from the ones used in basic skills testing. A handout with some instructions on filling in personal information, for instance, did not work; when many students in the first two pilot sessions simply transferred the sample names and numbers from the paper to their computer screen, she discarded the idea of using handouts even though they work well with native speakers. Also, it seemed that ESL students, rather than being distracted or annoyed by frequent checking from the proctor, usually welcomed and indeed required that intervention to get through the preliminary portions of the test (such as providing details of their educational background and reviewing sample questions).

During the pilot sessions, Solensky also had asked some students what they thought of the test after they finished. Some said that LOEP was easier than the EPT; others said that it was harder. Whatever their opinion about the difficulty of LOEP, several students liked the actual test-taking experience. One said that using the computer for placement made the test seem "more like college," while another claimed that he felt better prepared for the Test of English as a Foreign Language (TOEFL), which is now administered exclusively on computers. Comments like these reinforced the belief at the college that moving to LOEP for ESL testing was good for students and in keeping with NCC's mission of combining technology with teaching and learning.

Stage 2: Good-bye to the EPT (November 2002–January 2003)

Despite the lack of LOEP cut scores, the college decided to drop the EPT entirely when testing for the spring 2003 semester began in November. If all students took LOEP, a sampling much larger than that of the summer pilot would be collected and defined ranges or groupings of skill levels might be revealed. In the absence of definitive cut scores, the writing sample would continue to carry the greatest weight in placement. Unfortunately, this compromise plan had to be abandoned. Because of lengthy delays in setting up computers in the ESL testing center, the bulk of incoming ESL students (about 80 percent) were assessed with a paper-and-pencil test developed by the ESL department, not LOEP.

Just as frustrating were some staffing problems. The coordinator of the noncredit ESL program had taken another job at the end of the summer, and her position could not be refilled because of a statewide hiring freeze. Also, in order to conduct the additional test sessions, more proctors were needed, but contractual stipulations prevented the hiring of the best-qualified candidates: adjunct ESL instructors, who were already sensitive to the needs of ESL students. Solensky had to recruit other qualified proctors and then train them while testing was under way. Combined with the unpredictable progress of work in the ESL testing center, the uncertainties of staffing made it impossible to establish a testing schedule more than a few weeks ahead of time.

Nonetheless, giving up the EPT and putting ESL testing under the control of a new full-time coordinator for all college testing (Solensky) did bring distinct benefits. ESL testing was offered not just once or twice a week but at many times—during the day, on weekday evenings, and on Saturdays—on a schedule similar to that for testing of native speakers. As nearly all ESL test sessions were fully booked, it seemed that students appreciated the greater variety of test times, even if the schedule was not publicized well in advance. Furthermore, with sessions limited to twelve students each (the usual maximum for basic skills testing), proctors could give students greater attention, helping them with instruction on the computer and choosing essay prompts suited to their interests and levels of fluency. There are approximately thirty different prompts of varying levels of difficulty, which are updated periodically. Topics include family relationships, violence in the media, working and going to school, the role of technology, and so forth.

Finally, Solensky strove for greater parity not just in scheduling tests but also in treating incoming students. Other college applicants had long been able to make testing appointments over the phone; now the same option was extended to ESL students, who had previously been asked to come in person. Often, ESL students have friends or relatives call on their behalf; some bilingual staff members in admissions and the ESL department assist Hispanic students. In addition, ESL students were no longer required to produce identification at the time of the test, a demand not made of basic skills test takers.

Stage 3: The Arrival of the Computers (March–September 2003)

Although the long-awaited computers were installed in late December 2002, they could not be used extensively until all proctors had been trained on them. Training was not complete until March, the start of the testing cycle for summer and fall 2003 classes. From then on, except in rare instances such as the loss of the Internet connection, nearly all ESL students were tested with LOEP and the in-house essay.

With computers in place, students clicked their way through hundreds of LOEP tests, but the data, unfortunately, did not yield the expected cut scores. A brief analysis at the end of the testing cycle showed, for example, that for NCC's three highest credit classes, the average scores on Reading Skills were 103, 107, and 108—differences not great enough to be meaningful for placement. Since fall 2004, we have analyzed LOEP scores for noncredit and credit ESL levels and not been able to determine cut scores for all nine levels of both programs, except to note that students scoring below the 85–90 range are generally in noncredit classes and those scoring above 90 are generally in credit classes. The writing sample allows us to put students into the appropriate level in either program.

With computerized ESL testing, though, the college could expand its outreach to high school groups. Previously, on weekday mornings each spring, NCC admissions counselors had often invited seniors from local high schools to the campus for tours and placement testing. Such visits, however, could not include ESL students, because administering the EPT would simply have taken too long. The college's on-campus recruitment, therefore, did not target the many high school students in the area who are recent immigrants to this country. Once ESL testing went online, the admissions office could (and did) encourage guidance counselors to bring all interested students on group visits. Regardless of language background, each student could take the appropriate placement test alongside his or her classmates. During the spring of 2003, of the 167 high school seniors who came for group testing, 29 (or more than 17 percent) were ESL test takers.

Computerized ESL testing created a significant record-keeping problem. During the spring and summer of 2003, the number of test takers who had not submitted applications to the college rose dramatically—and the majority of them were ESL students. Solensky discovered the problem during the periodic uploading of transfer scores from the Accuplacer server to the college's Banner database. If students had not entered a college identification number or a Social Security number at the time of the test, their scores could not be matched to an existing record in Banner.

While investigating these so-called suspended scores further, Solensky found that in many cases the students had never completed an application to the college. One possible reason was that some students, especially those at the lowest ESL levels, simply did not understand college procedures or could not interpret the blank application form they received and, as a result, never bothered to complete it. The missing paperwork usually catches up with students, because they need to have a college identification number to enroll in classes. With a fair number of students who test but do not register, however, the college tries to ensure that applications are submitted before testing: the twenty-dollar application fee paid by students helps to cover the cost of online testing and proctor salaries. The admissions office therefore reverted to requiring ESL students to make testing appointments in person only (not over the phone) so that staff could check the status of the application. While allowing equal treatment of students in most respects, Web-based ESL testing also led the college to return to a different procedure for ESL appointments.

:: PROFESSIONAL RESONANCE

Accurate and timely placement testing is essential for the community college with its open enrollment philosophy. Even smaller institutions may be routinely testing hundreds, if not thousands, of new and returning students each semester. With ESL students, this is especially important, typically given the multiple levels into which a student can be placed. Most community college ESL programs routinely test multiple times during the preceding semester/term; thus, there is great need for a test that can be administered easily and frequently. Furthermore, it should be reliable, test a range of proficiency, and be administered in as secure an environment as possible.

Even though the computerized LOEP can only distinguish between four broad levels of proficiency—high beginning, low intermediate, high intermediate, and advanced—it meets the preceding criteria. Finer distinctions of the four proficiency levels can be done within each program (credit and noncredit) using a writing sample. In fact, the latter carries more weight than the LOEP test scores since writing is a productive instrument: students generate their own language from a prompt. At NCC the LOEP test scores are used primarily to reinforce placement based on the writing sample and identify students with weak grammar or reading comprehension.

:: INSTITUTIONAL CHALLENGES

Before the Adoption of LOEP

Questions of fairness, marginalization, and access to decision makers within the college were paramount for credit and noncredit ESL program administrators. If people in those programs felt that separate testing was not efficient, secure, or fair and that it relegated ESL to its own corner, how could the situation be rectified? Which deans and administrators would be most receptive, and would they grasp the concerns of ESL faculty and administrators and act on them?

During preliminary discussions about what to do with ESL testing, the dean of students acknowledged that the entire system of testing needed to be revamped: a new full-time testing coordinator would be hired, and this person would work closely with faculty and staff in the ESL department to move ESL testing under the umbrella of college-wide testing. The college recognized that ESL students represented a large portion (approaching 20 percent) of the student population and that it would be fairer and more efficient to test all incoming students through the same procedure, even if the ESL department would still be responsible for interpreting scores and making its own placements. In the end, the college listened, agreed to consolidate the testing, and asked the ESL credit director to serve on the search committee hiring the new testing coordinator.

After the Transition to LOEP

Although ESL testing is now under the jurisdiction of admissions, other attempts to integrate ESL students into admissions and registration procedures have been less successful. Placement testing is coordinated by the college's credit division, but ESL students may be eligible for either credit courses or the lower-level noncredit ones. Their level of fluency is not known until they take the placement test, and they cannot do that without submitting an application. A completed application, however, triggers the sending of letters from the credit division, asking, for example, for immunization records and high school transcripts, which noncredit students are not required to provide. For the students who end up placing into noncredit courses, such letters from the college can generate confusion and alarm. NCC has still not been able to adapt its student database and its admissions processes so that noncredit students are excluded from mailings and reports for credit students. NCC is one of twelve community colleges in Connecticut, all of which share the Banner system and adhere to the same policies on student records; however, there is great variation in the size of ESL programs, types of courses offered, and placement testing.

Since the summer of 2003, in fact, the only changes to ESL placement testing at the college have been minor refinements, such as the creation of new essay prompts. Many issues remain to be addressed, including the development of cut scores, even if they are only rough indicators of proficiency, to be used along with writing samples. The testing coordinator and the ESL department continue to work on these questions, but interest in them at higher levels of the college administration appears to have waned.

:: EXTENDING THE DIALOGUE

Placement testing continues to be an issue for many English language programs. Because of limited time, space, and resources, many community colleges must maximize the number of students tested and placed into appropriate levels. They may have to forgo more extensive testing such as individual oral interviews or listening comprehension (at NCC students may take, on average, 2 to 2½ hours [including testing orientation] to complete separate reading comprehension and usage sections as well as a writing sample).

On the other hand, each student learner is obviously more than the sum of his or her placement scores. Students often equate scores on placement tests with an accurate measure of their global language ability, rather than a means of putting them into the appropriate level class. Because there are many factors affecting placement that cannot routinely be taken into account, including previous educational achievement, length and nature of language study, and conditions under which the target language is used, instructors must further check and refine placement in the early weeks of a class, using additional writing samples, grammar checklists, or other diagnostic tools. ESL faculty and administrators must expect some replacements, especially when students or teachers question initial placement, which is done on an individual basis as the need arises. A few students are able to skip a level at the end of a semester, even though their initial placement exam showed weaker language skills. These are students who may have attended college in their home countries, been in the workforce for many years, or graduated from high school in the United States. The ESL director must approve all skips by looking at each student's writing portfolio.

Even though the ESL department acknowledges the benefit of seeing its placement testing brought under the college's own system, outstanding issues remain such as the following:

- getting ESL placements into the Banner system, where they would be available to more college personnel

- making sure that students register for the appropriate test (ESL versus English for native speakers)

- testing students by computer if they have little or no previous computer experience

- hiring, training, and supervising ESL-sensitive proctors

- screening students who are not interested in college-level courses but need placement testing

- getting misplaced students, such as those who end up in developmental English, into ESL classes

- accounting for discrepancies between LOEP scores and writing samples

- evaluating and placing ESL students who have U.S. public schooling or who have lived in the United States for many years

- adding and changing the mix of computer-based test sections (LOEP offers four multiple-choice sections and one online essay-writing section that we have not yet tried) and the implications of doing so

- allowing high-scoring ESL students to take the math placement test at the same time that they take the ESL test

- assessing the suitability of LOEP for students with limited English proficiency

:: CONTRIBUTORS

Craig Machado is the series editor for Perspectives on Community College ESL and has been ESL program director at Norwalk Community College, in Norwalk, Connecticut, in the United States, since 1999. He has extensive teaching and administrative experience in English as a second language and English as a foreign language and was a Fulbright scholar to the Czech Republic in 1997–98. He has also served as a member of the TESOL Publications Committee.

Suzanne Solensky is associate director of admissions at Norwalk Community College, where she oversees placement testing and retention projects. In previous higher education positions, she taught composition and literature and coordinated academic support services. A freelance writer for many years, she also served as managing editor for a philosophy journal.

CHAPTER 13

ESL in New York and San Diego: Lessons Learned in Diverse Settings

::

Ken Sheppard and JoAnn (Jodi) Crandall

:: FRAMING THE ISSUE

Immigrants increasingly come from countries in which English is not widely spoken, and many have limited prior education or literacy in their own languages. According to the U.S. Bureau of the Census (2003), over thirty-seven million adults spoke a language other than English. Of these, more than fifteen million were limited-English-proficient speakers who would need more English to participate fully in the country's social, economic, and political life. A third, or some five million, had completed less than a high school education (see Table 1).

Thus, the demand for adult English as a second language (ESL) and literacy instruction is high, while the ability of adult ESL programs to meet that demand is limited. Adult English language learners (ELLs) represent between 40 and 50 percent of those enrolled in federally funded adult education. Of the 42 percent in adult ESL in 2000, more than half were in beginning ESL or literacy classes. But they represent a small percentage of those needing or desiring adult ESL instruction, as evidenced by the long waiting lists for such classes in most metropolitan areas.

Adult ELLs are among the most persistent adult learners; many of those in adult basic education (ABE) or adult secondary education (ASE) were previously enrolled in adult ESL classes. As more immigrants continue to come to the United States and as the foreign-born population with limited English proficiency seeks access to greater employment or educational opportunities,

TABLE 1. Recent Immigrants: Level of Prior Education

Level of Prior Education	Percent of Total*
Less than high school**	33
Less than fifth grade	7.2
Between fifth and eighth grade	15
Between ninth and eleventh grade	10.8

SOURCE: U.S. Bureau of the Census (2003).
*37.2 million, 79 percent of whom are twenty-five years or older.
**More than twice the rate of native-born adults.

the need for adult ESL instruction is likely to grow. These immigrants will be served by state and local educational agencies; community or faith-based organizations; literacy or other volunteers; and increasingly, by community colleges, which offer the potential of providing instructional programs and support services to serve adult ELLs from literacy instruction through vocational and academic ESL programs.

However, providing appropriate programs and services to the diverse range of adult ESL students is a challenge. The adult ESL student may be a Vietnamese fisherman or Somali mother who has never attended school, a Nicaraguan or Bosnian young adult with limited or interrupted schooling, or an engineer from Russia or nurse from the Philippines with advanced education but limited English proficiency. Different programs evolve to meet the needs of these diverse students as the following descriptions of the adult ESL programs in New York and San Diego illustrate.

New York City, with more than seven million inhabitants, is home to a diverse array of ethnically defined communities. Many have deep roots in the city. They are identified with such neighborhoods as Chinatown, Brighton Beach, and Washington Heights. Their cultural institutions are decades old, and their leaders participate actively in the city's political life. In some of these neighborhoods, heritage language use has eroded; in others, it is very much alive. Joining these more established ethnic communities are a large number of newer communities, whose attitudes toward the city may be more ambivalent and whose understanding of how to access community services more limited. In these communities, more than 150 different heritage languages are spoken.

San Diego is a sprawling low-rise city roughly a fifth the size of New York City. While New York's population was shrinking in the 1980s, San Diego's population was booming. (Note, however, that in the 1990s, New York City's population increased substantially, including the immigrant population.) In San

Diego, a rising demand for housing among telecommunications and aviation workers led to the development of new bedroom communities to the south and east. At the same time, the city's foreign-born population grew to over 20 percent, according to the U.S. Bureau of the Census (2003), and a third of people in the surrounding county now speak a language other than English at home. Many are migrants from Mexico or Central America; others come from Asian countries. This influx has led, in some cases, to the creation of stable communities where the heritage language is widely spoken and ties to the mother country remain strong.

This chapter discusses how these two cities and their community colleges have met the demand for education among their diverse adult immigrant communities. In some ways, their stories are different because the communities and their needs differ. In other respects, despite differences in context, they are similar. Together, they offer valuable perspectives on adult ESL instruction in United States today.

In what follows, two institutions—the New York City College of Technology and the San Diego Community Colleges—are described with reference to four categories: assessment, articulation, challenges, and successes. Assessment refers to both the intake tests used to identify students and their levels of English proficiency, variously defined, as well as the exit tests used to assess their subsequent progress in relation to program goals. Articulation refers to a program's relationships or integration with the community and the college, on the assumption that these relationships might contribute to a student's willingness or ability to stay in school and pursue additional vocational or academic study.

∷ NARRATIVE

New York City College of Technology of The City University of New York

Overview of The City University of New York

The New York City College of Technology is one of the colleges of The City University of New York, commonly referred to as CUNY (KYOO-nee). CUNY serves more than 210,000 degree students and another 240,000 community adults each year. Each campus is quasi-independent, and therefore each college's ESL offerings are slightly different. However, in general, the university offers ESL instruction through five basic programs:

- credit courses for matriculated students still in need of academic ESL instruction

- low-cost, noncredit immersion classes for matriculated students who need intensive, preacademic ESL (CUNY Language Immersion Program [CLIP])

- fee-based continuing education classes open to the public

- publicly funded (by the federal government, New York State, and New York City) adult literacy programs providing free ESL and basic education/GED classes

- revenue-producing intensive classes for international students, many of whom do not matriculate at CUNY

Through these programs, the university provides a continuum of services to ELLs depending on their educational background and language learning goals. This chapter focuses primarily on the adult literacy programs and CLIP, specifically as they are implemented at the New York City College of Technology.

Both of these programs are loosely supervised by CUNY's central University Office of Academic Affairs. The adult literacy program, in existence for more than a quarter of a century, is offered on thirteen campuses. Funded by the federal government (through the Workforce Investment Act of 1998), the state, and the city, it serves about ten thousand community adult students a year, providing free instruction in ESL, basic education, and GED preparation.

CLIP, begun in 1995, was created to provide a voluntary option for matriculated university students with significant English language needs. The program is offered at nine campuses and serves about three thousand students a year in an intensive 25-hour-a-week instructional format. The program, supported by the university and very modest student fees, offers students up to a year of academic ESL preparation, leaving their financial aid allocation available for subsequent credit-bearing course work. Following CLIP, students are eligible to enroll in credit-bearing classes, which may include further ESL study.

The university's central office oversees the distribution of funding among the campuses for both programs. In addition, the office provides a framework for data management and support for curriculum and professional development. It has a cadre of staff developers who work closely with instructional staff to enhance teaching skills and develop instructional materials. Credit ESL courses at the various CUNY campuses vary widely. Students receive different types of instruction at different campuses, depending on their levels of preparation for higher education. Some colleges provide ESL writing almost exclusively, while others offer more comprehensive courses. Some have extensive instructional support programs, while others support students more modestly. Some offer specialized courses geared to CUNY's assessment of basic skills, integrated courses, bridge courses, and paired courses taught by instructors from more than one department; other colleges provide a more narrow range of courses.

Adult Literacy ESL and CLIP at New York City College of Technology

New York City College of Technology—or City Tech, as it is usually called—is situated along a broad avenue near the mouth of the Brooklyn Bridge and Brooklyn's administrative center, surrounded by a constant flux of commerce and traffic and ideally located to serve the needs of the borough's large immigrant population.

As a comprehensive college, City Tech confers both two- and four-year college degrees, in addition to providing an array of nondegree courses of study. It is one of nine CLIP sites, one of thirteen CUNY campuses providing adult literacy programs, and one of eight colleges offering both. The Division of Continuing Education at City Tech is home to both these programs. As adult literacy students improve their English language proficiency and determine that they wish to move toward college-level work, CLIP can be their next stop.

Adult Literacy Program

Eight hundred community adults study ESL in the literacy program (which also offers classes in basic education and GED preparation). These free classes are open to anyone in the community over the age of nineteen. The great majority of the ESL students in the adult literacy program are Spanish speakers, many from Mexico and the Dominican Republic. Others speak Arabic, Chinese, Haitian Creole, and Russian. Their educational backgrounds vary, ranging from those who have very low literacy in their native languages to those who hold university degrees. English language literacy is not formally assessed during intake, and discrete, ESL-focused literacy classes are not provided. Teachers try to address literacy needs once students are enrolled or refer students to other instructional programs as needed. Nevertheless, reading and writing pervade the curriculum.

At City Tech's adult literacy program, students take ESL for as long as they wish, repeating levels as needed. Once they complete the most advanced level, they are encouraged to move into GED classes, CLIP, or some other alternative. College-bound students learn about CLIP, a highly visible, minimally expensive, and increasingly popular way for students to transition into regular college courses.

The students' long-term goals for enrolling in ESL vary. They may have personal or employment-related reasons. Once they have learned enough English, some want to go into the GED program to qualify for jobs or to matriculate at the college and pursue degrees. Still others already have high school diplomas in hand and go directly into the college via CLIP or enrollment in credit ESL instruction.

Once classes have started, students are helped to define and refine their goals. Counselors and teachers help them explore their future options, including vocational training, employment opportunities, further credentials, college education, and/or citizenship. They also help students find additional information related to their goals and fill out needed forms.

Many ESL students in the adult literacy program stay at City Tech for more than a year, especially those who start out at the lowest levels of English language proficiency. There is frequent "opting in" and "opting out" of the program, as adult learners tend to other needs. Students may take a leave for health, personal, or family reasons and return in a later cycle. They may return to their home countries and then come back. Job schedules change, and students find different jobs. They move away, move back, and reenroll. This back-and-forth pattern is not surprising given the multiple demands on adult students' lives.

Assessment in Adult Literacy ESL

Placement in adult literacy ESL is determined at registration. Some students clearly know they need ESL and go directly into ESL classes. Others ask for GED but in fact need more English to benefit from the program. These students are gently nudged into ESL and tested for placement within that program.

In the past, all applicants took the New York State Placement Test for English as a Second Language Adult Students (NYSE Place); it was also used as a post-test. Recently, the program adopted the Basic English Skills Test (BEST) Plus,[1] a computer-adaptive oral interview. Therefore, students are assigned to one of the four levels of classes offered[2] on the basis of their speaking proficiencies (see Table 2), despite the emphasis on literacy in many of these ESL classes. Literacy levels are identified more finely by means of in-class reading and writing assignments during the first few days of class. This means that a teacher may start the term with students whose abilities to speak the language are comparable but whose abilities to read it are widely divergent. Because of this, reading and writing assessment at intake is under discussion.

As for a student's advancement, post-test scores are used in conjunction with teacher evaluations. This is a largely informal process: the instructors

---

[1] The BEST Plus is a new version of the Center for Applied Linguistics' (CAL's) BEST oral interview. Like the earlier test, BEST Plus is designed to assess a student's ability to engage in interpersonal communication in a face-to-face interview. The test uses pictures from everyday life and relatively simple language to stimulate the examinee's output. CUNY uses the computer-adaptive version of BEST Plus, which is scored on a computer: the input is delivered on a compact disc. As the examinee moves through the test, responding to each prompt in turn, the computer adjusts these prompts to the examinee's skill level as that is revealed in his or her responses. A test administrator uses a rubric to score each response and then inputs the score to tell the computer how to pitch the next prompt.

[2] These four levels cover the six National Reporting System (NRS) levels, which are used for reporting to the state and federal governments.

TABLE 2. ESL Placement in Adult Literacy at City Tech

NYSE Place Score	Class Level
0–15	I
16–26	II
27–34	III
35–54	IV

simply indicate where each student should be placed in the following cycle based on the students' oral, reading, and writing skills as evidenced in class. The recommendations are discussed with the program manager and the students themselves. A standard evaluation form and more explicit benchmarks are being developed, as discussed later in this chapter.

CLIP at City Tech

Unlike the ESL students in the adult literacy program, CLIP students must be admitted as matriculated students to one of the CUNY campuses. They then have the option to postpone enrolling in credit-bearing classes (ESL or otherwise) in favor of spending up to a year concentrating on developing their academic ESL skills. In addition, some ESL students in credit programs, having made insufficient progress in their course work, are referred to CLIP. Approximately four hundred students are served annually in City Tech's CLIP.

At CUNY, all students need to pass the ACT reading and writing tests before beginning their regular courses of study. ESL students who have not passed these assessments and opt to attend CLIP are reassessed on reading and writing instruments designed to discriminate more finely at the lower levels of language proficiency. They are then placed in one of six levels of instruction at CLIP. Skills are assessed at the beginning and end of each cycle of instruction, and students are promoted based on evaluations of portfolio materials, teacher recommendations, and test scores. Prior to returning to the credit side of the college to begin credit-bearing course work, students are retested on the university's ACT battery.

CLIP has a content-based instructional philosophy that engages students in extensive reading, along with written and oral response to a range of whole texts. The curricula, created by individual teachers within an overall programmatic framework, are designed to enhance students' academic literacies and help pave the way for their future success as college students. The content is generally interdisciplinary. Regular activities in a computer lab include work toward the completion of a research project that furthers the investigation of the particular content. As one example, in a course for intermediate students entitled "Around the World in Four-and-a-half Months," students read the Jules Verne (1874) classic *Around the World in Eighty Days* and the novel *Time and Again* by Jack Finney (1970). In conjunction with the former, the students use the Internet to plot their own routes around the world to see who can complete the virtual journey in the shortest time. They also research information about the cities and sites they pass on the way.

Articulation

City Tech has close ties to its community. This is a two-way street. College-based counselors refer students to Brooklyn's social service agencies and programs, and agencies refer clients to City Tech. The college also has an immigration clinic that provides information and support; this unit occasionally holds workshops for the adult literacy ESL classes. In addition, for adult learners, the adult literacy program offers an off-site English language and civics program.

As for university articulation, there are the regular meetings of managers of both CLIP and literacy programs as well as staff development workshops and seminars organized by CUNY's central office. The city's Literacy Assistance Center (LAC), a unique citywide technical support agency, holds managers' meetings, conducts staff development sessions, keeps staff abreast of events in the literacy field, advocates for literacy programs and students, and maintains a computerized data and reporting system.

Some, but not all, college services are available to students in the adult literacy program and CLIP through their official college IDs. Both have access to the library, but CLIP students, who have greater library research needs, have greater access. CLIP students in particular are provided with extensive counseling information related to college enrollment, including financial aid, academic planning, and courses of study.

Integration and cross-fertilization among noncredit ESL learning options at City Tech are enhanced by a single bridging administration. That office manages money, monitors students, and works with teachers on curricula and materials in both programs. Its director's role as manager-facilitator is evidence of the college's commitment to these students and their academic futures. Both programs also benefit from the director's interaction with the university's central office and directors of similar programs at other CUNY campuses and within City Tech itself. A very hands-on approach facilitates dialogue and sharing among teachers across programs.

Challenges

The challenge that the two programs share most is the reality of student lives that often make it difficult for students to devote the amount of time required for them to maximize their progress. In the adult literacy program, staff members wish for more full-time positions, greater access to computer labs for their students, and more hours available for paid staff development.

Another pressing need in this area is to develop clearer benchmarks to better match the operational descriptors used by the NRS and to help teachers plan their classes and assess student progress. Benchmarks include not only basic language skills such as pronunciation, vocabulary, grammar, and literacy skills to focus on at each level along the sequence but also functional skills that indicate the ways in which learners can use English, such as asking appropriate questions, explaining, and giving and understanding directions. Work along these lines has already begun. Additionally, formalization of articulation from one level to another and the use of portfolio evidence of a student's growth as a learner and his or her ability to express him- or herself in the new language should be addressed.

CLIP, on the other hand, has a highly formalized portfolio structure for tracking student writing. The persistent challenge is to make the transition of students from CLIP to credit-bearing course work as smooth as possible. A long-term goal is closer curricular articulation between CLIP and credit-bearing ESL.

Successes

Two of City Tech's successes are worthy of particular attention. First, while students in CLIP and the adult literacy programs do not pay student activity fees and thus do not have access to the full range of services available to students in credit programs, they do nevertheless feel that they are part of the college community. They use their college IDs to access the library, the bookstore, and lectures and art exhibits. Adult ESL students, even at the lowest levels, take a measure of pride in saying that they "go to college." For many of these adult students, the familiarity with the campus and its academic environment serves as an impetus for them to think of themselves as learners with definite goals, including college in their future.

Second, adult literacy ESL classes partially fulfill a community college's obligation to the broader community, but the college also receives benefits from meeting this obligation. Those enrolled in adult education are the parents, relatives, and neighbors of future or current students at the college or are themselves potential future students in the college's many programs. By teaching ESL, the college stimulates enrollment in all its instructional programs, supports families, and bolsters the community's economic development.

Both CLIP and the adult literacy program share a sense of pride and success related to actual classroom instruction. Both of the programs (adjusted for level of language proficiency and text difficulty, of course) share a similar instructional philosophy. Classes revolve around a theme—for example, Brooklyn history, immigration, or families and children. A planned course of study, related to the theme and flexible enough to respond to student interests, is required of each teacher. The use of a unifying theme encourages the integration of skills and provides an important opportunity to enhance students' general background knowledge. This "course of study" approach also demands that students enroll in class only at the start of a cycle so that the theme can be developed coherently over time. Students read material, discuss it, and write about it. They make presentations in class, have debates, and develop class Web sites. Source material is typically authentic—books, stories, videos, and articles—and workbooks are used only as supplemental texts. Classes also explore the city's resources, including museums, public libraries, and historical sites. Thus, in a variety of ways, students use real information in meaningful ways by collecting, sifting, sorting, reporting, summarizing, reorganizing, and evaluating it in light of their own experience.

Engagement with content and the language necessary to learn it, as well as the curricular connections to the city, are two elements that City Tech staffers point to in documenting their programs' successes.

San Diego Community Colleges

While City Tech is part of a large urban university, San Diego's adult education program is part of the community college system. Like CUNY, the system contains more than one satellite campus. The San Diego Community College District (SDCCD) includes three colleges that provide credit courses (City, Mesa, and Miramar Community Colleges) and San Diego Continuing Education, which provides noncredit courses in nine subject areas, including ESL. Through a delineation agreement with the K–12 system, the SDCCD provides adult education in the city of San Diego.

Four levels of credit ESL courses are offered through the English department at the three college campuses. Seven levels of noncredit ESL (adult education ESL) are offered at more than seventy locations through San Diego Continuing Education. ESL classes make up 42 percent of the noncredit program. The noncredit ESL classes are free of charge, while credit courses cost twenty-six dollars per credit hour. Students in credit courses are eligible for financial aid (Board of Governors Waivers and Pell grants).

Most of the funding for the noncredit classes comes from the state of California, roughly twelve million dollars in fiscal 2004. The noncredit ABE, ESL, and ASE programs, through the continuing education program, receive approximately one million dollars in federal funds through the Workforce Investment Act of 1998 for supplemental expenses (e.g., books, supplies, technology, instructional aides, staff development). These funds are allocated according to performance on standardized Comprehensive Adult Student Assessment System (CASAS) tests. The program operates under continual threat of reduced funding from the general fund because of persistent budget crises in California. In addition to ESL classes, the noncredit program offers classes in citizenship, ABE, GED/high school diploma preparation, business information technology, consumer science, vocational training, and classes for older adults. Former ESL students matriculate into many of these classes.

The students are predominantly of Mexican and Asian origins. However, other ethnic groups are present in significant numbers. As of fall 2003, there were one hundred or more students from twenty-eight countries; the newest students were a group of Somali Bantu refugees with little or no English language proficiency or literacy. On the whole, most students are enrolled in beginning-level ESL classes, and literacy levels vary widely across and within these classes.

In the noncredit program, there are seven levels of language proficiency as defined by the California Model Program Standards: beginning literacy, beginning low, beginning high, intermediate low, intermediate high, advanced low, and advanced high. The core courses offer an integrated skills approach, covering listening, speaking, reading, and writing in each course. Other special ESL classes that are offered include pronunciation, grammar, writing, and Test of English as a Foreign Language (TOEFL) preparation. The credit ESL program offers separate listening/speaking, reading, and writing courses at four different levels. These classes are more academic than the noncredit courses and have a greater emphasis on writing at all levels. Some noncredit and credit ESL courses overlap or cover similar material at a comparable level of language proficiency (as Table 3 indicates).

Students attend either the noncredit or credit program according to their goals. If they need English for everyday survival or vocational purposes or short-term skill improvements in listening, speaking, reading, or writing, they enroll in the noncredit program. If they are interested in degree or certain vocational certificate programs, they enroll in the credit program. Counselors in the noncredit program make regular presentations to ESL classes informing students of the educational options within the system.

Table 3. Noncredit and Credit Course Equivalents in the San Diego Community College District

Noncredit Levels	Credit Course Numbers
1–4	19
5	20
6	30
7	40

In general, the students at San Diego opt in and out of classes as employment opportunities emerge or dissipate and their plans change. A student may get a job after Levels 3–4, drop out, come back if the job ends or looks like a dead end, and drop out again if a new opportunity arises. It is not unusual for a student to complete Levels 1–4 and return later with more English to enroll in Levels 5–7 or the noncredit vocational ESL program and then matriculate to the credit program. A recent video shown to the board of trustees highlights an ESL student who attended an ESL class and then a citizenship class after which she got her citizenship. Then she attended the high school GED program and got her high school diploma—all in the noncredit program. After this she went to the credit side (City College) for two years and then to San Diego State University, where she received her bachelor's degree and teaching credential in May 2003, a process that took more than ten years.

Assessment

At registration, students at San Diego Continuing Education take a placement test that consists of a short oral test and a short reading test. Level 4 is the threshold level. If students test out at Level 4 or above, they qualify for vocational English as a second language, a program in which they study general English for the workplace for half the class and choose specific vocational modules to focus on for the second half of the class. This program serves as a great transition between ESL and the regular vocational classes offered within the noncredit program into such popular vocational programs as certified nursing assistant training, business information technology, and family home day care.

Additional testing—this time to satisfy funding guidelines—takes place after the students have been in class for three weeks. At that point, they are given the CASAS test mandated by the state, and they are given it again every ten weeks thereafter. In the view of many staff members, there is a mismatch between this test's purpose and San Diego's programmatic focus. While CASAS was designed for ABE and ESL programs, it stresses the receptive skills, reading and listening, not a student's ability to speak English. Thus, San Diego has to use other forms of assessment to measure gains in speaking and writing while, ironically, CUNY's test results in misplacements in literacy classes because it is a test of oral skills.

In all adult education programs, the issue of readiness for formal assessment arises often, as does the relationship between what is taught and measured and how scores are interpreted. San Diego and City Tech both illustrate the need for multiple measures to provide a more comprehensive picture of student strengths and needs.

Articulation

When credit students cannot fit classes into their schedules, or need additional instruction, they can attend noncredit classes, for example, in writing or pronunciation or conversation. Similarly, students in noncredit classes move to credit classes according to their needs and goals. Articulation and collaboration between the noncredit and credit programs is easier when these programs are neighbors or on the same premises. Proximity is important in the view of many staff members. Moving the noncredit ESL program onto the main campus at one of the centers has "been a wonderful thing," according to employees, since it has brought the programs into a closer day-to-day relationship and resulted in greater availability of resources and enhanced professional development among the adult ESL staff. Proximity has also paid off at City Tech.

San Diego Continuing Education also collaborates with community agencies to stretch dollars and serve those most in need. For example, it cosponsors classes with the city's housing commission, the latter providing space while the continuing education program absorbs the instructor's salary. The housing commission absorbs instructor costs if enrollment runs below the required average class size of twenty-six for the regular program. Similarly, continuing education works closely with K–12 schools to provide family literacy programs; the public schools provide space, child care, supplies, and a community assistant, while continuing education provides the instructors, coordination, and staff development.

Challenges

One major challenge relates to California's funding guidelines, which have sometimes felt like a straitjacket but, at the same time, have stimulated innovation. For example, the required class size can make it hard for the program to organize classes around specific learner needs and differences. Students with little or no prior literacy and those with more education may be assigned to the same classes to maintain the required average daily attendance rate of twenty-six students.

Shifts in California's political climate have also made program providers nervous. A rising antipathy to immigration and adult education has left the college's ESL staff feeling uncertain about the program's future. Even the state's faculty union president has suggested that cutting adult education is one way of reducing education budget shortfalls, since the state reimburses adult education at a lower rate than other college programs. Recent statewide legislation provides additional funds for noncredit programs, but it is still not equivalent to reimbursement for credit classes. Fortunately, the college has a new chancellor who supports the continuation of the noncredit program as a separate entity with its own administrative structure within the SDCCD.

Successes

San Diego is currently grappling with some problems that assail many programs. One is the question of whether to admit students continuously (open enrollment) or at fixed intervals. The latter policy gives the program more stability, but it means that it may also be more difficult to meet the state's average class size requirement that governs funding. Some San Diego sites are experimenting with "managed enrollment" in which students may join a class only at the start of a term.

Another concern in the San Diego program has been retention—how to keep students enrolled long enough to ensure learning gains and goal attainment. A study of classes with high retention rates last year was conducted, and it highlighted that key elements or strategies were similar in those classes. Providing staff development to other instructors on these strategies may also affect retention rates elsewhere and result in increased learning gains and goal attainment. More important, San Diego has learned to live with funding strictures and state regulations and turn them into opportunities.

∷ PROFESSIONAL RESONANCE

How do the Brooklyn and San Diego programs compare? Both have strong relations with their surrounding communities. Both not only offer classes off-site but also work hand-in-glove with community-based organizations and service agencies to ensure that their students receive all the services for which they qualify. Each college sees the community tie-in as a critical piece of its mission and worries about maintaining it.

Students generally enter ESL programs with the stated goal of learning or improving their English. Their immediate reasons may be personal, educational, or employment related, and these often change as the students begin to see how their improved English can open up new opportunities. For this reason, the tracking of student goals is done by teachers and counselors, who are best positioned to respond to these goals. Some goals are shared by many ESL students—parents wanting to assist their children in school or unemployed adults needing jobs—and these are typically addressed programmatically through classroom activities. (For example, the entire CLIP at City Tech is organized around the needs of students who have been admitted to the college but require academic English skills.) Other goals are individual and are best dealt with by offering students advice and assistance as needed. Some data are collected systematically to meet federal and state reporting requirements; however, each program's means of tracking students' goals and successes, and of addressing those goals, varies with the population served.

Both programs have an administrative structure that arches over and bridges adult education (including adult ESL) and academic ESL. Regardless of the formality of this arrangement, there is a lot of day-to-day contact among various faculties and cohesion in their planning and management that stems in part from their proximity.

Both programs have struggled with the need to regulate the constant ebb and flow of students into and through the program. The students do not constitute a stable population since, as immigrant adults, they have all the attendant pressures of family, employment, and mobility. But they are eager, if somewhat erratic, participants in adult education and far more persistent than most.

Neither program is satisfied with assessment instruments for placement or progress. The BEST Plus, used by City Tech's adult literacy program, is designed to measure listening and speaking among adults who might fall anywhere along a continuum of literacy skills. By comparison, San Diego's assessment is designed to measure receptive skills: listening and reading. In each case, the assessment is mandated by the state; the mandate does not provide the kind of information that programs need for placement or progress evaluation.

In the case of City Tech, the lack of a sensitive literacy assessment complicates placement. In the case of San Diego, the wide variety of tests, a mismatch between the tests and program needs, and the students' lack of familiarity with test formats generally make their use and interpretation problematic. Despite this, the tests continue to be used for high-stakes funding decisions. Both programs see an advantage in a test like BEST Plus, possibly in combination with other tests, but only City Tech has so far begun using it. And even that test is problematic, as individual administration can be time-consuming.

They both face one challenge that all public programs face: finding enough money to cover operating expenses while promoting professionalism, supporting program development, and keeping pace with innovations in the field. In a period of rapid change, when technology and innovation are the norm, these programs sometimes barely afford to deliver the basics. For example, computer literacy is now taken for granted in most community colleges, but too few adult education classrooms are wired for ready access, and few classes fully exploit computer-assisted learning and instruction.

On the other hand, the two programs differ in size. City Tech serves about one thousand students a year, while the San Diego system accommodates several times that. San Diego is the principal source of such instruction for the city as a whole, comprising several campuses, while City Tech is only one site in a vast CUNY network of colleges and programs. City Tech is embedded in a huge urban university; San Diego, in a community college system.

Professional support for these programs is also configured differently. City Tech is part of a network that includes an influential central office and organizations like the LAC. The Office of Academic Affairs' role may be top-down, but it also fosters lateral communication among programs, as does the LAC. There are meetings, staff development opportunities, conferences, workshops, instructional materials development sessions, and test recalibrations for CLIP. Staff developers fan out all over the city to work with instructors and suggest materials. San Diego's support is substantive but more informal. In addition to the cross-fertilization mentioned previously, professional development workshops are held at various locations in the city. In addition to attending the program's own staff development workshops, instructors attend workshops offered by regional resource centers affiliated with the statewide staff development program coordinated by the California Adult Literacy Professional Development Project (CALPRO), which provides training and technical assistance to local education and literacy providers. Noncredit faculty also have access to staff development activities offered by the credit program.

Articulation formulas vary in part because instructional alternatives vary. CUNY has an innovative immersion program, CLIP, offering students an intensive experience with the language at little cost. CLIP is the next stop for many students after adult education; shared facilities and administration facilitate the crossover.

No doubt, differences in funding account for different points of view. If the San Diego courses all acquired credit, students would have to pay for their courses, while New York City and the state of New York subsidize CUNY's ESL classes and services.

These differences mean that the two programs have met some of the same challenges differently, for example, in the area of curriculum. In general, CUNY courses have a looser, more thematic structure than San Diego's courses. CUNY faculty have the academic freedom to choose texts or materials appropriate for their classes. There is no mandated textbook. They use "authentic" material, sponsor museum visits, and encourage self-expression in a variety of media (e.g., journals, portfolios). Learning English, in their view, takes off from "strategic" engagement with text, an expanding understanding of the city and its resources, and self-discovery. Given this preference, the use of full-length texts (novels, histories, biographies) as well as stories and magazine or news articles is natural. The San Diego programs also encourage curriculum with a thematic focus and use according to student needs.

▪▪ INSTITUTIONAL CHALLENGES

While these programs, their goals, funding streams, and design are different, there can be little doubt that both are successful; however, their assessment systems are not the same.

Presumably, more data will be available in the future from the National

Reporting System for Adult Education,[3] including information about students' educational backgrounds or goals and how well they have achieved during and after their participation in adult ESL classes. As with other adult educational programs, currently not much is known about where the students wind up after they exit each program. In college? Nondegree programs? Elsewhere? Such information would help gauge the effect of program models and evaluate opportunities for adult ELLs in a larger context.

Extensive federal and state regulations or institutional change can have a stifling effect on programs by instilling an atmosphere of fear and uncertainty, but they are not all bad. Some programs thrive and innovate under these stresses. For example, City Tech staff members have made the CLIP tie-in work. Similarly, efforts at San Diego to meet a state attendance requirement have resulted in a better understanding of student motivation.

Synergies result from proximity and articulation. San Diego discovered that its program ran better once it shared premises with the credit program. That sharing has made it easier to move students back and forth. Similarly, City Tech benefits from its proximity to CLIP and other programs. Evidence is also available of an advantage for a centralized administrative structure for adult ESL by promoting communication, articulation, and service integration. The converse is also true: colleges whose ESL programs are scattered or balkanized often have lower transitional rates. Finally, a strong college commitment to the integration of ELLs can make a positive difference.

∷ EXTENDING THE DIALOGUE

Models for adult ESL programs within community colleges differ, because of distinct contexts, students, funding sources, policies, and institutional cultures (for more information, see Crandall and Sheppard 2004). In communities as disparate as Brooklyn and San Diego, instructional programs are bound to look different. Some of these differences frustrate comparison. However, there are common lessons to be drawn. The following features most likely account for the effectiveness of these programs:

- close collaboration with community-based organizations
- a cohesive administrative structure for all ESL programs

[3] The National Reporting System for Adult Education is an outcomes-based reporting system for the state-administered, federally funded adult education programs. Theoretically, the system "will improve the public accountability of the adult education program by documenting its ability to meet federal policy and programmatic goals" by using "a common set of outcome measures" and "enable states to correlate effective practices and programs with successful outcomes," but there are many problems with the system, and, so far, the promise has remained unfulfilled (National Reporting System for Adult Education n.d.).

- an ongoing program of professional development for all staff

- a commitment to advocating for the needs of immigrant students

- clear articulation and transition among programs

In addition, there are independent variables relevant to criteria of program effectiveness, in particular, the rate of student transition into degree programs, which may deserve attention. These include the following:

- the use of appropriate measures and tests for identifying students' goals and abilities at intake and throughout the program

- an institutional commitment at the highest level to long-term ESL training and transition

Despite the differences of these two programs and the contexts in which they have developed and grown, each opens a window on key current features of effective adult ESL in a community college context.

▪▪ ACKNOWLEDGMENTS

This chapter is part of a larger study of relations between ESL and degree programs at community colleges (see Crandall and Sheppard 2004). We would like to thank the Council for the Advancement of Adult Literacy for its support, as well as Gretchen Bitterlin and Donna Price Machado at SDCCD and Leslee Oppenheim and Joan Manes at CUNY.

▪▪ CONTRIBUTORS

Ken Sheppard is a language acquisition specialist at the National Foreign Language Center at the University of Maryland, College Park, in the United States, where he is responsible for training and assessment materials. Previously, he was TOEFL associate director, a project director at the Center for Applied Linguistics, and director of intensive English at Fordham University.

JoAnn (Jodi) Crandall is professor of education at the University of Maryland Baltimore County, where she also directs the PhD program in language, literacy, and culture and teaches in the ESL/bilingual MA program. Previously she was vice president of the Center for Applied Linguistics, where she established the National Clearinghouse on ESL Literacy.

References

Accuplacer OnLine technical manual. 2003. New York: College Board.

Althusser, L. 1971. *Lenin and philosophy, and other essays.* London: New Left Books.

Anderson, T. 2004. Language education classes offer global appeal. *Employee Benefit News* 76 (September 15). http://www.findarticles.com/p /articles/mi_km2922/is_200409/ai_n6929046.

Angelo, T. A., and P. K. Cross. 1993. *Classroom assessment techniques: A handbook for college teachers.* 2nd ed. San Francisco: Jossey-Bass.

Aronowitz, S., and H. A. Giroux. 1993. *Education still under siege.* 2nd ed. Westport, CT: Bergin & Garvey.

Atwell, N. 1998. *In the middle: New understanding about writing, reading, and learning.* 2nd ed. Portsmouth, NH: Boynton/Cook.

Auerbach, E. 1999. Teacher, tell us what to do. In *Critical literacy in action: Writing words, changing worlds,* ed. I. Shor and C. Pari, 31–52. Portsmouth, NH: Boynton/Cook.

Ayala, G. E., T. Thornton, and K. St. Amand. 2005. Curriculum reformation at a Canadian university school of English: An integrated and community-based pedagogical vision. Panel session presented at the annual TESL Canada Conference, Ottawa, Ontario.

Ayers, W., J. Hunt, and T. Quinn, eds. 1998. *Teaching for social justice.* New York: New Press.

Babbitt, M. 2001. Making writing count in an ESL learning community. In *Academic writing programs,* ed. I. Leki, 49–60. Alexandria, VA: TESOL.

Bagnall, R. G. 2000. Lifelong learning and the limitations of economic determinism. *International Journal of Lifelong Education* 19:20–35.

Bandura, A. 1981. Self-referent thought: A developmental analysis of self-efficacy. In *Social cognitive development: Frontiers and possible futures,* ed. J. H. Flavell and L. Ross, 200–239. New York: Cambridge University Press.

———. 1986. *Social foundations of thought and action: A social cognitive theory.* Englewood Cliffs, NJ: Prentice Hall.

Bates, L., J. Lane, and E. Lange. 1993. *Writing clearly.* Boston: Heinle & Heinle.

Benesch, S. 2001. *Critical English for academic purposes.* Mahwah, NJ: Lawrence Erlbaum.

Bernstein, T. 2005. WIDA standards: What are they and how do they affect us? *MATSOL Currents* 29 (2): 11.

Bigelow, B. 1998. The human lives behind the labels: The global sweatshop, Nike, and the race to the bottom. In *Teaching for social justice,* ed. W. Ayers, J. Hunt, and T. Quinn, 21–38. New York: New Press.

Block, D. 2003. *The social turn in second language acquisition.* Edinburgh, Scotland: Edinburgh University Press.

Bloome, D. 1989. Locating the learning of reading and writing in classrooms: Beyond deficit, difference, and effectiveness models. In *Locating learning: Ethnographic perspectives on classroom research,* ed. C. Emihovich, 87–114. Norwood, NJ: Hampton Press.

Bowles, S., and H. Gintis. 1976. *Schooling in capitalist America: Educational reform and the contradictions of economic life.* New York: Basic Books.

Brandt, D., and K. Clinton. 2002. Limits of the local: Expanding perspectives on literacy as a social practice. *Journal of Literacy Research* 34:337–56.

Brint, S. G. 2003. Few remaining dreams: Community colleges since 1985. *The ANNALS of the American Academy of Political and Social Science* 586 (1): 16–37.

Brint, S. G., and J. Karabel. 1989. *The diverted dream: Community colleges and the promise of educational opportunity in America, 1900–1985.* New York: Oxford University Press.

Brinton, D. M., M. A. Snow, and M. B. Wesche. 1989. *Content-based second language instruction.* Boston: Heinle & Heinle.

Britton, J. 1982. *Prospect and retrospect: Selected essays of James Britton.* Ed. G. M. Pradl. Montclair, NJ: Boynton/Cook.

Brown, H. D. 1994. *Principles of language learning and teaching.* 3rd ed. Englewood Cliffs, NJ: Prentice Hall Regents.

Brown, J. D. 1995. *The elements of language curriculum.* Boston: Heinle & Heinle.

Bruffee, K. A. 1993. Collaboration, conversation, and reacculturation. In *Collaborative learning: Higher education, interdependence, and the authority of knowledge,* ed. K. A. Bruffee, 15–27. Baltimore: Johns Hopkins University Press.

———. 1995. Sharing our toys: Cooperative learning versus collaborative learning. *Change* (January/February): 12–18.

Burbules, N. C., and C. A. Torres. 2000. *Globalization and education: Critical perspectives.* New York: Routledge.

Byrns, J. 1997. *Speak for yourself: An introduction to public speaking.* New York: McGraw-Hill.

Caesar, J. 1987a. Dangerous work. In *About our jobs,* 20. Philadelphia: La Salle University, Urban Studies and Community Services.

———. 1987b. The washroom technician. In *About our jobs,* 5. Philadelphia: La Salle University, Urban Studies and Community Services.

Campbell, D. M., and L. S. Harris. 2001. *Collaborative theme building: How teachers write integrated curriculum.* Needham Heights, MA: Allyn & Bacon.

Campbell, J., and B. Moyers. 1988. *Joseph Campbell and the power of myth with Bill Moyers.* DVD. Burlington, VT: Mystic Fire Video.

Canagarajah, A. S. 1993. Critical ethnography of a Sri Lankan classroom: Ambiguities in student opposition to reproduction through ESOL. *TESOL Quarterly* 27:601–26.

———. 1999a. On EFL, teachers, awareness, and agency. *ELT Journal* 53 (3): 207–14.

———. 1999b. *Resisting linguistic imperialism in English teaching.* Oxford: Oxford University Press.

Canale, M., and M. Swain. 1980. Theoretical bases of communicative approaches to second language teaching and testing. *Applied Linguistics* 1:1–47.

Casey, C. 2000. *Interviews–A low-level ESOL curriculum about work.* New York: City University of New York Adult Literacy Program.

Castleton, G. 2002. Workplace literacy as a contested site of educational activity. *Journal of Adolescent and Adult Literacy* 45 (7): 556–67.

Celce-Murcia, M., D. Brinton, and J. M. Goodwin. 1996. *Teaching pronunciation: A reference for teachers of English to speakers of other languages.* Cambridge: Cambridge University Press.

Christie, F. 2002. *Classroom discourse analysis: A functional perspective.* London: Continuum.

Cisneros, S. 1998. *The house on Mango Street.* Read by the author. Random House Audio. Audio cassette.

Clark, B. R. 1960. *The open door college: A case study.* New York: McGraw-Hill.

Clatsop County Commission on Children and Families. 2004. *Clatsop County comprehensive plan: 2004 Phase III update*. Clatsop, OR: Clatsop County Commission on Children and Families.

Cohen, B. 2000. *USDA community food security assessment toolkit*. Washington, DC: U.S. Department of Agriculture. http://www.ers.usda.gov/publications /efan02013/efan02013a.pdf

Collins, J., and R. K. Blot. 2003. *Literacy and literacies: Texts, power, and identity*. Cambridge: Cambridge University Press.

Collins, M. 1991. *Adult education as vocation: A critical role for the adult educator*. London: Routledge.

Comber, B. 1997. *Managerial discourses: Tracking the local effects on teachers' and students' work in literacy lessons*. ERIC Document Reproduction Service No. ED444206. http://www.eric.ed.gov.

Conway, M. A., J. M. Gardiner, T. J. Perfect, S. J. Anderson, and G. M. Cohen. 1997. Changes in memory awareness during learning: The acquisition of knowledge by psychology undergraduates. *Journal of Experimental Psychology* 126 (4): 393–413.

Crandall, J., and K. Sheppard. 2004. *Adult ESL and the community college*. Working Paper 7, Council for Advancement of Adult Literacy. http://www .caalusa.org/eslreport.pdf.

Cross, P. 1985. Determining missions and priorities for the fifth generation. In *Renewing the American community college: Priorities and strategies for effective leadership*, ed. W. L. Deegan, D. Tillery, and ERIC Clearinghouse for Junior Colleges, 34–48. San Francisco: Jossey-Bass.

Cross, P., and M. H. Steadman. 1996. *Classroom research: Implementing the scholarship of teaching*. San Francisco: Jossey-Bass.

Cummins, J. 1980. The entry and exit fallacy in bilingual education. *NABE Journal* 4:25–60.

Curtis, C. P. 2000. *Bud, not buddy*. Read by J. Avery. Listening Library. Audio cassette.

Darrah, C. 1992. Workplace skills in context. *Human Organization* 5:264–73.

De Avila, E. 1997. *Setting expected gains for non and limited English proficient students*. NCBE Resource Collection Series, no. 8. http://www.ncela.gwu.edu /pubs/resource/setting/index.htm.

Deegan, W. L., D. Tillery, and ERIC Clearinghouse for Junior Colleges. 1985. *Renewing the American community college: Priorities and strategies for effective leadership*. San Francisco: Jossey-Bass.

Dougherty, K. J. 1994. *The contradictory college: The conflicting origins, impacts, and futures of the community college.* Albany: State University of New York Press.

Dubin, F., and E. Olshtain. 1986. *Course design.* Cambridge: Cambridge University Press.

Edwards, M., and B. Weber. 2003. Food insecurity and hunger in Oregon: A new look. Working Paper AREC 03-104, Department of Agriculture and Resource Economics, Oregon State University.

Egan-Robertson, A., and J. Willett. 1998. Students as ethnographers, thinking and doing ethnography: A bibliographic essay. In *Students as researchers of culture and language in their own communities,* ed. A. Egan-Robertson and D. Bloome, 1–32. Cresskill, NJ: Hampton Press.

Eggins, S. 1994. *An introduction to systemic functional linguistics.* London: Pinter.

Faltis, C., and S. Hudelson. 1998. *Bilingual education in elementary and secondary school communities: Toward understanding and caring.* Boston: Allyn & Bacon.

Fantini, B. C., and A. E. Fantini. 1997. Artifacts, sociofacts, mentifacts: A sociocultural framework. In *New ways of teaching culture,* ed. A. E. Fantini, 57–61. Alexandria, VA: TESOL.

Finney, J. 1970. *Time and again.* New York: Simon & Schuster.

Fox, R. N. 1996. Intensive ESL program spring 1996 outcomes. Institutional Research Report No. 114. Office of Institutional Research, Kingsborough Community College, Brooklyn, New York.

Freire, P. 1998. *Teachers as cultural workers: Letters to those who dare teach.* The Edge, Critical Studies in Educational Theory. Boulder, CO: Westview Press.

Gabelnick, F., J. MacGregor, R. Matthews, and B. Smith, eds. 1990. *Learning communities: Creating connections among students, faculty, and disciplines.* New Directions for Teaching and Learning, no. 41. San Francisco: Jossey-Bass.

Gebhard, M. 1999. Debates in SLA studies: Redefining classroom SLA as an institutional phenomenon. *TESOL Quarterly* 36:544–57.

Gee, J. P. 1992. *The social mind: Language, ideology, and social practice.* New York: Bergin & Garvey.

———. 1996. *Social linguistics and literacies: Ideology and discourses.* New York: Routledge/Falmer.

Giroux, H. A. 1988. *Teachers as intellectuals: Toward a critical pedagogy of learning.* Critical Studies in Education Series. Granby, MA: Bergin & Garvey.

Gonzales, V., P. Bauerle, and M. Felix-Holt. 1996. Theoretical and practical implications of assessing cognitive and language development in bilingual children with qualitative methods. *The Bilingual Research Journal* 20 (1): 93–131.

Graves, K. 2000. *Designing language courses: A guide for teachers.* Scarborough, Ontario, Canada: Heinle & Heinle.

Gutiérrez, K., L. Stone, and J. Larson. Forthcoming. Hypermediating in the urban classroom: When scaffolding becomes sabotage in narrative activity. In *Literacy and power,* ed. C. D. Baker, J. Cook-Gumperz, and A. Luke. Oxford: Blackwell.

Halliday, M. A. K. 1994. *An introduction to functional grammar.* 2nd ed. New York: Routledge.

Hargreaves, A. 1994. *Changing teachers, changing times: Teachers' work and culture in the postmodern age.* London: Cassell.

———. 2003. *Teaching in the knowledge society: Education in the age of insecurity.* New York: Teachers College Press.

Harklau, L., K. M. Losey, and M. Siegal. 1999. *Generation 1.5 meets college composition: Issues in the teaching of writing to U.S.-educated learners of ESL.* Mahwah, NJ: Lawrence Erlbaum.

Hart, K. D. 1994. Understanding literacy in the Canadian business context: Conference Board of Canada study. In *Basic skills for the workplace,* ed. M. C. Taylor, G. R. Lewe, and J. A. Draper, 2–32. Malabar, FL: Kreiger.

Hasan, R., and G. Williams. 1996. *Literacy in society.* London: Longman.

Hunsberger, B. 2004. Oregon drops down the jobless list. *The Oregonian,* May 22.

Jenkins, J. 2002. A sociolinguistically based, empirically researched pronunciation syllabus for English as an international language. *Applied Linguistics* 23 (1): 83–103.

Karabel, J. 1972. Community colleges and social stratification: Submerged class conflict in American higher education. *Harvard Educational Review* 42:521–62.

Kasper, L. F. 2000. *Content-based college ESL instruction.* Mahwah, NJ: Lawrence Erlbaum.

Kelley, E. F. 1993. The non-native English speaking student in the community college developmental English classroom: An ethnographic study. PhD diss., University of Massachusetts (Amherst).

Kern, R. 2000. *Literacy and language teaching.* Oxford: Oxford University Press.

Kincheloe, J. L. 1995. *Toil and trouble: Good work, smart workers, and the integration of academic and vocational education.* New York: Peter Lang.

King, J. R., and D. G. O'Brien. 2002. Adolescents' multiliteracies and their teachers' needs to know: Toward a digital détente. In *Adolescents and literacies in a digital world,* ed. D. E. Alvermann, 40–50. New York: Peter Lang.

Kurin, R. 1997. *Reflections of a culture broker: A view from the Smithsonian.* Washington, DC: Smithsonian Institution Press.

Lanham, R. 1994. The economics of attention. In *Proceedings of the 124th annual meeting of the Association of Research Libraries.* Washington, DC: Association of Research Libraries. http://www.arl.org/arl/proceedings/124/ps2econ.html.

Larsen-Freeman, D., and M. H. Long. 1991. *An introduction to second language acquisition research.* London: Longman.

Levin, J. 2001. *Globalizing the community college: Strategies for change in the twenty-first century.* New York: Palgrave.

Levy, J. 1995. Intercultural training design. In *Intercultural sourcebook: Cross-cultural training methods volume 1,* ed. S. M. Fowler and M. G. Mumford, 1–15. Yarmouth, ME: Intercultural Press.

Lewis, T. 1997. America's choice: Literacy or productivity? *Curriculum Inquiry* 27 (4): 391–422.

Lipton, J. n.d. Inside the actors studio. New York: Bravo. http://www.bravotv .com/Inside_the_Actors_Studio/guests/A-F.shtml.

Luke, A. 1998. Getting over method: Literacy teaching as work in "new times." *Language Arts* 75 (4): 305.

Luna, A. 2005. A training model for TAA/WIA funded students with basic needs. Paper presented at the annual meeting of the Texas Administrators of Continuing Education for Community/Junior Colleges, Austin, Texas.

Luna, G., and D. Cullen. 1995. *Empowering the faculty: Mentoring, redirected and renewed.* ASHE-ERIC Higher Education Report, no. 3. Washington, DC: Graduate School of Education and Human Development, George Washington University.

MacDonald, B. 1987. *The state of education today: Record of the first C.A.R.E. conference.* Norwich, England: University of East Anglia.

MacGregor, J., J. L. Cooper, K. A. Smith, and P. Robinson, eds. 2000. *Strategies for energizing large classes: From small groups to learning communities.* New Directions for Teaching and Learning, no. 81. San Francisco: Jossey-Bass.

Mager, R. 1962. *Preparing instructional objectives.* Palo Alto, CA: Fearon.

Marginson, S. 1997. *Markets in education.* St. Leonards, New South Wales, Australia: Allen & Unwin.

Martin, I. 2001. Lifelong learning—For earning, yawning, or yearning? *Adults Learning* 13 (2): 14–17.

Marton, F., and R. Saljo. 1976. On qualitative differences in learning: Outcomes and processes. *British Journal of Educational Psychology* 46:4–11.

Matthews, C. 1994. *Speaking solutions.* White Plains, NY: Prentice Hall Regents.

Mayher, J. S., N. Lester, and G. M. Pradl. 1983. *Learning to write/writing to learn*. Portsmouth, NH: Boynton/Cook.

McAndrew, D. A., and T. J. Reigstad. 2001. *Tutoring writing: A practical guide for conferences*. Portsmouth, NH: Boynton/Cook.

McKenna, B., and P. Graham. 2000. Technocratic discourse: A primer. *Journal of Technical Writing and Communication* 30 (3): 219–47.

McNeil, J. 1996. *Curriculum: A comprehensive introduction*. 5th ed. New York: John Wiley & Sons.

Mendonça, M., and V. Franco. 1998. *Sweating for a T-shirt*. DVD. San Francisco: Global Exchange.

Mikulecky, L. 1990. National adult literacy and lifelong learning goals. *Phi Delta Kappan* 72 (4): 304–9.

Mlynarczyk, R. W., and M. Babbitt. 2002. The power of academic learning communities. *Journal of Basic Writing* 21 (1): 71–89.

Morley, J., ed. 1994. *Pronunciation pedagogy and theory: New directions, new views*. Alexandria, VA: TESOL.

Mosisa, A. T. 2002. The role of foreign-born workers in the U.S. economy. *Monthly Labor Review* 125 (5): 3–14.

National Assessment of Adult Literacy. 2005. *A first look at the literacy of America's adults in the 21st century*. Washington, DC: U.S. Department of Education, National Center for Education Statistics. http://nces.ed.gov/NAAL/PDF/2006470_1.PDF.

National Reporting System for Adult Education. n.d. About the NRS. http://www.nrsweb.org/asp.

New London Group. 2000. A pedagogy of multiliteracies. In *Multiliteracies: Literacy learning and the design of social futures*, ed. B. Cope and M. Kalantzis, 9–38. London: Routledge.

Nunan, D., and C. Lamb. 1996. *The self-directed teacher: Managing the learning process*. Cambridge: Cambridge University Press.

Paltridge, B. 2001. *Genre and the language learning classroom*. Ann Arbor: University of Michigan Press.

Pannu, R. 1996. Neo-liberal project of globalization: Prospects for democratization of education. *The Alberta Journal of Educational Research*, 32 (2): 87–101.

Paybarah, A., and T. Lin. 2003. Immigration success: Four immigrants who made it in Queens. Immigrant's Guide, *Queens Tribune*, December 25–31.

Pennycook, A. 1994. *The cultural politics of English as an international language.* Harlow, England: Longman.

———. 2001. *Critical applied linguistics: A critical introduction.* Mahwah, NJ: Lawrence Erlbaum.

Peterman, D. 1999. Business and education partnerships in community colleges. *Community College Journal of Research and Practice* 23 (7): 683–86.

Peters, M., J. Marshall, and P. Fitzsimons, P. 2000. Managerialism and educational policy in a global context: Foucault, neoliberalism, and the doctrine of self-management. In *Globalization and education: Critical perspectives,* ed. N. C. Burbules and C. A. Torres, 109–32. New York: Routledge.

Phillipson, R. 1992. *Linguistic imperialism.* Oxford: Oxford University Press.

Portland State University. 1996. Adult literacy estimates. Portland, OR: Portland State University. http://www.casas.org/lit/litcode/Detail.CFM ?census__AREAID=2402.

Pritchard, J. 2004. One Mexican dying a day. *The Rearguard* 6 (7). http://www .therearguard.pdx.edu/issues/Vol6_iss7_april04.

Rafael, V. L. 2000. *White love and other events in Filipino history.* Durham, NC: Duke University Press.

Rajagopalan, D. 2004. On being critical. *Critical Discourse Studies* 1 (2): 261–63.

Ramanathan, V. 2002. *The politics of TESOL education: Writing, knowledge, critical pedagogy.* New York: Routledge Falmer.

Resnick, S. A., and R. D. Wolff. 1987. *Knowledge and class: A Marxian critique of political economy.* Chicago: University of Chicago Press.

Richardson, J., and C. Richard. 1990. Community colleges: Democratizing or diverting? *Change* 22 (4): 52–53.

Rodby, J. 1992. *Appropriating literacy: Writing and reading in English as a second language.* Portsmouth, NH: Boynton/Cook.

Saljo, R. 1984. Learning through reading. In *The experience of learning,* ed. F. Marton, D. Hounsell, and N. Entwistle, 89–105. Edinburgh, Scotland: Scottish Academic Press.

Schleppegrell, M. J. 2004. *The language of schooling: A functional linguistics perspective.* Mahwah, NJ: Lawrence Erlbaum.

Schunk, D. H., and A. R. Hanson. 1985. Peer models: Influence on children's self-efficacy and achievement. *Journal of Educational Psychology* 77:313–22.

Shaw, K. M., and J. A. Jacobs. 2003. *Community colleges: New environments, new directions.* Thousand Oaks, CA: Sage.

Shor, I., and C. Pari. 1999. *Critical literacy in action: Writing words, changing worlds.* Portsmouth, NH: Boynton/Cook.

Smith, B. L., J. MacGregor, R. Matthews, and F. Gabelnick. 2004. *Learning communities: Reforming undergraduate education.* San Francisco: Jossey-Bass.

Southern Illinois University Edwardsville. n.d. Classroom assessment techniques. Southern Illinois University Edwardsville. http://www.siue.edu/~deder/assess /catmain.html.

Spangenberg, G. 2004. Foreword to *Adult ESL and the community college,* by J. Crandall and K. Sheppard. Working Paper 7, Council for Advancement of Adult Literacy. http://www.caalusa.org/eslreport.pdf.

Spring, J. H. 1998. *Education and the rise of the global economy.* Mahwah, NJ: Lawrence Erlbaum.

Stein, S. 2000. *Equipped for the future content standards: What adults need to know and be able to do in the 21st century.* Washington, DC: National Institute for Literacy.

Strevens, P. 1987. The nature of language teaching. In *Methodology in TESOL: A book of readings,* ed. M. Long and J. Richards, 10–25. Boston: Heinle & Heinle.

Tagg, J. 2003. *Learning paradigm college.* Bolton, MA: Anker.

Taylor, B. 1987. Teaching ESL: Incorporating a communicative, student-centered component. In *Methodology in TESOL: A book of readings,* ed. M. Long and J. Richards, 45–60. Boston: Heinle & Heinle.

Teachers of English to Speakers of Other Languages (TESOL). 1997. *ESL standards for pre-k–12 students.* Alexandria, VA: TESOL.

———. 2003. *Standards for adult education ESL programs.* Alexandria, VA: TESOL.

Test Publications. n.d. University of Michigan, English Language Institute. http://www.lsa.umich.edu/eli/testpub.htm#EPT.

Tierney, R. J. 1999. *How to write to learn science.* Arlington, VA: National Science Teachers Association.

Tillett, B., and M. N. Bruder. 1985. *Speaking naturally.* Cambridge: Cambridge University Press.

Tilove, J. 2004. The new sun belt: White Americans, Latino immigrants take flight for their new frontier. *The Oregonian,* February 26.

Tinto, V. 1987. *Leaving college: Rethinking the causes and cures of student attrition.* Chicago: University of Chicago Press.

———. 1997. Classrooms as communities: Exploring the educational character of student persistence. *The Journal of Higher Education* 68 (6): 599–623.

Tinto, V., A. Goodsell Love, and P. Russo. 1994. *Building learning communities for new college students: A summary of research findings of the collaborative learning project*. National Center on Postsecondary Teaching, Learning, and Assessment. University Park: Pennsylvania State University.

U.S. Bureau of the Census. 2000. State and county QuickFacts: Clatsop, Oregon. http://quickfacts.census.gov/qfd/states/41/41007.html.

U.S. Bureau of the Census. 2003. Language use and English-speaking ability: 2000. *Census 2000 brief*. http://www.census.gov/prod/2003pubs/c2kbr-29.pdf.

Veel, R., and C. Coffin. 1996. Learning to think like an historian: The language of secondary school history. In *Literacy in society*, ed. R. Hasan and G. Williams, 191–231. London: Longman.

Verne, J. 1874. *Around the world in eighty days*. New York: Scholastic.

Vygotsky, L. S. 1978. *Mind in society: The development of higher psychological processes*. Trans. and ed. M. Cole, V. John-Steiner, S. Schribner, and E. Souberman. Cambridge, MA: Harvard University Press.

Wells, A., S. Carnochan, J. Slayton, R. Lee Allen, and A. Vasudeva. 1998. Globalization and educational change. In *International handbook of educational change*, ed. A. Hargreaves, 322–48. Boston: Kluwer Academic.

White, R. 1987. Teaching the passive. In *Methodology in TESOL: A book of readings*, ed. M. Long and J. Richards, 298–303. Boston: Heinle & Heinle.

Wiggins, G. P., and J. McTighe. 1998. *Understanding by design*. Alexandria, VA: Association for Supervision and Curriculum Development.

Willett, J. 1995. Becoming first graders in an L2: An ethnographic study of L2 socialization. *TESOL Quarterly* 29:473–503.

Willis, P. E. 1981. *Learning to labor: How working class kids get working class jobs*. New York: Columbia University Press.

Yalden, J. 1987. *Principles of course design for language teaching*. Cambridge: Cambridge University Press.

Zamel, V., and R. Spack, eds. 2003. *Crossing the curriculum: Multilingual learners in college classrooms*. Mahwah, NJ: Lawrence Erlbaum.

Zwerling, L. 1986. Lifelong learning: A new form of tracking. In *The community college and its critics*, ed. L. Zwerling, 53–60. San Francisco: Jossey-Bass.

Index

Page numbers followed by an *f*, *n*, or *t* indicate figures, tables, or footnotes.

A

Absenteeism, 136
Academic culture, 11. *See also* Culture
Academic Systems (software), 129
Accuplacer OnLine Technical Manual, 188
Accuplacer test, 126, 188–189. *See also* Levels of English Proficiency (LOEP)
Achievement tests, 94–95
ACTFL. *See* American Council on the Teaching of Foreign Languages (ACTFL)
Active learning, 173–174
Active listening, 157–158
Activities
　interview project, for writing skills, 135–148, 141*f*
　journaling, 66–67
　"My Life in a Bag," 13–14, 14
Adjunct language instruction, 117
Adult Education and Family Literacy, 81
Adult learners, curriculum planning and, 95
AEFL. *See* Adult Education and Family Literacy
Age of Reform, 23
Agriculture, Department of, 78

Alamo Community College District, 96
Allison, H. A., 1–2, 47, 60
Althusser, L., 23
American Association of Community Colleges, 93
American Association of Higher Education, 125
American Council on the Teaching of Foreign Languages (ACTFL), 101
Anderson, S. J., 65
Anderson, T., 93
Angelo, T. A., 71, 72
Apple, M., 28
Arlington Adult Learning System: The Arlington Education and Employment Program, 99–100
Aronowitz, S., 23
Around the World in Eighty Days (Verne), 208
Artifacts, cultural, 64–65
Assessment sheet, oral, 43*f*
Assessment Techniques, Classroom (CATs), 71–72
Attendance, in vocational ESL program, 86
Atwell, N., 138, 139
Auerbach, E., 33
Austin Community College District, 107
Australian critical pedagogy, *vs.* North American, 28*n*1
Autonomy, learner, 156

student placement in, 63–64
student responses to, 68
Internet
  effective use of, 59–60
  in ESL instruction, 127–129,
      159–160, 162–164, 165
  in Japanese ESL instruction,
      154–159
  right answers and, 58
  use of, in first language, 153
  use tracking, 56–57
Interpretation
  culture and, 13
  "My Life in a Bag" activity and, 14
Interview project, for writing skills,
    135–148, 141*f*
*Interviews: A Low-Level ESOL
    Curriculum about Work* (Casey),
    140

J

Jacobs, J. A., 24
Japan, ESL instruction in, 151–154,
    154–159
Japanese Americans, internment of, 15
Japanese Ministry of Education,
    Culture, Sports, Science, and
    Technology, 164
Jenkins, J., 156
Journaling, 66–67

K

Kamat, S., 43
Karabel, J., 23, 24
Kasper, L. F., 51
Kelley, E. F., 28
Kelley, J., 192
Kern, R., 39
Kincheloe, J. L., 89
King, J. R., 49, 53, 54, 58, 59
Kingsborough Community College,
    61
Kurin, R., 10–11

L

Labor, sweatshop, 29–33
LAC. *See* Literacy Assistance Center
    (LAC)
LaGuardia Community College, 136,
    149
Lamb, C., 119
Lane, J., 148
Lange, E., 148
Language proficiency, 94–95
Language skills, perception of
    employees due to, 87–88
Lanham, R., 54, 56
Larsen-Freeman, D., 25
Larson, J., 35*n*3
LCHC. *See* Lower Columbia Hispanic
    Council
Learner autonomy, 156
Learning
  active, 173–174
  deep, 65
Learning communities, 65–66
Lee Allen, R., 42
Legg, B., 173
Lenhardt, L., 2, 77, 91
Lester, N., 138, 142
Levels of English Proficiency (LOEP),
    188–189, 189–195, 196–197
Levin, J., 42
Levy, J., 14
Lewis, T., 88, 89
Lieske, C., 2, 151, 166
Lin, T., 144
Linguistics, systemic functional, 39*n*5
Linguistic tradition, 25
Lipton, J., 138, 142
Listening, active, 157–158
Literacy
  critical, 29–33, 40
  of national population, 78
  program at City Tech, 205–207,
      207*t*
  Volunteer Literacy Tutor program,
      81–82

Tragedies, in student personal lives, 98

Transfer *vs.* vocational students, at community colleges, 23–24

Transformative pedagogy, 17. *See also* Pedagogy

Tyson, M., 2, 77, 87, 91

▋▋ U

University of Maryland, 218
University of Massachusetts, 29, 43
University of Michigan, 187
University of York, 123
U.S. Council for Advancement of Adult Literacy, 93
U.S. Labor Department Trade Adjustment Assistance, 96

▋▋ V

Vasuveda, A., 42
Veel, R., 28n1
Venkatesh, U., 1, 7, 9, 12–13, 15–16, 21
Verne, J., 208
VLT. *See* Volunteer Literacy Tutor (VLT) program
Vocabulary, in vocational ESL, 83–85
Vocational ESL, 82–90
Vocational *vs.* transfer students, at community colleges, 23–24
Volunteer Literacy Tutor (VLT) program, 81–82
Vygotsky, L. S., 58, 117

▋▋ W

Walters, B., 140
WebCT (software), 129

Weber, B., 78
Wells, A., 42
Wesche, 116
White, R., 156
"White love," 41
WIA. *See* Workforce Investment Act (WIA)
WIDA Engligh Language Proficiency Standards, 172
Wiggins, G. P., 34
Willett, J., 25, 43
Williams, G., 39, 39n5, 40
Willis, P. E., 23
Winfrey, O., 140
Wolff, R. D., 23, 43
Workforce Investment Act (WIA), 96, 204, 210
Workplace literacy, 82–90, 104–105, 151–152. *See also* Continuing Education Training Network (CETN)
Writing, interview project for, 135–148, 141f
Writing Clearly (Bates, Lane, & Lange), 148
Writing programs, computer, 129–132

▋▋ Y

Yalden, J., 160
York, University of, 123

▋▋ Z

Zamel, V., 70
Zwerling, L., 24